ArchiCAD 19 – The Definitive Guide

Dive into the wonderful world of Building Information Modeling (BIM) to become a productive ArchiCAD user

Scott H. MacKenzie

Adam Rendek

BIRMINGHAM - MUMBAI

ArchiCAD 19 – The Definitive Guide

First published: June 2015

Production reference: 1250615

Published by Packt Publishing Ltd.
Livery Place
35 Livery Street
Birmingham B3 2PB, UK.

ISBN 978-1-84969-762-0

www.packtpub.com

Cover image by Artie Ng (artherng@yahoo.com.au)

Credits

About the Authors

Scott H. MacKenzie started working in the AEC (architecture, engineering, and construction) industry way back in 1988. His first role was as a manual draftsman, where he drew with ink on Mylar. Soon afterwards, he became a CAD operator. He loves creating, drawing, and managing construction documents. He worked with several different CAD programs and became a CAD manager in 1994. In 2003, he started using his first BIM program. Scott was convinced at that time that BIM was a much better way to draw, document, and manage drawing sets. Fast forward to today, and he says to you, "There is no project too small for the use of BIM (ArchiCAD). Those other CAD programs are stuck in 20th century technology."

He spent the first 12 years of his career producing electrical, HVAC, and plumbing drawings. Then, in 2000, he jumped over to the architecture side and has been there ever since.

Back in 2007, he was asked by Graphisoft to update *ArchiCAD for AutoCAD Users* to match the current version of ArchiCAD.

I would like to thank my wife, Karen, for her support and belief that I could complete this project. Despite all the distractions in our life, such as major house repairs, selling our house after the repairs were complete, and then moving from Columbus, Ohio, to Manhattan, it has finally happened!

I also want to thank my friend, a well-esteemed professional peer and colleague Adam Rendek. Without Adam, this book would have been only half as good as it is and would have taken much longer to finish.

Also, I thank Packt Publishing for giving me this opportunity and working with me through all my issues.

Adam Rendek moved to San Francisco to pursue his career in design and construction after graduating from the Budapest University of Technology and Economics with a master's degree in architecture and building engineering. He has worked on numerous large projects, both in Europe and the United States, including the Palace of Arts in Budapest—recipient of the 2006 FIABCI Prix d'Excellence—and the UCSF Mission Bay Hospital project in San Francisco.

In addition to his professional work, he taught a lecture series on digital presentation and building information modeling at U.C. Berkeley in 2005 and 2006. Adam also worked on a research project that explores optimization opportunities in the energy modeling workflow and developed solutions to build life cycle and operations management in the past 3 years. He published several papers on building information modeling (BIM) and energy modeling and presented at a major conference in the United States and Europe.

He is currently working on the BIM implementation of a large public organization (San Francisco International Airport) on behalf of DPR Consulting. His responsibilities include client stakeholder engagement as well as the development of technology implementation strategies. Adam collaborated with the Lawrence Berkeley National Laboratories in a research project, identifying optimal data exchange for energy modeling purposes. He was a consultant for IDEO, Adobe Systems, Autodesk, and Graphisoft on product development for the AEC industry.

About the Reviewers

Hristina Altavanska is a junior interior designer who is eager to explore the design field and pursue her career in retail and commercial design all over the world. She is a person with interests in different cultures and languages and uses her free time expanding her knowledge in these areas.

Jengel Ansip is the owner and manager of a small architecture studio in Estonia and an ArchiCAD consultancy web-based service in Australia.

He has over 10 years of experience in ArchiCAD BIM modeling and building designs as an architectural technician. He has also worked in architectural firms in Australia and Switzerland and has designed houses in many other countries.

Jengel has also helped many firms implement BIM and has trained people to use ArchiCAD.

Michael T. Chang was born and raised in Long Beach, California. As a game enthusiast, he regularly played *The Sims*, which sparked off his interest in architecture. He began his architectural education in the fall of 2008 at California College of the Arts, located in San Francisco, California. Struggling with the rigor of the program at CCA, he stayed focused, persevered through his studies, and graduated in May 2012, earning a bachelor's of architecture. Currently, he resides in the Southern California area and will be pursuing his postgraduate degree, masters of architecture II, at University of California, Los Angeles in the fall.

Brice Desportes is a young Franco-Canadian architect, currently based in Denmark. His hunger to improve led him to Canada and all over Europe, starting with France, Czech Republic, the Netherlands, and Denmark, where he undertook a master's degree in sustainable architecture. An award-winning person, he has worked for several years in different fields, such as architecture and planning, furniture design, and 3D visualizations, and has always proven himself an essential member of his team.

Animes Fyz Sarkar is a senior BIM manager, with over 9 years of experience in virtual construction and BIM. He is a civil engineer by profession and a DIY enthusiast by heart. As both a service provider and a BIM service user, he has successfully developed, managed, and implemented BIM on more than 100 commercial, residential, infrastructure, and mixed-use projects across the globe.

I am grateful to my mother and father for everything, my brother for being a mountain of support, and my wife for bringing me back to the journey called life.

I am also thankful to all my teachers. And I do not need to thank my friends.

www.PacktPub.com

Support files, eBooks, discount offers, and more

For support files and downloads related to your book, please visit www.PacktPub.com.

Did you know that Packt offers eBook versions of every book published, with PDF and ePub files available? You can upgrade to the eBook version at www.PacktPub.com and as a print book customer, you are entitled to a discount on the eBook copy. Get in touch with us at service@packtpub.com for more details.

At www.PacktPub.com, you can also read a collection of free technical articles, sign up for a range of free newsletters and receive exclusive discounts and offers on Packt books and eBooks.

https://www2.packtpub.com/books/subscription/packtlib

Do you need instant solutions to your IT questions? PacktLib is Packt's online digital book library. Here, you can search, access, and read Packt's entire library of books.

Why subscribe?

- Fully searchable across every book published by Packt
- Copy and paste, print, and bookmark content
- On demand and accessible via a web browser

Free access for Packt account holders

If you have an account with Packt at www.PacktPub.com, you can use this to access PacktLib today and view 9 entirely free books. Simply use your login credentials for immediate access.

Table of Contents

Preface

Your whole experience of creating an architectural design and conveying that design via construction documents can be a fun, challenging, aggravating, or an enlightening experience. Many factors come into play to determine the success of your project, such as the people involved and the established procedures used, but the design tools you use in the process can greatly affect your success.

Graphisoft introduced their true 3D design software for a personal computer at the Hanover Fair in Germany back in 1984. By 1986, the program was named ArchiCAD (Version 2.0) for the Apple Macintosh operating system. The first Windows version of ArchiCAD was released in 1993 for Version 4.16. Since then, ArchiCAD has been available for both the Macintosh and Windows operating systems. ArchiCAD 19, released in 2015, is the culmination of the industry's evolving technology, new features, improved process workflow, and a graphic user interface that has been evolving ever since that first unveiling in 1984.

Learning a new software program can be enjoyable if the program is fun to use and somewhat intuitive. Experienced CAD users that start using a BIM (Building Information Modeling) program such as ArchiCAD enjoy the intelligent interaction between elements and the 3D model environment.

If you are a 2D CAD user, you will appreciate ArchiCAD's ability to keep everything in one file, instead of needing to have separate files for each floor (story). Modeling tools generate 3D elements by default, even when you draw within a 2D view. Elements such as doors and windows clean up automatically when moved along a wall. Changes made to the elements in a plan view will update automatically in the corresponding section and the elevation views. You are going to love it! This reason is enough to stop using your CAD program and move to ArchiCAD.

You will need to draw your major design elements only once, because the virtual model drives the documentations. You will learn that this is all a part of the virtual building environment inside ArchiCAD.

If you are already a BIM user with an understanding of all the abilities mentioned here, you will learn about the unique features that ArchiCAD offers. These features include special ways to control your viewing environment, numerous selection modes, flexible element filtering, and robust modeling tools.

What this book covers

Chapter 1, Project Setup and Modeling a Residential Project, helps you to get started using ArchiCAD by creating your first project. You will get an introduction to the ArchiCAD graphic user interface (GUI), as you learn about project settings and how they drive your project environment. Then, you will see how easy it is to model walls, doors, windows, and a roof for your new house!

Chapter 2, Objects, Drafting, and Annotation – A Residential Project, will teach you how to create your own custom objects to add to your new house. This chapter will introduce you to the tools used for text creation and 2D line work. You will feel right at home with the tools in this chapter, because they are very similar to all the basic tools in any standard CAD program.

Chapter 3, Documentation – A Residential Project, will get into forming the finished look of your project. You will learn about views, how to manipulate what is displayed on your drawings, and how to control the way it is graphically displayed. Then, you will learn about creating sheets and the super easy way to put views on them.

Chapter 4, Project Setup and Modeling Part I – A Healthcare Building Project, will help you set up what will be used as the shell and core model for your commercial building. In this chapter, you will dig a little deeper into ArchiCAD's project environment settings, and learn to use more advanced modeling tools. This will provide the framework for your new building.

Chapter 5, Project Setup and Modeling Part II – A Healthcare Building Project, will cover creating the interiors model to be used together with the shell and core model created in the previous chapter. You will get the project settings put in place, and link the shell and core model in. Then, you will model all the interior walls, and have fun inserting furniture, casework, and appliances.

Chapter 6, Objects, Drafting, and Annotation – A Healthcare Building Project, will dig deeper into making your own custom objects. You may find that creating your own custom objects it a lot of fun, and your favorite thing to do. In this chapter, you will also learn about the other annotation tools available in ArchiCAD, as well as advanced detail creation.

Chapter 7, Documentation – A Commercial Project, will teach you more about view creation, view management, sheet creation, and drawing management. This chapter will help ensure that you fully understand how to control the look and feel of your drawings. You may not realize it at first, but this knowledge is essential to a successful project.

Chapter 8, Work Sharing with ArchiCAD, will teach you about data extraction, and the many different ways to incorporate different types of drawing formats into your projects. Also, it will teach you how to export your work into multiple different file formats for other parties to utilize in their work. You will find that ArchiCAD is second to none in this category.

Chapter 9, Visualization and Model Management, will be fun when learning about rendering, animations, and virtual environment fly-through models. We end the book with model management and best practices. Model management may sound boring, but it will help you keep your project in good shape.

What you need for this book

A basic understanding of architecture and to be proficient with a 2D CAD software program, such as AutoCAD Lite, or exposure to a BIM program, such as Revit.

Who this book is for

This book is for architects, architectural technicians, and construction professionals who are familiar with 2D CAD, such as AutoCAD Lite, or have some exposure to a 3D BIM package, such as Revit. No experience with ArchiCAD is required. If you want to learn the skills needed for architectural drawing production in the real world, then this book is for you.

Conventions

In this book, you will find a number of styles of text that distinguish between different kinds of information. Here are some examples of these styles, and an explanation of their meaning.

New terms and **important words** are shown in bold. For example, the words that you see on the screen, in menus, or dialog boxes, appear in the text as, "clicking on the **Next** button moves you to the next screen."

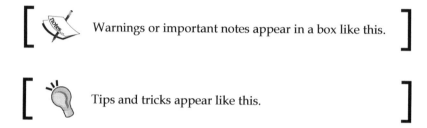

> Warnings or important notes appear in a box like this.

> Tips and tricks appear like this.

Reader feedback

Feedback from our readers is always welcome. Let us know what you think about this book—what you liked or may have disliked. Reader feedback is important for us to develop titles that you really get the most out of.

To send us general feedback, simply send an e-mail to feedback@packtpub.com, and mention the book title via the subject of your message.

If there is a topic that you have expertise in and you are interested in either writing or contributing to a book, see our author guide on www.packtpub.com/authors.

Customer support

Now that you are the proud owner of a Packt book, we have a number of things to help you to get the most from your purchase.

Downloading the example code

You can download the example code files for all Packt books you have purchased from your account at http://www.packtpub.com. If you purchased this book elsewhere, you can visit http://www.packtpub.com/support and register to have the files e-mailed directly to you.

Errata

Although we have taken every care to ensure the accuracy of our content, mistakes do happen. If you find a mistake in one of our books—maybe a mistake in the text or the code—we would be grateful if you would report this to us. By doing so, you can save other readers from frustration and help us improve subsequent versions of this book. If you find any errata, please report them by visiting http://www.packtpub.com/submit-errata, selecting your book, clicking on the **errata submission form** link, and entering the details of your errata. Once your errata are verified, your submission will be accepted and the errata will be uploaded on our website, or added to any list of existing errata, under the Errata section of that title. Any existing errata can be viewed by selecting your title from http://www.packtpub.com/support.

Piracy

Piracy of copyright material on the Internet is an ongoing problem across all media. At Packt, we take the protection of our copyright and licenses very seriously. If you come across any illegal copies of our works, in any form, on the Internet, please provide us with the location address or website name immediately so that we can pursue a remedy.

Please contact us at copyright@packtpub.com with a link to the suspected pirated material.

We appreciate your help in protecting our authors, and our ability to bring you valuable content.

Questions

You can contact us at questions@packtpub.com if you are having a problem with any aspect of the book, and we will do our best to address it.

1

Project Setup and Modeling a Residential Project

Our journey into ArchiCAD 19 begins with an introduction to the graphic user interface, also known as the GUI. As with any software program, there is a menu bar along the top that gives access to all the tools and features. There are also toolbars and tool palettes that can be docked anywhere you like. In addition to this, there are some special palettes that pop up only when you need them.

After your introduction to ArchiCAD's user interface, you can jump right in and start creating the walls and floors for your new house. Then you will learn how to create ceilings and the stairs. Before too long you will have a 3D model to orbit around. It is really fun and probably easier than you would expect.

The ArchiCAD GUI

The first time you open ArchiCAD you will find the toolbars along the top, just under the menu bar and there will be palettes docked to the left and right of the drawing area. We will focus on the three following palettes to get started:

- **The Toolbox palette**: This contains all of your selection, modeling, and drafting tools. It will be located on the left hand side by default.
- **The Info Box palette**: This is your context menu that changes according to whatever tool is currently in use. By default, this will be located directly under the toolbars at the top. It has a scrolling function; hover your cursor over the palette and spin the scroll wheel on your mouse to reveal everything on the palette.
- **The Navigator palette**: This is your project navigation window. This palette gives you access to all your views, sheets, and lists. It will be located on the right-hand side by default.

These three palettes can be seen in the following screenshot:

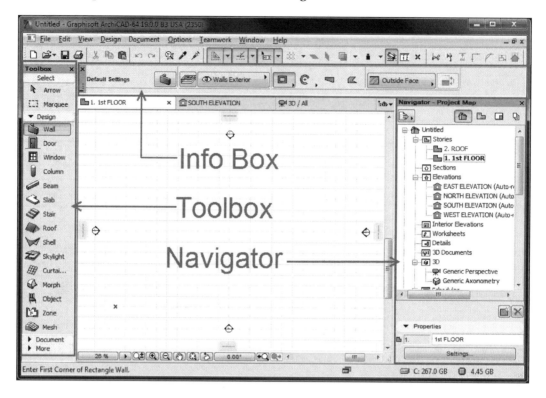

All of the mentioned palettes are dockable and can be arranged however you like on your screen. They can also be dragged away from the main ArchiCAD interface. For instance, you could have palettes on a second monitor.

Panning and Zooming

ArchiCAD has the same panning and zooming interface as most other **CAD (Computer-aided design)** and **BIM (Building Information Modeling)** programs. Rolling the scroll wheel on your mouse will zoom in and out. Pressing down on the scroll wheel (or middle button) and moving your cursor will execute a pan.

Each drawing view window has a row of zoom commands along the bottom. You should try each one to get familiar with each of their functions.

View toggling

When you have multiple views open, you can toggle through them by pressing the *Ctrl* key and tapping on the *Tab* key. Or, you can pick any of the open views from the bottom of the **Window** pull-down menu.

Pressing the *F2* key will open a 2D floor plan view and pressing the *F3* key will open the default 3D view.

Pressing the *F5* key will open a 3D view of selected items. In other words, if you want to isolate specific items in a 3D view, select those items and press *F5*.

> The function keys are second nature to those that have been using ArchiCAD for a long time. If a feature has a function key shortcut, you should use it.

Project setup

ArchiCAD is available in multiple different language versions. The exercises in this book use the USA version of ArchiCAD. Obviously this version is in English. There is another version in English and that is referred to as the International (INT) version. You can use the International version to do the exercises in the book, just be aware that there may be some subtle differences in the way that something is named or designed.

When you create a new project in ArchiCAD, you start by opening a project template. The template will have all the basic stuff you need to get started including layers, line types, wall types, doors, windows, and more.

The following lesson will take you through the first steps in creating a new ArchiCAD project:

1. Open ArchiCAD.
2. The **Start ArchiCAD** dialog box will appear. Select the **Create a New Project** radio button at the top.
3. Select the **Use a Template** radio button under **Set up Project Settings**.
4. Select **ArchiCAD 19 Residential Template.tpl** from the drop-down list. If you have the International version of ArchiCAD, then the residential template may not be available. Therefore you can use **ArchiCAD 19 Template.tpl**.
5. Click on **New**. This will open a blank project file.

Project Settings

Now that you have opened your new project, we are going to create a house with 4 stories (which includes a story for the roof). We create a story for the roof in order to facilitate a workspace to model the elements on that level. The template we just opened only has 2 stories, so we will need to add 2 more. Then we need to look at some other settings.

Stories

The settings for the stories are as follows:

1. On the Navigator palette, select the Project Map icon .
2. Double click on **1st FLOOR**.
3. Right click on **Stories** and select **Create New Story**.
4. You will be prompted to give the new story a name. Enter the name BASEMENT.
5. Click on the button next to **Below**.
6. Enter 9ʹ into the **Height** box and click on the **Create** button. Then double click on **2. 2nd FLOOR**.
7. Right click on **Stories** and then select **Create New Story**.
8. You will be prompted to give the new story a name. Enter the name ROOF.
9. Click on the button next to **Above**.
10. Enter 9ʹ into the **Height** box and click on the **Create** button.

Your list of stories should now look like this

- **3. ROOF**
- **2. 2nd Floor**
- **1. 1st Floor**
- **-1. BASEMENT**

> The International version of ArchiCAD (INT) will give the first floor the index number of 0. The second floor index number will be 1. And the roof will be 2.

Now we need to adjust the heights of the other stories:

1. Right click on **Stories** (on the **Navigator** palette) and select **Story Settings**.

2. Change the number in the **Height to Next** box for **1st FLOOR** to 9'.

3. Do the same for **2nd FLOOR**.

Units

On the menu bar, go to **Options | Project Preferences | Working Units** and perform the following steps:

1. Ensure **Model Units** is set to **feet & fractional inches**.

2. Ensure that **Fractions** is set to **1/64**.

3. Ensure that **Layout Units** is set to **feet & fractional inches**.

4. Ensure that **Angle Unit** is set to **Decimal degrees**.

5. Ensure that **Decimals** is set to **2**.

You are now ready to begin modeling your house, but first let's save the project. To save the project, perform the following steps:

1. Navigate to the **File** menu and click on **Save**. If by chance you have saved it already, then click on **Save As**.

2. Name your file `Colonial House`.

3. Click on Save.

Renovation filters

The Renovation Filter feature allows you to differentiate how your drawing elements will appear in different construction phases. For renovation projects that have demolition and new work phases, you need to show the items to be demolished differently than the existing items that are to remain, or that are new.

The projects we will work on in this book do not require this feature to manage phases because we will only be creating a new construction. However, it is essential that your renovation filter setting is set to **New Construction**. We will do this in the first modeling exercise.

Selection methods

Before you can do much in ArchiCAD, you need to be familiar with selecting elements. There are several ways to select something in ArchiCAD, which are as follows:

Single cursor click

Pick the Arrow tool from the toolbox or hold the *Shift* key down on the keyboard and click on what you want to select. As you click on the elements, hold the *Shift* key down to add them to your selection set. To remove elements from the selection set, just click on them again with the *Shift* key pressed.

There is a mode within this mode called Quick Selection. It is toggled on and off from the **Info Box** palette. The icon looks like a magnet. When it is on, it works like a magnet because it will stick to faces or surfaces, such as slabs or fill patterns. If this mode is not on, then you are required to find an edge, endpoint, or hotspot node to select an element with a single click. Hold the *Space* button down to temporarily change the mode while selecting elements.

Window

Pick the Arrow tool from the toolbox or hold the *Shift* key down and draw your selection window. Click once for the window starting corner and click a second time for the end corner.

 This works just as windowing does in AutoCAD. *Not* as Revit does, where you need to hold the mouse button down while you draw your window.

There are 3 different windowing methods. Each one is set from the **Info Box** palette:

- **Partial Elements**: Anything that is inside of or touching the window will be selected. AutoCAD users will know this as a Crossing Window.

- **Entire Elements**: Anything completely encapsulated by the window will be selected. If something is not completely inside the window then it will not be selected.

- **Direction Dependent**: Click and window to the left, the **Partial Elements** window will be used. Click and window to the right, the **Entire Elements** window will be used.

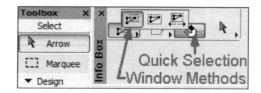

Marquee

A marquee is a selection window that stays on the screen after you create it. If you are a MicroStation CAD program user, this will be similar to a selection window. It can be used for printing a specific area in a drawing view and performing what AutoCAD users would refer to as a Stretch command.

There are 2 types of marquees; single story (skinny) and multi story (fat). The single story marquee is used when you want to select elements on your current story view only. The multi-story marquee will select everything on your current story as well as the stories above and below your selections.

The Find & Select tool

This lets ArchiCAD select elements for you, based on the attribute criteria that you define, such as element type, layer, and pen number. When you have the criteria defined, click on the plus sign button on the palette and all the elements within that criterion inside your current view or marquee will be selected.

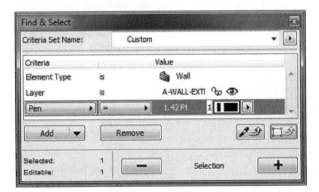

 The quickest way to open the Find & Select tool is with the *Ctrl + F* key combination

Modification commands

As you draw, you will inevitably need to move, copy, stretch, or trim something. Select your items first, and then execute the modification command. Here are the basic commands you will need to get things moving:

- **Adjust (Extend)**: Press *Ctrl* + - or navigate to **Edit | Reshape | Adjust**
- **Drag (Move)**: Press *Ctrl* + *D* or...navigate to **Edit | Move | Drag**
- **Drag a Copy (Copy)**: Press *Ctrl* + *Shift* + *D* or navigate to **Edit | Move | Drag a Copy**
- **Intersect (Fillet)**: Click on the **Intersect** button on the Standard toolbar or navigate to **Edit | Reshape | Intersect**
- **Resize (Scale)**: Press *Ctrl* + *K* or navigate to **Edit | Reshape | Resize**
- **Rotate**: Press *Ctrl* + *E* or navigate to **Edit | Move | Rotate**
- **Stretch**: Press *Ctrl* + *H* or navigate to **Edit | Reshape | Stretch**
- **Trim**: Press *Ctrl* or click on the **Trim** button on the Standard toolbar or navigate to **Edit | Reshape | Trim**. Hold the *Ctrl* key down and click on the portion of wall or line that you want trimmed off. This is the fastest way to trim anything!

 Memorizing the keyboard combinations above is a sure way to increase your productivity.

Modeling – part I

We will start with the wall tool to create the main exterior walls on the 1st floor of our house, and then create the floor with the slab tool. However, before we begin, let's make sure your **Renovation Filter** is set to **New Construction**.

Setting the Renovation Filter

The Renovation Filter is an active setting that controls how the elements you create are displayed. Everything we create in this project is for new construction so we need the new construction filter to be active.

To do so, go to the **Document** menu, click on **Renovation** and then click on **04 New Construction**.

Using the Wall tool

The **Wall** tool has settings for height, width, composite, layer, pen weight and more. We will learn about these things as we go along, and learn a little bit more each time we progress into to the project.

1. Double click on **1. 1st Story** in the **Navigator** palette to ensure we are working on story 1.

2. Select the **Wall** tool from the **Toolbox** palette or from the menu bar under **Design | Design Tools | Wall**.

3. Notice that this will automatically change the contents of the **Info Box** palette. Click on the wall icon inside **Info Box**. This will bring up the active properties of the wall tool in the form of the **Wall Default Settings** window. (This can also be achieved by double clicking on the wall tool button in **Toolbox**).

4. Change the composite type to **Siding 2x6 Wd. Stud**. Click on the wall composite button to do this.

Creating the exterior walls of the first story

To create the exterior walls of the 1st story perform the following steps:

1. Select the **Wall** tool from the **Toolbox** palette, or from the menu bar under **Design | Design Tools | Wall**.

2. Double click on **1. 1st Story** in the **Navigator** palette to ensure that we are working on story 1.

3. Select the **Wall** tool from the Toolbox palette, or from the menu bar under **Design | Design Tools | Wall**.

4. Change the composite type to be **Siding 2x6 Wd. Stud**. Click on the wall composite button to do this.

5. Notice at the bottom of the **Wall Default Settings** window is the layer currently assigned to the wall tool. It should be set to **A-WALL-EXTR**.

6. Click on **OK** to start your first wall.

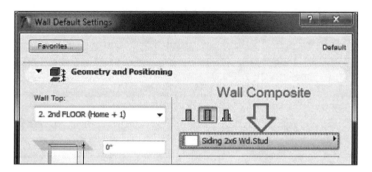

7. Click near the center of the drawing screen and move your cursor to the left, notice the orange dashed line that appears. That is your guide line. Keep your cursor over the guide line so that it keeps you locked in the orthogonal direction. You should also immediately see the **Tracker** palette pop up, displaying your distance drawn and angle after your first click. Before you make your second click, enter the number 24 from your keyboard and press *Enter*. You should now have 24-0" long wall.

If your Tracker palette does not appear, it may be toggled off. Go up to the **Standard** tool bar and click on the **Tracker** button to turn it on.

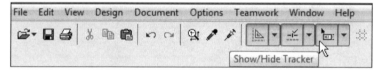

8. Select this again and make your first click on the upper left end corner of your first wall. Move your cursor down, so that it snaps to the guideline, enter the number 28, and press the *Enter* key.

9. Draw your third wall by clicking on the bottom left endpoint of your second wall, move your cursor to the right, snapped over the guide line, type in the number 24 and press *Enter*.

10. Draw your fourth wall by clicking on the bottom right end point of your third wall and the starting point of your first wall. You should now have four walls that measure 24'-0" x 28"-0, outside edge to outside edge.

11. Move your four walls to the center of the drawing view and perform the following steps:

    a. Click on the **Arrow** tool at the top of the **Toolbox**.

    b. Click outside one of the corners of the walls, and then click on the opposite side. All four walls should be selected now.

    c. Use the Drag command to move the walls. The quickest way to activate the Drag command is by pressing *Ctrl + D*. The long way is from the menu bar by navigating to **Edit | Move | Drag**.

    d. Drag (move) the walls to the center of your drawing window.

    e. Press the *Esc* key or click on a blank space in your drawing window to deselect the walls.

 You can select all the walls in a view by activating the **Wall** tool and pressing *Ctrl + A*.

You are now ready to create a floor with the slab tool. But first, let's have a little fun and see how it looks in 3D (press the *F3* key):

1. From the **Navigator** palette, double click on **Generic Axonometry** under the 3D folder icon.

2. This will open a 3D view window. Hold your *Shift* key down, press down on your scroll wheel button, and slowly move your mouse around. You are now orbiting!

Play around with it a little, then get back to work and go to the next step to create your first floor slab. Press the *F2* key to get back to a 2D view.

[You can also perform a 3D orbit via the **Orbit** button at the bottom of any 3D view window.]

Creating the first story's floor with the Slab tool

The slab tool is used to create floors. It is also used to create ceilings. We will begin using it now to create the first floor for our house. Similar to the **Wall** tool, it also has settings for layer, pen weight and composite. To create the first story's floor using the **Slab** tool, perform the following steps:

1. Select the **Slab** tool from the **Toolbox** palette or from the menu bar under **Design | Design Tools | Slab**.

2. This will change the contents of the **Info Box** palette. Click on the Slab icon in **Info Box**. This will bring up the **Slab Default Settings** (active properties) window for the **Slab** tool.

3. As with the **Wall** tool, you have a composite setting for the slab tool. Set the composite type for the slab tool to **FLR Wd Flr + 2x10**.

4. The layer should be set to **A-FLOR**.

5. Click **OK**.

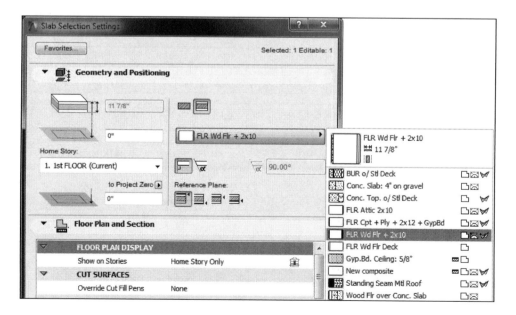

6. You could draw the shape of the slab by tracing over the outside lines of your walls but we are going to use the Magic Wand feature. Hover your cursor over the space inside your four walls and press the space bar on your keyboard. This will automatically create the slab using the boundary created by the walls. Then, open a 3D view and look at your floor.

> Instead of using the tool icon inside the **Info Box** palette, double click on any tool icon inside the **Toolbox** palette to bring up the default settings window for that tool.

Creating the exterior walls and floor slabs for the basement and the second story

We could repeat all of the previous steps to create the floor and walls for the second story and the basement, but in this case, it will be quicker to copy what we have already drawn on the first story and copy it up with the **Edit Elements by Stories** tool. Perform the following steps to create the exterior walls and floor slabs for the basement and second story:

1. Go to the **Navigator** palette and right click over Stories, select **Edit Elements by Stories**. The **Edit Elements by Stories** window will open.
2. Under **Select Action**, you want to set it to **Copy**.
3. Under **From Story**, set it to **1. 1st FLOOR**.
4. In the **To Story** section, check the box for **2nd FLOOR** and **-1. BASEMENT**.
5. Click on **OK**.
6. You should see a dialog box appear, stating that as a result of the last operation, elements have been created and/or have changed their position on currently unseen stories. Whenever you get this message, you should confirm that you have not created any unwanted elements.

> Click on the **Continue** button. Now you should have walls and a floor on three stories; **Basement, 1st FLOOR**, and **2nd FLOOR**.
>
> The quickest way to jump to the next story up or the next story down is with the *Ctrl* + Arrow Up or *Ctrl* + Arrow Down key combination.

Basement element modification

The floor and the walls on the **BASEMENT** story need to be changed to a different composite type. Do this by performing the following steps:

1. Open the **BASEMENT** view and select the four walls by clicking on one at a time while holding down the *Shift* key.

2. Right click over your selection and click on **Wall Selection Settings**. Change the walls to the **EIFS on 8" CMU** composite type. Then, click on **OK**.

3. Move your cursor over the floor slab. The quick selection cursor should appear. This selection mode allows you to click on an object without needing to find an edge or endpoint. Click on the slab.

4. Open the **Slab Selection Setting** window but this time, do it by pressing the *Ctrl + T* key combination. Change the floor slab composite to **Conc. Slab: 4" on gravel**. Click on **OK.**

The *Ctrl + T* key combination is the quickest way to bring up an element's selection settings window when an element is selected.

Open a 3D view (by pressing the *F3* key) and orbit around your house. It should look similar to the following screenshot:

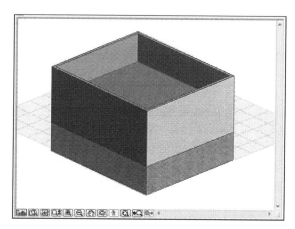

Adding the garage

We need to add the garage and the laundry room, which connects the garage to the house. Do this by performing the following steps:

1. Open the **1st FLOOR** story from the project map.

2. Start the **Wall** tool. From the **Info Box** palette, set the wall composite setting to **Siding 2x6 Wd. Stud**.

3. Click on the upper-left corner of your house for your wall starting point. Move your cursor to the left, snap to the guide line, type 6'-10", and press *Enter.*

4. Change the **Geometry Method** setting on **Info Box** to **Chained.** Refer to the following screenshot:

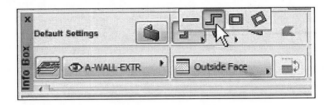

5. Start your next wall by clicking on the endpoint of your last wall, move your cursor up, snap to the guideline and type **5'**, and press *Enter.*

6. Move your cursor to the left, snap to grid line, type in 12'-6", and press *Enter.*

7. Move your cursor down, snap to grid line, type in 22'-4", and press *Enter.*

8. Move your cursor to the right, snap to grid line and double click on the perpendicular west wall (double pressing your *Enter* key will work the same as a double click).

Now we want to create the floor for this new set of walls. To do that, perform the following steps:

1. Start the **Slab** tool.

2. Change the composite to **Conc. Slab: 4" on gravel**.

3. Hover your cursor inside the new set of walls and press the *Space* key to use the magic wand. This will create the floor slab for the garage and laundry room.

There is still one more wall to create, but this time we will use the Adjust command to, in effect, create a new wall:

1. Select the 5'-0" wall drawn in the previous exercise.

2. Go to the **Edit** menu, click on **Reshape**, and then click on **Adjust**.

3. Click on the bottom edge of the perpendicular wall down below. The wall should extend down. Refer to the following screenshot:

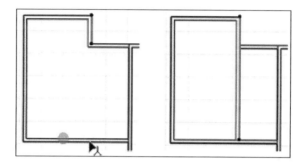

4. Then Change to a 3D view (by pressing *F3*) and examine your work.

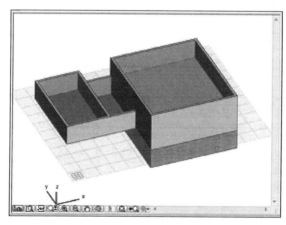

The 3D view

 If you switch to a 3D view and your new modeling does not show, zoom in or out to refresh the view, or double click your scroll wheel (middle button). Your new work will appear.

Modeling – part II

Now we are ready to create the interior walls. Open the **1st FLOOR** view from the project map, and perform the following steps:

1. Start the wall tool, change the composite to **Wall Wd 2x4 + 5/8" Gyp.Bd.**

2. Draw your interior walls on the first floor according to the following plan:

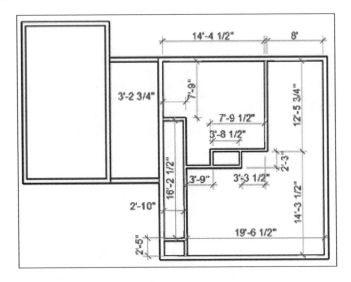

Second floor walls

We are going to create the interior walls on the second floor. Some of the walls on the second story align with walls on the first story. We will use the **Trace and Reference** feature to display the walls on the story below. Revit users will know this as the underlay property of the view.

Open the **2nd FLOOR** view and go to the **View** menu, click on **Trace** to toggle on the Trace mode. This should display the floor below in a halftone by default. The image that follows shows the second floor walls to be drawn and the wall below in a halftone.

 Other ways to toggle the Trace mode on and off are with the keyboard combination *Ctrl + F2*, the **Trace** button on the **Standard** toolbar, and the button on the **Trace and Reference** palette.

Draw the walls of the second floor according to the dimensions shown in the following diagram. Use the locations of the wall below as a guide for the second floor walls that are aligned.

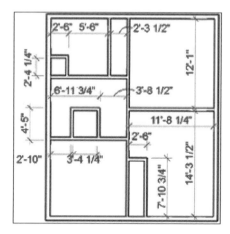

Open a 3D view. It should look like the image that follows:

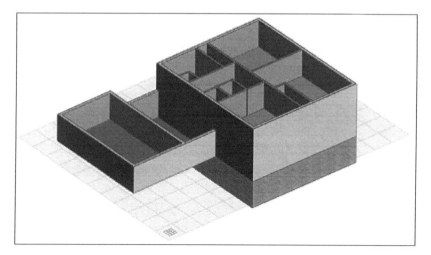

Modification II – pet palette

Another way to modify something is to use the pet palette. After you select an item, click on an endpoint or edge of that element. This will bring up the pet palette for that type of element. The pet palette is essentially an on-demand toolbar that is specifically designed for the type of element you select. It can have commands such as move, rotate, stretch, etc. Following are a few examples according to element type and what part of the element is clicked on.

Ceilings

All the walls and floors in our house are drawn. Now it is time for us to model the ceilings. This house has typical gypsum board ceilings at 8'-0" above the finished floor. We will put them in the first and second floor stories. The basement ceiling will be exposed to the floor above.

First, we need to create a composite for a 5/8" gypsum board to be used by the slab tool as the ceiling material.

Creating a composite type

Perform the following steps to create a composite type:

1. On the menu bar navigate to **Options | Element Attributes | Composites**. The **Composite Structures** window will open. Click on the **New** button.
2. Enter Gyp.Bd. Ceiling: 5/8" as the name.
3. Change the building material to **Gypsum Board** and the thickness to **5/8"**.

4. This composite is designed to be used for slabs and walls. At the bottom right, click on the **Roof** and **Shell** buttons so they are un-selected, leaving the **Wall** and **Slab** tool selected.

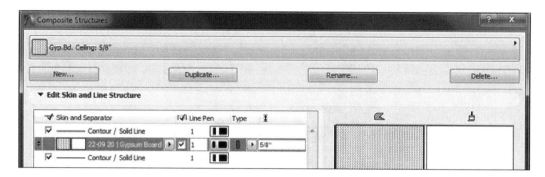

First floor ceilings

We will start modeling the ceilings on the first floor by drawing slabs in every room except the garage and the stairwell. However, before we start modeling the ceilings, we need to assign a composite type to the ceiling.

1. Open the **1st FLOOR** viewpoint from project map on the **Navigator** palette. Start the **Slab** tool from the **Toolbox** palette.

2. On the **Info Box** palette, change the composite to **Gyp.Bd. Ceiling: 5/8"**.

3. Change the layer to **A-CLNG**.

4. Set the **Reference** level to **Height and Home Offset**. In the height offset box, enter 8'-0".

5. Use the Magic Wand (*Space*) and click inside each room one at a time. This will create a 5/8" gypsum board ceiling inside each room at a height of 8'-0".

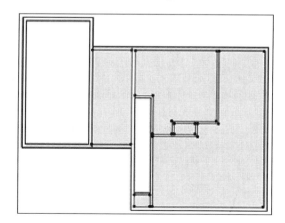

The skinny room on the first floor to the left is where the stairs to the second floor are going to be. The ceiling over this area needs to be modified to match the wall above on the second floor.

6. Turn on the **Trace** feature from the standard toolbar. Click on the down arrow at the right of the **Trace** button. Choose **Reference | Above current story**.

7. Select the ceiling, click on the top edge and drag it down to the first edge of the wall above. Refer to the following sequence of images:

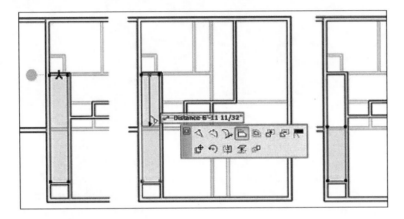

Second floor ceilings

Now we are ready to create the ceilings on the second floor. Perform the following steps:

1. Open the **2nd FLOOR** viewpoint from the Project Map.

2. Start the slab tool. Keep the same settings used for the 1st floor. Use the Magic Wand (*spacebar*) to create a ceiling in every room on the 2nd floor.

Open a 3D view to check your work.

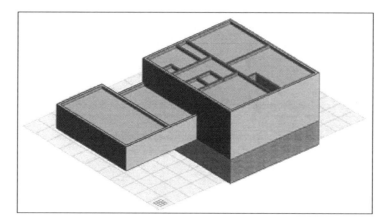

Roofs

You are now ready to model two gable style roofs for our house. One roof over the garage and laundry room, and the second over the second floor. The **Roof** tool is very dynamic; it can create a complete gable or hip style roof in one step. Or you can create separate individual panels.

The following exercise will step you through the creation of your first roofs!

1. Open the **1st FLOOR** view and start the **Roof** tool from the tool box.

2. Change **Construction Method** to **Rotated Rectangular Hip/Gable**. Change the overhang offset to 1'-0". Look at the following image:

This construction method requires 3 clicks. Select the upper-left corner of the garage, then click on the bottom left corner, and then the bottom-right hand corner. Refer to the following image:

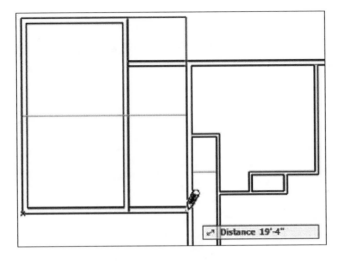

1. The overhang on the right edge is penetrating the second floor and needs to be pulled back. Select the roof, click on the right edge (the pet palette will pop up, the offset edge button will be selected), then drag the edge over to the edge of the wall to the left. Take a look at the following image:

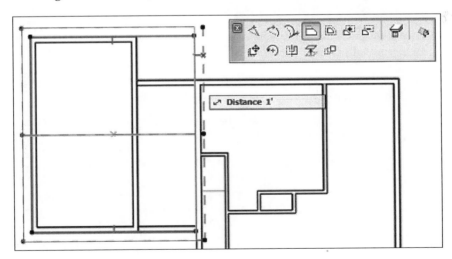

2. Open the **2nd FLOOR** view. Click on the **Roof** tool; use the same method as before. Click on the upper left corner of the second floor wall, then click on the lower left corner, and then on the lower right corner.

You now have 2 roofs, but the pitch needs to be adjusted for our house's design:

1. Open the **WEST ELEVATION** viewpoint from Project Map
2. Select one of the roofs. Click on the top point and hold the cursor down so the pet palette pops up.
3. Click on the **Elevate Horizontal Ridge** button from the pet palette. Drag your cursor up, enter 1 from your keyboard and press *Enter*. This should bring up the ridge by 1'-0".
4. Repeat steps 2 and 3 for the other roof.

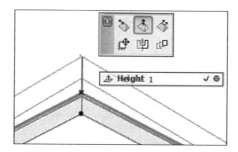

Open a 3D view. You will see that your roofs are added but there is a gap at the gable ends that needs to be filled.

Trimming walls with roofs

Your task is to change the height of the 3 walls that will fill the gable end of each roof, then trim the walls using the roofs as a cutting plane:

1. Open the 3D window, orbit to the west side of the house and select the west wall of the garage.
2. With the wall selected, go to the **Info Box** palette and change the **Top** setting to **3. Roof**. Use the following image as a guide:

3. Right-click on wall (the wall is still selected), from the right-click menu select **Connect... | Trim Elements to Roof/Shell**.

    a. Click on the roof over the garage to use it as your trim element.

    b. Click on the lower portion of the wall to select what part to keep.

    c. Click on a blank area of the screen to complete the command.

Next, you want to do the same to the second floor walls at the gable ends of the second floor roof. However, this time when you change the height of the wall, the process is different because there is no story above **3. Roof**.

Perform the following steps to trim the second story walls to the second story roof. When finished, your exterior walls will be complete.

1. Select one of the second floor walls that need to be trimmed to the second floor roof. From the **Info Box** palette, change the **Bottom** and **Top** setting to **Top and Home Offsets**. Set the top height to 9'-0". Refer to the following image:

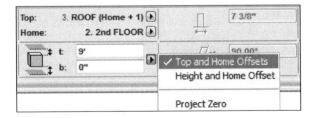

2. Select the same wall and right click on it. From the right-click menu select **Connect... | Trim Elements to Roof/Shell**.

    a. Click on the roof over the second floor to use as your trim element.

    b. Click on the lower portion of the wall to select what part to keep.

    c. Click on a blank area of the screen to complete the command.

3. Repeat steps 1 and 2 for the other second floor wall.

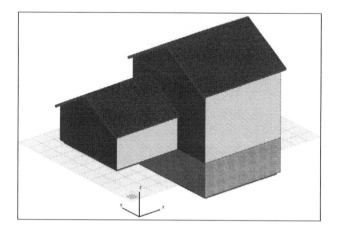

Cutting the roof

There is a portion of the roof over the garage that will need to have a piece cut out of it. It is the area above the back door of the laundry room. ArchiCAD makes it easy to cut holes out of roof objects. You will start by activating the **Roof** tool, then select the roof and draw the portion of the roof to be subtracted. To demonstrate this feature, perform the following steps.

1. Open **1st FLOOR** from the project map.

2. Start the **Roof** tool, then hold the *Shift* key down and select the roof over the garage (it is vital that you start the **Roof** tool before you select the roof).

3. Click on the outside corner of where the east garage wall and the North house wall intersect. Make your second click at the end of the wall, where it intersects with the west wall of the house. Drag your cursor up past the edge of the overhang and click. This should create the notch as shown in the following images:

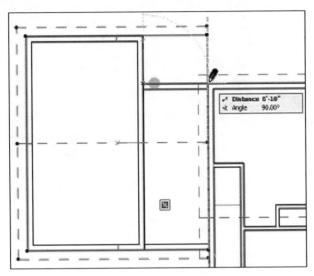

The first step in cutting the notch in the roof

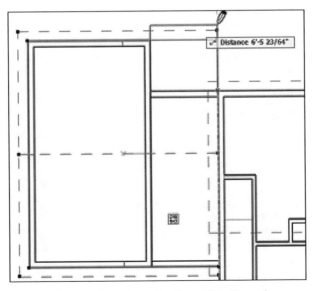

The second step in cutting the notch in the roof

° The 2D plan view will still show the northeast corner of the roof, but if you open a 3D window, you will see that it is not there.

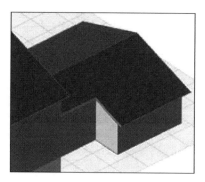

Layers

We have briefly touched upon using layers in the steps leading to this point. As we go further, you will need to learn how to manage your layers. We will go deep into layer management in later portions of this book, but we will have a quick primer on layers to keep you productive.

Similar to how layers work in CAD programs, you can turn them on, off, and lock them. Any element is subject to the on/off/lock status of the layer it is placed on. However, layers in ArchiCAD do not control elements the same way as they do in AutoCAD or MicroStation.

Open the Layer Settings manager window with a *Ctrl + L* key combination. Or you could also open it from the menu bar by navigating to **Document | Layers | Layer Settings**.

Look at the screenshot taken from the layer settings manager. You will see the eyeball icon column; it shows the layer (on) or hides the layer (off). The concept for the lock icon is the same. We will discuss the other columns later in the book.

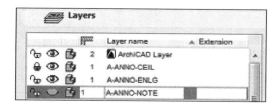

Hide a layer by selection: select an item that is on a layer you want to hide and right click, then select **Layers...** | **Hide Layer**.

Managing layers with the Quick Layers palette

The **Quick Layers** palette is an excellent tool for performing quick little layer tasks such as hiding the layer of a selected object, hiding all the layers that your selected object is on, or locking a selected item's layer. See the features list, palette, and legend notes that follow:

    a.   Toggle between shown and hidden layers

    b.   Toggle between unlocked and locked layers

    c.   Hide the selection's layer(s)

    d.   Lock the selection's layer(s)

    e.   Unlock the selection's layer(s)

    f.   Hide all layers other than the ones selected (isolate selected objects' layers)

    g.   Lock all the layers not selected

    h.   Undo and Redo for any of the commands executed on the Quick Layers palette. Lock all layers other than the ones selected

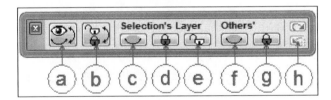

Site

All of the major modeling tasks have been completed. But the house is floating in space and we need to put it on something. So, let's start on creating the site. We will use the Mesh command to create the terrain for the house to sit on:

1.   Open **1st FLOOR** from the project map.

2.   From **Toolbox**, click on the **Mesh** tool.

3.   Change the construction method to rectangle.

4. Create a 150' x 150' rectangle to surround the house: after your first click point, enter 150 on the keyboard, then press the *Tab* key and enter 150 again, then press *Enter*. This will create a site mesh. Select the mesh, then drag and center it around the house.

5. You need to cut a hole in the mesh to accommodate the basement. Click on the **Mesh** tool icon again and select the mesh that you just created.

6. Click on the upper-right outside corner of the house, then with your second pick, click on the exterior left front corner of the house. A window will pop up for specifying new mesh points. Select the radio button for **Create Hole**. Leave the fit specification as **Fit to User Ridges**. Click on **OK**.

Zones (rooms)

Let's go back inside the house and add the room elements, known as zones. Zones contain information that feeds room tags and provides data that can be used for BIM data extraction.

We need to add zones to all the room spaces. The following steps will walk you through the process by starting at the bottom story, in the basement:

1. Open **BASEMENT** from the project map.

2. Start the **Zone** tool from **Toolbox**. On the **Info Box** palette, do the following:

    a. Set the construction method to **Rectangular**.

    b. Enter the name **BASEMENT** in the room name box.

    c. Enter 001 in the room number box.

3. Click on the top left inside corner of the basement room and then on the lower right hand inside corner. Then click on the center of the room (the hammer icon will appear). You should now see a room tag that has the room name, number, and area.

4. Open the **Layer Settings** manager (*Ctrl + L*) and hide the following layers: **A-CLNG, A-FLOR, A-ROOF,** and **L-SITE**. This will keep us from accidently selecting items on those layers, or you could lock them instead.

5. Open the **1st FLOOR** from the project map and start the **Zone** tool. On the **Info Box** palette, click on the **Floor Plan Contour Line** icon to turn it on, and set the pen to 5. Change **Construction Method** to **Polyline**.

6. Change the name in the **Name** box to **DINING**. Draw the zone boundary of the **DINING** room according to the following diagram:

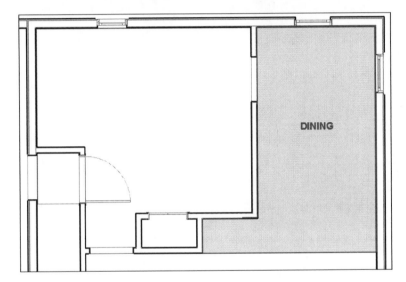

7. Change the name in the **Name** box to **KITCHEN**. Change the construction method to **Inner Edge**. Click inside the kitchen room and the zone will automatically find the walls and use them as a boundary.

8. Finish the remaining rooms on the first floor (shown in the following diagram) with any of the construction methods used previously.

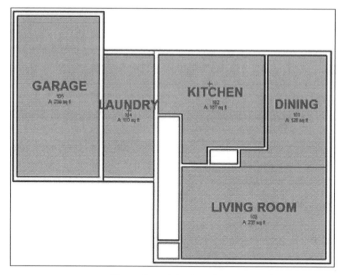

Floor plan of the first floor

9. Do the same for the rooms on the second floor according to the image of the second floor that follows:

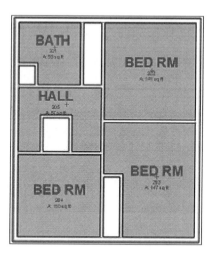

Floor plan of the second floor

 Zone numbers will automatically increase with each new zone created. You can select a zone after it has been created and change the number if you need to.

Lists

Now that you have created most of your rooms, you may want to know the square footage of each one and see them in a list. Go to the project map and scroll down to **Lists**. Expand **Lists** by clicking on the plus sign, then expand **Zones**.

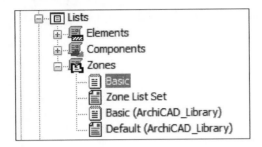

Double click on **Basic**. This will open a list of all the zones you just created. Refer to the following screenshot:

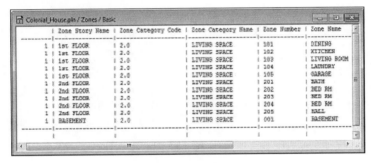

The list of created zones

Zone categories

Notice that all the rooms are in the **LIVING SPACE** zone category. This is not what we want for **Garage**, or **Laundry Room**, or probably even the **BASEMENT**. Perform the following steps to change the category of the zones that we don't want in the **LIVING SPACE** category.

1. Open **1st FLOOR.** and select the **GARAGE** zone.

2. In Info Box change the zone category from **2.0 LIVING SPACE** to **3.1 Garage**.

3. Select the **LAUNDRY** zone and change the zone category to **3.0 UTILITY**.

4. Select the **BASEMENT** zone and change the zone category to **2.2 Unconditioned Space**.

Closets are zones too

You are almost done with inserting your zones. All that is left to do is to add zones for the closets and the stairs from the first floor to the second floor.

1. Open **2nd FLOOR**.

2. Start the **Zone** tool and set the zone category to **0.10 Storage**. Change the room name to **CLOSET**. The value for **Construction Method** is set to **Inner Edge**.

3. Create a zone inside each one of the empty rooms on the second floor. The room numbers will start from where you left off on the second floor before.

4. Open **1st FLOOR**. Change the room number in the Info Box to **106**. Create a zone inside the small rectangle room at the top of the living room, and do the same for the small room on the lower-left side of the living room.

5. Set the zone category in the Info Box to **2.0 LIVING SPACE**. Change the room name to **STAIRS**. Click inside the remaining empty space above the front closet.

Doors

It is time for us to start adding doors to our house. If you have used CAD for as long time you will quickly learn to love how doors work inside of ArchiCAD. When you place a door, it will automatically attach itself to a wall. From there you can move the door along the wall and the line work will automatically cleanup. Within each door object are parameters that can control size and appearance.

Before you begin, hide the following layers: **A-AREA-IDEN**, **A-ROOF**. This will make it easier to work on our doors. Perform the following steps:

1. Let's start on the first floor. Click on the **Door** tool inside the **Toolbox** palette. Look at the **Info Box** palette and **D1 Entrance 19** should be the default door that is ready to be inserted.

2. Zoom in on the southwest corner of the house. Hover your cursor over the bottom edge of the south exterior wall, which is just to the right of the front closet. You will see the Mercedes cursor and an outlined representation of the door opening appear, along with a sun symbol that signifies the exterior side of the door. Click once on the wall to place the door in it.

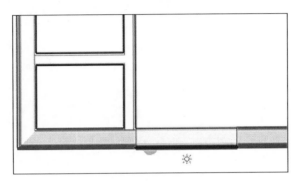

3. As you move your cursor around you will see how it changes where the door leaf will be placed. Click on it one more time when you have the door opening outside to the left. Notice how a door tag is automatically inserted.

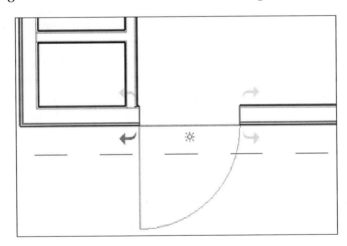

4. Insert another door in the upper-left corner of the laundry room.

You have now placed your first two doors. They are exterior doors, so now we need to place interior doors and openings. We will continue working on the first floor:

1. Double click on the **Door** tool icon inside the **Toolbox** palette. This will open the **Default Door Settings** window. In the library pane on the upper left, under **Linked Libraries**, click on Empty Door **Openings 19** folder. Click on **Arch Top Door Opening 19**. Click on the **OK** button.

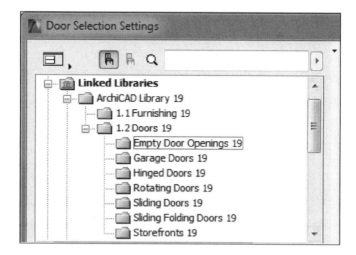

2. Place a door opening at the bottom of the stairs, and two in the kitchen.

3. Double click on the **Door** tool icon again to change the door type to **D1 Garage 2 19**, from under **08 30 00 Specialty Doors and Frames 19\Garage Doors 19**. Place the garage door at the center of the south wall of the garage.

4. Double click on the **Door** tool icon to change the door type to **D1 19** from under **08 11 00 Wood Doors 19\Wood Internal Doors 19**. Insert the door in the kitchen by the laundry room.

5. Double click on the **Door** tool icon to change the door type to **D1 Bifold 19** from under **08 30 00 Specialty Doors and Frames 19\Bifold Doors 19**. Insert the door at the closet at the bottom of the stairs and the closet in the Kitchen. In the **Info Box** palette, change the door opening width to 2'-6". Refer to the screenshot of **Info Box** that follows:

6. Open the second floor. Double click on the **Door** tool icon to change the door type to **D1 19** from under **08 11 00 Wood Doors 19\Wood Internal Doors 19.** Insert doors for all 3 bedrooms and the bathroom.

7. Using the same settings as discussed in the preceding step, change the door width to 1'-8", and place a door in the bathroom for the closet.

8. Double click on the **Door** tool icon to change the door type to **Sliding Folding Multipanel Door 19** from under **Sliding Folding Doors 19**. Change the width to 5'-0". Insert doors for the long closet in the 2 bedrooms on the right. Refer to the mages that follow to check your work:

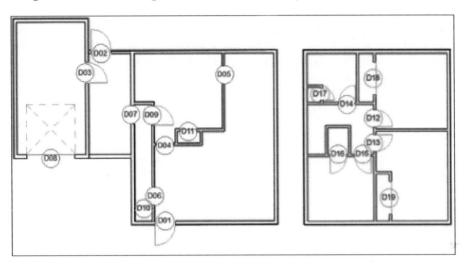

1st Floor   2nd Floor

Windows

Similar to doors, windows automatically snap to walls and have changeable parameters that control size and appearance. But it is important to note that doors and windows require a wall to act as a host because they cannot exist on their own. This means that the door and windows assume the layer of the wall. This is why you don't see a layer setting in **Info Box** when the window or door tool is active.

Let's add windows to our house, starting on the first floor:

1. Start the **Window** tool from the **Toolbox** palette. The default settings should be door **W Double Hung 19**, width 2'-6", height 5'. Look at the image of the **Info Box** palette that follows:

2. Use the following plan as a guide and place 2 windows in the living room, 2 in the dining room, 1 in the kitchen, 1 in the laundry room, and 1 in the garage. Placing windows works just like placing doors, refer to steps 2 and 3 in the *Doors* exercise done earlier.

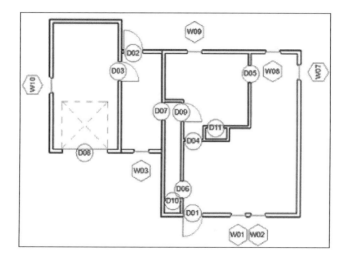

3. Open the second floor. Using the same settings as we used earlier, place windows in each room according to the following image.

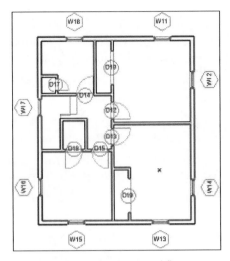

The layout for the second floor

Stairs

The **Stair** tool is a tool that involves a good amount of setup before you actually place a stair, because stairs are always unique and contain many components. For our project we need 2 stairs. One to get to the 2nd floor from the first floor and one to get to the basement from the first floor.

Before we get started, we will want to alter our view to give us a better view. Specifically, we want to turn off the window and door tags. We will do this by changing the current model view options:

1. Go to the menu bar, navigate to **Document | Set Model View | Model View Options**.

2. Select the **Presentation-Solid** model view option combination.

3. Click on **OK**.

Create your first stair

Perform the following steps to create your first stair:

1. Open the basement viewpoint from the project map on the **Navigator** palette. Toggle on the **Trace** feature from the **Standard** tool bar at the top of your screen. Turn on the first floor for tracing.

    a. Click the drop down portion of the **Trace** button, and select **Reference | Above Current Story**.

2. Start the **Stair** tool. Set the construction method to **Diagonal** and the **Home** story to **-1. BASEMENT** on the **Info Box** palette.

3. Click on the Stair icon to open the **Stair Default Setting** window. Change the stair type to **Stair Straight 19**. Then, go to the **Preview and Position** section. Then, perform the following steps:

    a. Rotate the preview to match the image that follows.

    b. Set the insertion point to the lower right corner of the stair.

    c. Uncheck the **Mirror Library Part** box.

    d. Change the height to 9 '. Click on **OK**.

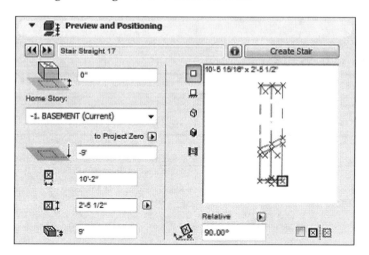

4. You will make two clicks to define the width and length of the stair. Click on the inside corner of the opening above for your first click and the bottom edge of the door above, as per the image that follows:

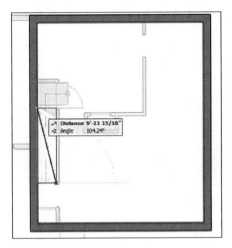

5. Toggle off the trace and your plan should look similar to the following image.

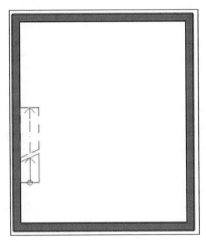

Create your second stair

The stair going up to the second floor is not of a typical design. It is an L-shaped stair with a landing. The landing is at the top and the L portion is only 2 risers. In this situation we will use the **Create Stair** tool to create a new stair object. Perform the following steps to create your second stair:

1. Open the **1st FLOOR** view. Click on the **Stair tool** icon in the **Toolbox** palette. Then from the **Info Box** palette, click on the **Create Stair** button.

2. Select **L-Run with Landing**. Click on **OK**.

3. This will open a settings window. The **Geometry** and **Flight** settings will be shown. Make the following changes:

   a. Total height: 9 ' | push the lock button.

   b. Flight width: 2 ' - 9 " | push the lock button.

   c. Lower part length: 13 '.

   d. Number of risers of the lower side to 13.

   e. Number of risers of the upper side to 2 | push the lock button.

   f. Offset of lower walking: 1 '.

g. Offset of upper walking: 1'.

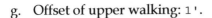

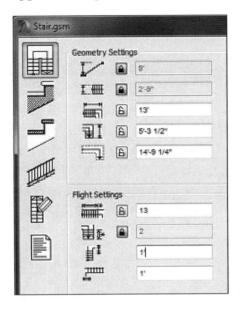

4. Click on the **Structure and Landing** settings button on the left-hand side.

    a. Change all four surface materials under Attributes to **06 | W Pine H.**

    b. Change the section fill to vectorial fill **06 | Wood Siding.**

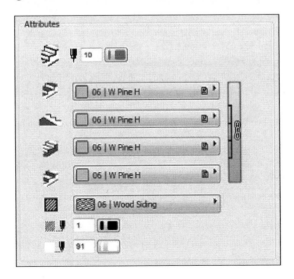

5.   Click on the **Tread Settings** button on the left.

  a.   Change all three surface materials under Attributes to **06 | W Pine H**.

  b.   Change the section fill to vectorial fill **06 | Wood Siding**.

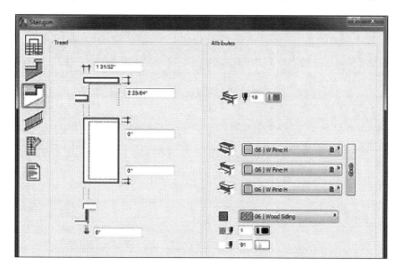

  c.   Click on the **Railing Settings** button on the left-hand side.

  d.   Change the **Railing Setting** selection to **No railing**.

  e.   Click on the **Symbol Settings** button to the left.

  f.   Change the **2D Detail Level** type to **Type 9**.

  g.   Click on OK. The **Save Stair** window will open, prompting you to name your new stair. Enter the name Stair Custom 1 and click on **Save**.

6. Click on the **1st Floor** plan view to insert the stair. Then, drag it into position as shown in the following diagram:

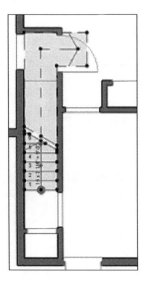

Slab modification

In order for the stairs to get from the first floor to the second floor, you will need to cut a hole in the floor slab on the second floor. Now that you have modelled all the interior walls, you have a template to use as a guide to make the hole.

1. Open the **2nd Floor** viewpoint from the project map. Toggle on the **Trace** feature and change the reference to **1st Floor**.

2. Make sure the bathroom entry door is placed at the far right, up against the wall.

3. Start the **Slab** tool and then select the floor slab (it is vital that the **Slab** tool is active while the slab is selected). Change the construction method to **Polygon**.

In this step we will define the boundary of the hole to be cut in the slab. Make your first click on the bottom edge of the bathroom wall, where it intersects the stair below. Trace the outline of the stair below and along the edge of the second floor walls as shown in the following diagram. Toggle off the **Trace** feature and your floor should as in the following diagram:

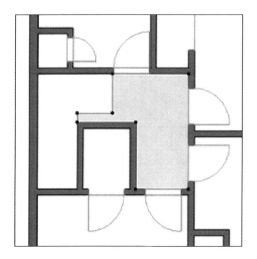

4. Do the same for the floor on the first floor according to the diagram that follows. This will allow access to the basement stair to reach the first floor.

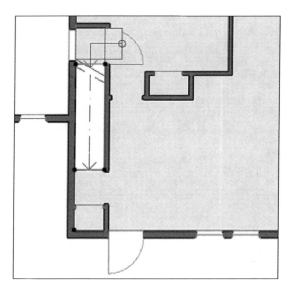

Stair Modification

Open the **1st Floor** viewpoint. Select the stair, open the **Stair Selection Settings** (*Ctrl + T*). Under **Parameters**, change the **2D Symbol Type** to **Type 8**. This will remove the line work for the second floor representation.

Summary

In this chapter you were introduced to the ArchiCAD **Graphical User Interface (GUI)**, project settings and learned how to select stuff. You created all the major modeling for your house and got a primer on layers. Now you should have a good understanding of the ArchiCAD way of creating architectural elements and how to control their parameters. In the next chapter you will be introduced to objects such as casework, plumbing fixtures, and furniture; as well as the drafting and annotation tools.

2
Objects, Drafting, and Annotation – A Residential Project

In this chapter, you will populate your house with ArchiCAD objects such as casework, plumbing fixtures, furniture and more. You will also learn how to create your own custom objects. You will start using the tools used for text creation and 2D line work. Here is a list of the main topics we will learn about:

- Objects — furniture and casework to populate the rooms in the house
- Annotation — text and dimensions
- The **Mesh** tool
- The **Beam & Column** tool

Objects

Objects in ArchiCAD are akin to blocks in AutoCAD, cells in MicroStation, or families in Revit. Objects can be furniture, casework, appliances, plumbing fixtures, and more. In *Chapter 1*, *Project Setup and Modeling a Residential Project*, you created your own custom stair object. However, that was with the special stair-building interface, exclusive to the **Stair** tool. The interface is different for creating other types of objects.

Your house is ready for the interior fit-out. In other words, you need to insert the stuff to sit, work, eat, and sleep on. We will go through each room, starting with the rooms on the second floor and work our way down.

Bathroom

Your bathroom will need a casework, sink, and bathtub. The first thing we need to do is create a layer for the casework. Then, we will add the vanity with a sink and countertop.

The casework layer

Before we start inserting casework, we will have to create a layer specifically for placing the casework on. Do so by performing the following steps:

1. Open the **Layer Settings** window by pressing *Ctrl + L*. Click on the **New** button at the upper-right corner of the window. The **New Layer** dialog box will open. Enter A-CSWK in the **Name** box. Click on **OK**.

2. The new layer will appear in the list at the right (the layer should appear as selected). In the **Layer Combinations** pane on the left-hand side, click on the closed eyeball icon next to the **Enlarged Plan**, **Floor Plan**, and **Section** layer combinations. This will unhide the **A-CSWK** layer in those layer combinations.

Vanity

Next, we will add the vanity for the bathroom. It has a sink and base cabinet with a single door. To add the vanity for the bathroom, perform the following steps:

1. Double-click on the object icon in the **Toolbox** palette and set the layer at the bottom to **A-CSWK**.

2. In the upper-left pane of the **Object Default Settings** window, navigate to **ArchiCAD Library 19 | 12 Furnishing 19 | 12 30 00 Casework 19**. Select the object named **Cabinet Base Single Door 19**.

3. Look at the **Preview and Positioning** window and rotate the cabinet to be 270°. Click on the lower-right hotspot to designate the insertion point. Click on **OK** and place the cabinet on the right-hand side wall of the bathroom.

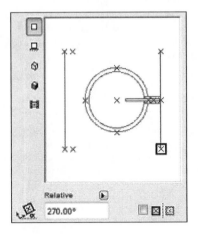

Notice that the cabinet is missing the end panels. We need to add the end panels and make some other changes.

4. Select the cabinet and open the **Object Selection Settings** window (*Ctrl + T*). Expand the **Parameters** section and make the following changes:

   a. Cabinet: **Toe Setback** = 4"; **Toe Height** = 4".

   b. End panels: Left End Panel = **On**; Right End Panel = **s**

   c. Counter: Backsplash Height = **4"**; Overhang to Front of Cabinet = **1"**, Overhang to Left of Cabinet = **1"**; Overhang to Right of Cabinet = **1"**

   d. Tap: = **Style 4**

   e. 2D Representation: Edge Visibility in 2D = **Both**

Your cabinet will look like the following 2D and 3D images:

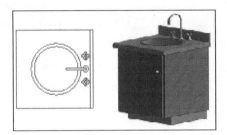

Mirror

The mirror for the vanity will need to be inserted on the wall. It can be found in the ArchiCAD library, under **Toilet, Bath and Laundry Accessories**.

- Double-click on the object icon in the **Toolbox** palette. In the upper-left pane of the **Object Default Settings** window, navigate to **ArchiCAD Library 19 | 10 Specialties 19 | 10 28 00 Toilet, Bath and Laundry Accessories 19**. Select the object named **Mirror 19**.

- Look at the **Preview and Positioning** window and rotate the cabinet to be 270°. Click on the middle hotspot to designate the insertion point. Click on **OK** and place the mirror on the wall, centered over the vanity.

Toilet

The toilet needs to be placed in the bathroom, up against a wall. However, before you place it, you will have to change the layer by performing the following steps:

1. Double-click on the object icon in the **Toolbox** palette and set the layer to **A-FLOR-FIXT**.

2. In the upper-left pane of the **Object Default Settings** window, navigate to **ArchiCAD Library 19 | 22 Plumbing 19 | 22 40 00 Plumbing Fixtures 19 | Toilets**. Select the object named **WC 19**.

3. Look at the **Preview and Positioning** window and rotate the cabinet to be 270°. Click on the middle-right hotspot to designate the insertion point. Click on **OK** and place the toilet on the right-hand side wall, above the vanity.

Tub

Finally, we will place the bathtub in. It goes up against the bathroom west wall. To place the bathtub in, perform the following steps:

1. Double-click on the object icon in the **Toolbox** palette. Keep the layer set to **A-FLOR-FIXT**. In the upper-left pane of the **Object Default Settings** window, navigate to **ArchiCAD Library 19 | 22 Plumbing 19 | 22 40 00 Plumbing Fixtures 19 | Tubs**. Select the object named **Bathtub 19**.

2. Place the tub in the lower-left corner of the bathroom above the closet.

Bedrooms

Each of your bedrooms will need furniture and a bed. We will use the search feature this time to find what we need. Then, we will rotate our objects on screen.

Beds

1. Click on the object icon in the **Toolbox** palette. Go to the **Info Box** palette and change the layer to **A-FURN**. Click on the object button in the **Info Box** palette to open the **Object Default Settings** window.

2. At the upper-left part of the **Object Default Settings** window, click inside the search box. Enter the word Bed. Select the bed that you would like to use and place a bed in each bedroom.

3. The beds are not sized as per the standard US sizing convention. Use the following table to size your beds according to your needs:

      ◦ **Single**: 39" x 75"

      ◦ **Double**: 54" x 75"

      ◦ **Queen**: 60" x 78"

      ◦ **King**: 72" x 80"

The image of the **Preview and Positioning** window shown here is set for a queen size bed:

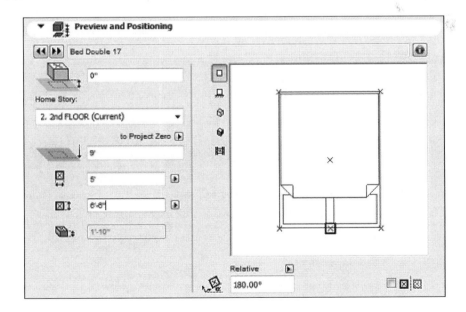

Furniture

Add the furniture that you would like to have in each bedroom, such as a wardrobe, night stand (end table), and desk with a chair, using the methods explained earlier. Refer to the following example diagram of a finished second floor:

Kitchen

Your kitchen will have casework, appliances, furniture, and a sink. Some of the casework goes on the floor and some goes on the wall.

The kitchen casework – base cabinets

Some of the cabinetry that goes on the floor contains drawers. Other cabinetry provides a container for appliances. The following steps will get you started with the base cabinets:

1. Open the first floor viewpoint and zoom in on the kitchen. Start the **Object** tool and open the **Object Default Settings** window. Set the layer to **A-CSWK**.

2. Navigate to **ArchiCAD Library 19 | 12 Furnishings 19 | 12 30 00 Casework 19**. Place the following casework items as instructed here:

    ° **Cabinet Base Corner L 19**: Place this in the upper-left corner of the kitchen

    ° **Cabinet Base MultiDrawer 19**: Place this in the upper-left corner, to the right of the corner cabinet

- ○ **Cabinet Base Double Door 19**: Place this on the wall, midway between the window and the dining room wall

3. Navigate to **ArchiCAD Library 19 | 11 Equipment | 11 33 00 Residential Equipment 19**. Place the following casework equipment items as instructed here:

   - ○ **Refrigerator Side by Side 19**: Place this in the lower-left corner of the kitchen, below the cabinet base corner object
   - ○ **Range Electric 03 19**: Place this on the top wall of the kitchen, between the cabinets
   - ○ **Cabinet Base Dishwasher 19**: Place this in the upper-right corner of the kitchen

4. Move the base cabinet with the sink up against the dishwasher. Move the electric range against the base cabinet with the sink. Then, move the multi-drawer cabinet against the electric range.

5. This will leave you with a gap at the bottom and right-hand side of the corner base cabinet. Select the corner base cabinet. Click on a black dot hotspot at the bottom of the cabinet and drag it down to the refrigerator. Do the same for the right-hand side of the cabinet and drag it over to snap to the multi-drawer cabinet.

6. Select all kitchen objects except the refrigerator and electric range. Open the selection settings window (*Ctrl + T*). Go to the **Parameters** section and make the following changes:

   - ○ For the cabinet, set the following values: **Toe Height** = 4"; **Toe Setback** = 4"
   - ○ For the counter set the following values: **Backsplash Height** = 4"
   - ○ Click on **OK**

7. Select the cabinet that has the sink (**Cabinet Base Double Door 19**) and open the object selection settings. Go to the **Parameters** section and turn on the **Left End Panel,** under the **End Panels** heading. Under the **2D Representation** parameter, change **Edge Visibility** in 2D to **Left**.

8. Select the multi-drawer cabinet (**Cabinet Base MultiDrawer 19**) and open the object selection settings. Go to the **Parameters** section and turn on the **Right End Panel,** under the **End Panels** heading. Under the **2D Representation** parameter, change **Edge Visibility** in 2D to **Right**.

9. Select the corner cabinet (**Cabinet Base Corner L 19**) and open the object selection settings. Go to the **Parameters** section and turn on the **Left End Panel,** under the **End Panels** heading. Under the **2D Representation** parameter, change **Edge Visibility** in 2D to **Left**.

10. Select the electric range and open the object selection settings. Go to the **Parameters** section and turn on the back splash.

Your plan view will look like the following diagram:

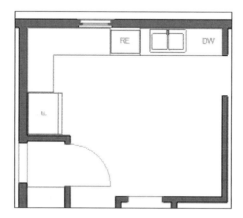

View the kitchen in 3D with a single floor marquee and then perform the following steps:

1. Click on the marquee tool icon in the **Toolbox** palette. From inside the **Info Box** palette, set the selection method to **Single Floor**.

2. Draw the marquee window around the perimeter of the kitchen.

3. Press the *F5* key. Your 3D view will look like the following diagram:

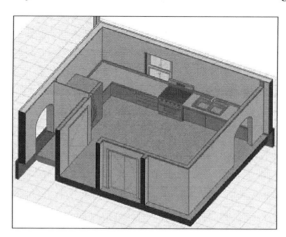

Notice how the window in the kitchen is too large for the case work.

4. Select the window; change the height to 3'-6" and width to 2'-0".

The kitchen casework – wall cabinets

The floor-based cabinetry is in! Now, you can install the wall cabinets by performing the following steps:

Navigate to **ArchiCAD Library 19 | 12 Furnishings 19 | 12 30 00 Casework 19**. Place the following casework items as instructed here:

*   **Cabinet Wall Corner L 19**: Change the width and length to 2'-2" and place it in the upper-left corner of the kitchen.

*   **Cabinet Wall Double Door 19**: Change the **Left End** parameter to **On**. Change the **Edge Visibility** parameter to **Left** and place it on the wall between the refrigerator and corner wall cabinet, snapped to the corner wall cabinet.

*   **Cabinet Wall Single Door 19**: Change the width to 1'-10". Turn on the **Right End Panel** parameter and change the **Edge Visibility** parameter under **2D Representation** to **Right**. Place it on the north wall, snapped to the right of the corner wall cabinet.

*   **Cabinet Wall Double Door 19**: Change the width to 2'-0". Turn on the **Left Panel** and **End Panel**. Change the **Edge Visibility** parameter under **2D Representation** to **Left** and place it on the wall at the upper-right corner, over the dishwasher.

*   **Cabinet Wall Double Door 19**: Change the width to 2'-2". Change the **b:** height to 6'-6" and **h:** height to 1'-0" (refer to the following screenshot of the **Info Box** palette). Turn on the **Left End Panel** and **Right End Panel**. Change the **Edge Visibility** parameter under **2D Representation** to **Both** and place it on the wall, centered over the electric range.

See the 3D view of the wall cabinets in the kitchen shown here:

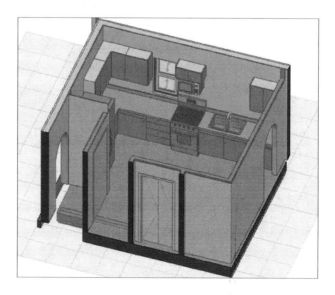

Dining room

You need to add a table and chairs with the **Object** tool by performing the following steps:

1. Double-click on the **Object** tool icon and set the layer to **A-FURN**.

2. Navigate to **ArchiCAD Library 19 | 12 Furnishings 19 | 12 58 00 Residential Furniture 19**. Place the following furniture items as instructed here:

    ° **Dining Table 01 19**: Change the width to 3'-0" and length to 5'-0". Place it in the center of the dining room. Rotate it so the short ends are north and south.

    ° **Chair 02 19**: Place it at the top and center of the dining room table. Use the **Mirror a Copy** command (*Ctrl + Shift + M*) to create a copy at the bottom of the table:

        a. Select the chair, press *Ctrl + Shift + M*, and click on the two mid points on the long 5' ends of the table to define the mirroring axis.

        b. Place four more chairs at the table; two each on the long sides of the table

c. Notice in the 2D plan view, the chairs appear to be above the table. Perform the steps shown in the following screenshot to graphically lift the table over the chairs. Select the table, right-click on it, and navigate to **Display Order | Bring to Front**:

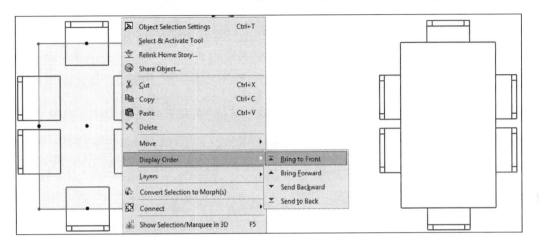

 The **Display Order** feature allows you to control the stacking priority of the elements in your view. In other words, it lets you control what's on top.

Living room

You need to create a fireplace, add tables, chairs, and sofa with the **Object** tool. Perform the following steps:

1. Navigate to **ArchiCAD Library 19 | 10 Specialties 19 | 10 30 00 Fireplaces and Stoves 19**. Select **Fireplace-Traditional 19**. Then, perform the following steps:

    a. In the **Preview and Positioning** pane, change the rotation to **270**. Change the insertion point to the lower-left corner.

    b. Change the **Surface** parameter **Cover** to **1 (04 | B Running Bond)**.

    c. Change the layer to **M-HVAC**.

    d. Click on **OK**. Place the fireplace on the east wall, 5'-6" from the inside of the bottom-right corner of the living room.

2. Navigate to **ArchiCAD Library 19 | 10 Specialties 19 | 10 30 00 Fireplaces and Stoves 19**. Select **Prefabricated Chimney Single 19**. Then, perform the following steps:

    a. Change the **Style** parameters **Top Cleaning Door** to **Off** and change **Top Cover** to **Off**.

    b. Change the height to 23', which will automatically change to **23'-3 19/64"**. It is fine so we can keep it.

    c. Change the **Surface** parameter of **Structure** to **1 (04 | B Running Bond)**.

    d. Click on **OK**. Then, place it on top of the exterior portion of the fireplace and center it.

3. Navigate to **ArchiCAD Library 19 | 12 Furnishings 19 | 12 50 00 Furniture 19 | 12 51 00 Office 19 | Tables-Office 19**. Then, perform the following steps:

    a. Set the layer to **A-FURN** and select **Desk 19**.

    b. Change the width to 3'-8".

    c. Place it against the wall at the top of the living room, against the vertical wall of the kitchen closet.

4. Navigate to **ArchiCAD Library 19 | 12 Furnishings 19 | 12 50 00 Furniture 19 | 12 52 00 Seating**.

    Place one sofa and four chairs of your choice in the living room; including a chair for the desk.

5. Navigate **to ArchiCAD Library 19 | 12 Furnishings 19 | 12 58 00 Residential Furniture 19 | Tables-Coffee 19**.

    Place one or more tables of your choice into the living room.

Laundry room

You need a washer, dryer, wall cabinets, and table in your laundry room. It is where clothes are cleaned, and a place to keep coats and cleaning supplies. Perform the following steps for the laundry room:

1. Navigate to **ArchiCAD Library 19** | **12 Furnishings 19** | **12 30 00 Casework 19** and set the layer to **A-CSWK**. Place the following casework items as instructed here:

   ○ **Cabinet Tall Double Door 19**: In the **Parameters** pane, under **End Panels**, turn on the **Right End Panel**. In the **2D Representation** pane, set the **Edge Visibility** in 2D to **Right**. Place it in the lower-left corner of the laundry room.

   ○ **(2) Cabinet Base MultiDrawer 19**: Place the first against the tall cabinet. Place the second to the right. Change the **End Panels** parameter on the second cabinet to show the right **End Panel** and set the **Edge Visibility** in the 2D parameter to **Right**.

   ○ **Cabinet Wall Triple Door 19**: In the **Preview and Positioning** pane, change the width to 4'-0" and height to 2'-0". Change the **End Panels** parameter to show the right end panel and set the **Edge Visibility** in the 2D parameter to **Right**. Place it to the right of the tall cabinet (over the top of the multi-drawer cabinets).

2. Use the search feature at the upper-left of the **Object Selection Settings** window to find and insert the following objects:

   ○ **Book Shelf 01 19**: Place it against the west wall and the second multi-drawer cabinet.

   ○ **Wall Mount Table 19**: Change the width to 3'-0" and depth to 1'-6". Place it against the east wall 6" above the door.

3. Use the search feature at the upper-left corner of **Object Selection Settings** window to find and insert the following objects:

   ○ **Washer 19**: In the **Parameters** pane under **Laundry Storage**, turn this **On**. Change the layer to **A-EQMT**. Place the washer in the upper right-hand corner of the laundry room 6" off the east wall and about 2" from the north wall.

     ○   **Dryer 19**: In the **Parameters** pane under **Laundry Storage**, turn this **On**. Place the dryer below the washer:

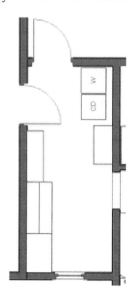

Basement

Your basement will have a work sink, water heater, furnace, and glass block windows. Use the search feature at the upper-left corner of the **Object Selection Settings** window to find and insert the following details:

- **Gas Furnace 19** and **Gas Water Heater 19**: Set the layer to **A-EQMT**. Place the furnace and water heater in the upper right-hand side corner of the basement. Start with a 6'-0" offset from the north wall and 12" from the east wall.

- **Mop Sink 19**: Set the layer to **A-FLOR-FIXT**. Under the **Parameters** pane, set the **Rim** to **On**. Change the **Tap style** to **Style 1** or something you prefer. Place the sink against the north wall, at the center.

- **W Glass Block Wall 19**: In the **Preview and Positioning** pane, set the width to 2'-8 5/8", height to 2'-5/8", and **Header to Story** -1 to 9'-0".

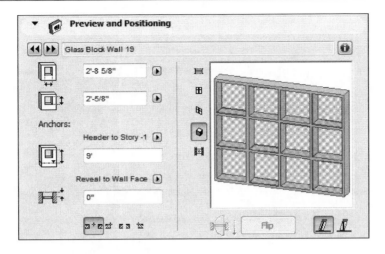

Then, perform the following steps:

1. In the **Parameters** pane under **Structural Dimensions**, enter the following:

    ◦ **Block Thickness:** 3 5/8"

    ◦ **Block Joint Thickness:** 3 3/8"

    ◦ **No. of Horiz. Blocks:** 4

    ◦ **No. of Vert. Blocks:** 3

    ◦ **Block Width:** 7 3/8"

    ◦ **Block Height:** 7 3/8".

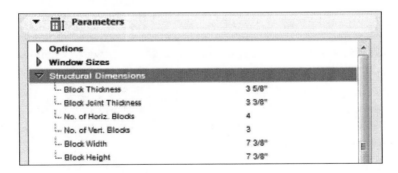

2. Place two glass block windows on the north wall, one on the west wall, and one on the east wall, as shown here:

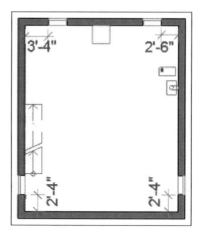

Mesh 2

If you try to look at your new basement windows in a 3D view, you will not see them because the mesh you created in the last chapter is blocking the view. The mesh is acting as the Earth that your house is sitting on. So, we need to move the Earth away from the windows to create a light well for the basement. To do this, we will create new points on the mesh. Each point on a mesh has an elevation height assigned to it. We will change the elevation heights on the new points we will create (after they are created):

1. Unhide the **L-SITE** layer and hide the **A-DIMS** and **A-ROOF** layers. Open the **Basement** viewpoint from the project map. Set the **Model View** option to **Detailing+No Fill (Document | Set Model view)**. Zoom in on the northwest corner of the house, at the kitchen window.

2. We will use the **Line** tool as a temporary guide to layout our point locations on the site mesh for an 18" wide light well. Click on the **Line** tool inside the **Toolbox** palette. Go to the **Info Box** palette and change the geometry method to **Chained** and set the layer to **L-SITE**.

3. Make the starting point of your line on the upper-left corner of the basement window. Notice that the cursor will change to a check mark to signify the endpoint snap. Before you make your second point, you will use the keyboard to create the first line segment by performing the following steps:

    a. Enter 18" (this will appear in the **Tracker** palette).

    b. Press the *Tab* key, enter 90, and press *Enter*.

    c. Hold the *Shift* key down and click on the upper-right corner of the window. This will make a perfect parallel line offset from the window.

    d. Let go of the *Shift* key and double-click on the upper-left corner of the window.

The following screenshot shows you what steps b and c look like:

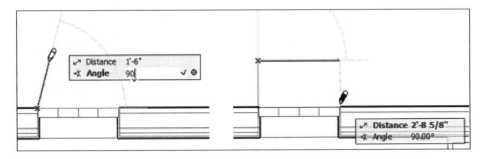

4. Create an offset copy of the lines you just drew and select all three lines. Click and hold on one of the lines; this will bring up the pet palette. Click on the **Offset** icon. Tap the *Ctrl* key to invoke the copy command. Bring your cursor to the inside of the widow well, type `1"`, and press *Enter*. You now have the lines that you need to guide us in creating the new mesh points.

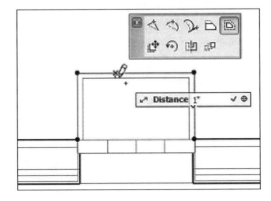

5. We have to do the same for the remaining basement windows. You can copy the lines you made, over to each window location but that can be a bit cumbersome. We will take this opportunity to create our first object:

    a. Select the six lines that you created and navigate to **File | Libraries and Objects | Save Selection As... | Object**.

    b. Enter the name for your object, such as `Window Well Guide Lines` and click on **Save**. You have created your first object!

    c. Start the **Object** command and set the layer to **L-SITE**. Your new object will be the current object, ready for insertion and if not, use the search feature. Place one at each window. Delete the original lines that were used to create your object and replace them with your new object.

6. Open the first floor viewpoint from the project map. Since the mesh was created on the first floor, this is where we need to edit the site mesh. Turn on the **Trace** feature (*Alt + F2*). Set the reference to **Below Current Story**. You will now see the lines you created on the basement level.

7. Activate the **Mesh** tool. Select the mesh. Go to the **Info Box** palette and set the geometry method to **Rectangular**. Zoom in on the northwest window. Click on an outside corner of the outermost corner of your guide object and then click on the opposite corner in the window. A dialog box will pop up. Click on the **Add New Points** radio button and then click on **OK**. Do the same for the innermost points. Refer to the following screenshot:

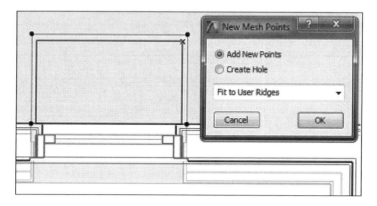

8. You have created the new points for one window well, now you need to change the elevation height in the four innermost points. Select the mesh. Click on one of the four inner points. The pet palette will appear. Click on the **Elevate Mesh Point** button. The **Mesh Point Height** dialog box will appear. Enter -2 and click on **OK**. Do this for the three other inside points. Switch to a 3D view (*F3*) and see your work.

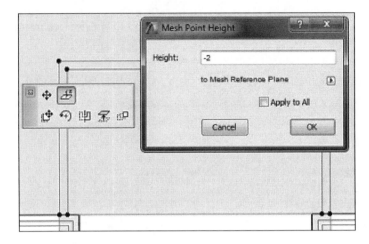

9. Repeat steps seven and eight for the other three window wells.

 Holding the *Shift* key down in ArchiCAD works like pressing the *F8* key in AutoCAD for Ortho mode and is similar to checking the Constrain box on the options bar in Revit.

See the 3D view of a window well in the following screenshot:

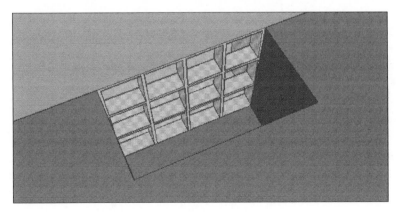

The Beam & Column tool

Your basement also needs to have a little bit of structural support that we did not complete in the first chapter. We need to put a beam down the center and single column near the center of the room. You can do so by performing the following steps:

1. Open the Basement viewpoint from the project map. Unhide the **A-BEAM** layer and start the **Beam** tool from the **Toolbox** palette. Click on the **Beam** icon in the **Info Box** palette to open the **Beam Default Settings** window. Change the beam type to **W8X31**. Change the beam height to 8" and change the reference line offset to the home story to 8'-8".

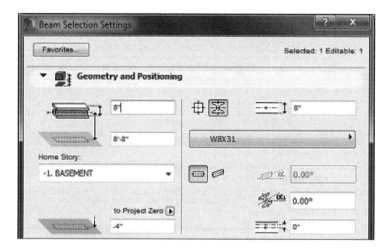

2. Draw the beam by making a start point at the west wall above the stairs and end point at the east wall:

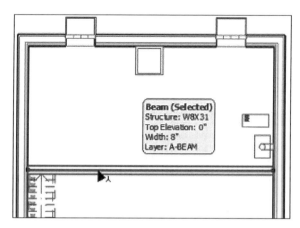

3. Go to the **Toolbox** palette and click on the **Column** tool. Open the **Column Selection Settings** window. Change the structure method to **Circular**. Change the value for **Building Material** to **41-30 20 | Steel**. Change the top offset to `-8"`. Refer to the following screenshot; place the column at the midpoint of the beam.

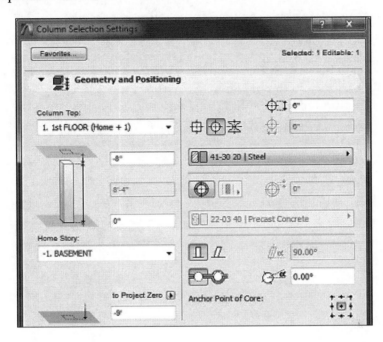

Draw a 2D marquee around the beam and press *F5* to view your work in 3D.

Garage

Your garage will need some heavy duty shelving. You can add this by performing the following step:

1. Use the search feature in the upper-left corner of the **Object Selection Settings** window to find and insert the following details:

    ○   **Book Shelf 02 19**: Set the layer to **A-CSWK**. In the **Preview and Positioning** pane, change the width to 5 ' - 7 ½". Under the **Parameters** pane, change the number of shelves to 5. Under **Structural Dimensions**, change the **Frame Width** to 2 ", and the **Bottom Shelf Height** to 4 ". Place two book shelves on the north wall of the garage, next to each other. They should both fit with about ¼" extra space.

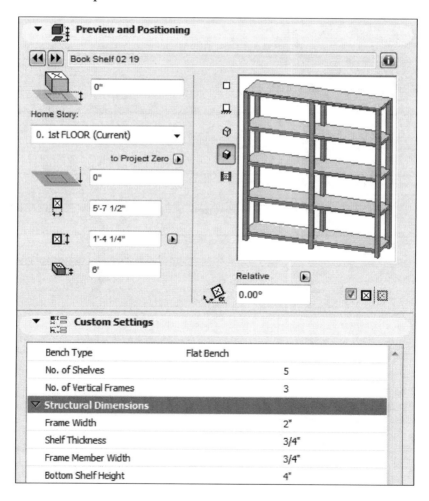

Annotation

Annotation is the text notes, labels, tags, and dimensions on your drawings. In ArchiCAD, the annotation adjusts its size based on your drawing scale. The following is a set of exercises for the main annotation types that you will use in ArchiCAD.

The Text tool

When you use the **Text** tool in ArchiCAD, you are essentially creating paragraphs. These paragraphs are referred to as **text blocks**. If you are an AutoCAD user, you will think of them as Mtext elements. You can format the text block as a whole or have differing formats within the same text block.

ArchiCAD uses the point system to measure the size of text (and also millimeters). The size is also blind to the drawing scale. In other words, it does not matter what scale your view is at; your text will always be the same point size. Another important thing to note is that a text's pen assignment has no effect on the printed thickness. But we can address that in a later chapter.

The following is an exercise to add text blocks to aid in the identification of elements on the first floor:

1. Open the first floor viewpoint from the project map and set the view scale to ¼"=1'-0". Zoom in on the living room.

2. Start the **Text** tool in the **Toolbox** palette. Look at the **Info Box** palette; it contains the standard formatting tools. Set the layer to **A-ANNO-TEXT**. Set the text height to 6.75. Change the arrowhead height to 4.

3. The next step is to define the width of the text block that you want to place by windowing the text block boundary with two cursor clicks (also referred to as a rubber band rectangle). Do this over the coffee table object:

   a. The text format palette will appear

   b. Type in COFFEE TABLE

   c. Finish the text block by clicking anywhere outside of the text editor or by pressing *Ctrl + Enter*

4. Create text blocks for other objects in the living and dining rooms, such as **WORK DESK** and **DINING ROOM TABLE**.

5. If your text block disappears after you have placed it on an object, you can find and select your text block with a window selection, change the display order property of your text block, and bring it to the front (right-click on it and then navigate to **Display Order | Bring to Front**).

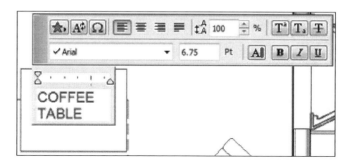

Edit existing text blocks

To edit a text block after it has been placed, perform the followings steps:

1. Activate the **Text** tool.
2. Select the text block with the arrow tool by clicking on an end, or midpoint, hot spot, or with a partial elements window.
3. Click inside the text block. The text editor will appear.

An alternative to these steps is to turn on the quick select feature and double-click on the text block. Then, the text editor will appear.

The Label tool

The **Label** tool is essentially the same as the text tool with a built-in leader function and a connection to the objects. You start by drawing the leader (pointer) with three clicks. Then, you draw the rubber band rectangle to define the width of the text block:

1. Zoom in on the kitchen.
2. Start the **Label** tool in the **Toolbox** palette. Go to the **Info Box** palette and set the layer to **A-ANNO-TEXT**. Set the text height to 6.75. Change the arrowhead height to 4.
3. Click your first of the three leader points on the dishwasher to define the label pointer and then draw the rectangle to define the text block width. Type in DISHWASHER.

4. Create text labels for the electric range and the refrigerator.

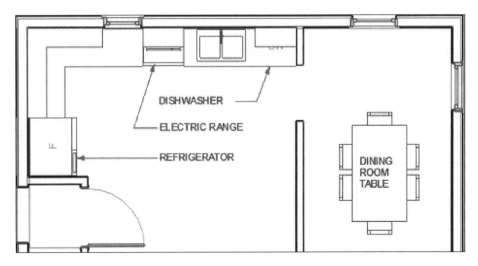

Go through the rest of the house and place the text blocks and labels where appropriate.

> Instead of grabbing the scroll bar on the **Info Box** palette with your cursor, hover over the **Info Box** palette and use the scroll wheel on your mouse to scroll through all the settings.

The Dimension tool

Dimensions are created by first defining the reference points to be dimensioned, then placing the dimension line. The **Dimension** tool has an associative function that connects to elements (via reference points) and it will change automatically when the elements are moved, although you can opt to make a dimension static via the **Info Box** palette or the **Dimension Selection Settings** window.

Dimensions are composed of five main components as shown here:

 a. Dimension point
 b. Dimension line
 c. Dimension unit
 d. Marker
 e. Witness line

The following screenshot is a graphic representation of the preceding dimension type list:

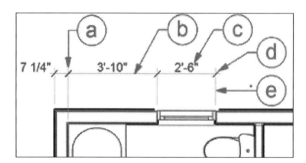

Creating your first dimension

Perform the following steps to create your first dimension:

1. Hide the **A-ANNO-NOTE** layer and unhide **A-DIMS**. Open the first floor viewpoint and zoom in on the kitchen, at the pantry closet.

2. Select the **Dimension** tool in the **Toolbox** palette. Go to the **Info Box** palette and change the font size to 6.75.

3. Click on the bottom two inside corners of the pantry closet. With each click, the pencil cursor will turn black to signify that you are at an endpoint. A successful click will leave behind a temporary symbol called a reference point that looks like a circle with a cross inside.

4. Double-click above and in-between your first two clicks to place the dimension line. This will bring up the hammer cursor; move it to where you want your dimension line. Click one more time to place the dimension line.

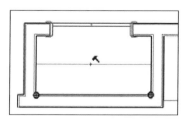

Go through the rest of the house and create dimensions. Refer to the wall modeling exercises in *Chapter 1, Project Setup and Modeling a Residential Project,* and place your dimensions according to those plan views.

Editing existing dimensions

To delete a dimension unit segment, hold the *Shift* key down, select a witness line, and then press the *Delete* key.

To add a dimension unit, select the dimension line, hold the *Ctrl* key down, and click on a point to be dimensioned. Or select the dimension, click on the dimension line and the pet palette will appear. Then, click on the **Insert/Merge Dimension Point** button and then click on a new point.

To edit the length of the witness line, select the dimension and click on the dimension line. The pet palette will appear. Then, click on the **Edit Length of witness line** button. Finally, click to place the new witness line endpoint.

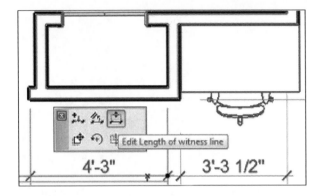

To override the text value with your own custom text, select the dimension unit text. Go to the **Info Box** palette and change **Measured Value** to **Custom Text**. Clear the box that has **<MeasuredValue>** and type in your own custom text.

Summary

In this chapter, you populated your house with furniture, casework, and plumbing fixtures. Along the way, you learned more about the dynamics of objects and their many changeable parameters. We took a step back into a little modeling, by modifying the mesh (landscape) object in order to accommodate for the low basement windows. You were introduced to the drafting tools, text tools, and **Dimension** tool.

We are ready to take the next step and learn how to control the look of your drawing elements and create construction documents that are referred to as layouts and also known as sheets!

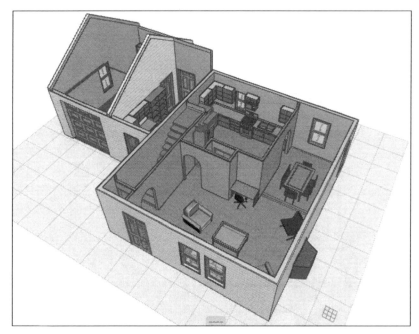

A screenshot of a 3D perspective view of the first floor

3
Documentation – A Residential Project

So far, we have focused on creating things. Now, it's time to focus on controlling how these things are displayed. In this chapter, you will learn about graphic controls and sheet setup. This is an extremely important topic to comprehend because understanding how to control your graphics is the key to good-quality drawings. The topics we will cover in this chapter are as follows:

- The project workflow
- View Map and Layout Book
- Layer Combinations
- Elevations & Sections
- Enlarged Plans
- Annotation
- Schedules

The project workflow

Once you understand the project workflow in ArchiCAD, you will know how to produce excellent drawings. Let's start with the fundamentals. The workflow in ArchiCAD can be divided into four steps, which are as follows:

1. **Creation**: modeling, objects, drafting, and annotation
2. **Graphic Control**: view control (layers, model view options, and view scale)
3. **Documentation**: sheets
4. **Collaboration**: printing and file exports

Take a look at the workflow legend, as follows:

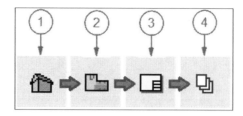

These steps are managed in ArchiCAD within the **Navigator** palette and the **Organizer** palette:

1. Navigate to **Project Map | Creation**, as shown in this screenshot:

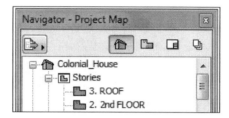

2. Go to **View Map | Graphics & Creation**, as shown in the following screenshot:

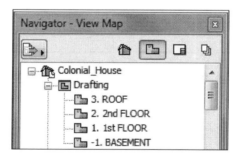

3. Then, navigate to **Layout Map | Documentation**, as shown in this screenshot:

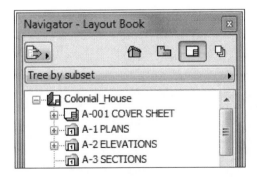

4. Next, go to **Publisher | Collaboration**, as shown here:

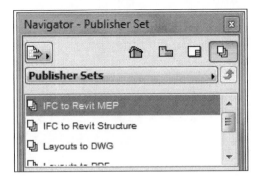

View Map

The view map is where you control the graphic display of your drawings. It is also where you organize all your drawing views. A well-configured view map will ensure a well-managed project.

When you open the view map for the first time, you will see several folders already present there. Each one has its own purpose and view settings. Each view contains settings for layer combination, scale, pen set, model view options, and more.

The View Map palette

The view map palette is where you create and manage your views. Before you begin creating views, you should be familiar with the features of the palette. Refer to the following legend that is used in the following screenshot:

a. **View Settings**

b. **Save Current View**

c. **New Folder**

d. **Clone a Folder**

e. **Delete**

f. **View ID & View Name**

g. **Layer Combination**

h. **Scale**

i. **Model View Options Combination**

Use the preceding list to match the items to the following screenshot:

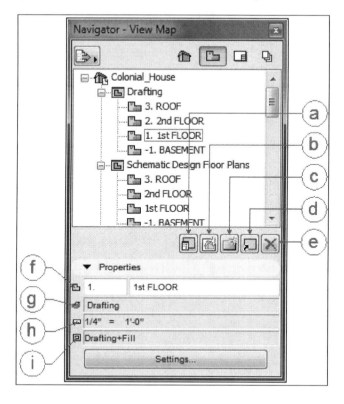

Project views

What you see in project map is the result of what just happens to be the current view setting, that is, model view option or layer combination. What you see in a **View Map** view is controlled and saved within that view's settings. When you open multiple views from within the project map, the view settings stay the same. As soon as you open a view from **View Map**, you will get the opened view's view settings.

Layer combinations

Click on the view map folder named **CD Floor Plans**. This is where your floor plans for the complete building are kept, which will be placed on your sheets. Open the first floor plan and notice that the layer combination assigned to the view is **Floor Plan**. There are a couple layers that need to be unhidden and saved to the **Floor Plan** layer combination, which can be done by performing the following steps:

1. Open the layer settings manager window (*Ctrl + L*).
2. Select the **Floor Plan** layer combination from the left pane.
3. From the right pane, unhide the **A-EQMT** and **A_FURN** layers.
4. Then, click on the **Update** button.
5. Finally, click on **OK**.

There will inevitably be annotation items overlapping each other, which shouldn't be the case. To improve the clarity of your drawings, go through the first floor, second floor, and basement views. Then, move the room tags, dimensions, and text away from each other.

To move the door tags, select the door, click on the hot spot at the center of the tag and drag it, as shown in the following screenshot. The same process works for the window tags.

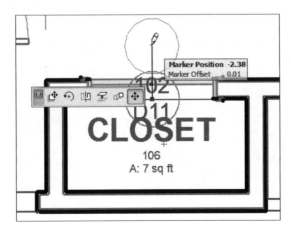

The ceiling plan views

You need to create a set of views for your ceiling plans to show the locations of your lights. Ceiling plans are graphically different from regular floor plans. Because of this, we need a separate set of views that have their own model views. This situation calls for the creation of a clone folder.

Cloning a folder

A clone folder is a complete copy of a viewpoint category from the project map, such as stories, sections, or elevations, with its own view settings saved. Here is how to create one for your ceiling plans:

1. From the view map, click on the **Clone a Folder** button. The **Clone a Folder** configuration window will appear.

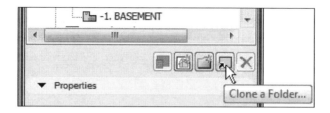

2. In the **Identification** panel, click on **Stories**, change the **Name** setting to **Custom** and enter CD Ceiling Plans in the text box. (CD stands for construction documents).

3. In the **General** panel, change **Layer Combination** to **Reflected Ceiling Plan**, set the Scale to 1/4" = 1'-0", the model view options to **Reflected Ceiling Plan**, and **Renovation Filter** to **04 New Construction**.

4. In the 2D/3D Documents panel, change the zooming to **Fit in window**.

5. Click on the **Clone** button.

6. Find the new folder in **View Map**; select it and drag it up to the position just below CD floor plans.

Layer preparation for reflected ceiling plans

There will be a couple of layers you will want to hide in the **Reflected Ceiling Plan** layer combination. Hide the following layers:

*   **A-ANNO-TEXT**
*   **A-DIMS**

Use the same process explained earlier in this chapter to update a layer combination.

Lighting

Light fixture objects in ArchiCAD are called Lamps. Now that you have your ceiling views ready, you can insert the lamp objects you need to light the inside of your house. They are as follows:

1. Open the second floor view under the **CD Ceiling Plans** folder.

2. Click on the **Lamp** tool on the **Toolbox** palette (located under the **More** panel). Click on the **Lamp** setting button on the **Info Box** palette.

3. Navigate to **26 Electrical 19 | 26 51 00 Interior Lighting 19** and select **Ceiling Lamp 19**.

4. Under the **Parameters** panel, change the Style to **Type 2**.

5. Under the **Parameters** panel, click on **Show Text**, and then enter the letter A in the text box.

6. Place one in the center of each bedroom.

The following screenshot shows the **Lamp** option:

Use the following list and plan the following drawings to finish placing light fixtures in the house:

- **Ceiling Lamp 19: Show Text** = A

  Bedrooms, Hallways, and Living Room

- **Chandelier 19: Show Text** = B

  Dining Room

- **Fluorescent Lamp 19** : **Show Text** = C1 (2' x 4 '), **C2** (2' x 2')
  Laundry Room (2' x 2'), Garage (2 'x 4), and Basement (2' x 4')

- **Halogen Recessed 19**: **Show Text** = D
  Kitchen

- **Recessed Spot 19**: **Show Text** = E
  Kitchen

- **Wall Lamp 19**: **Show Text** = F, **Style 9**
  Bathroom

The following screenshot shows the reflected ceiling plan of the basement:

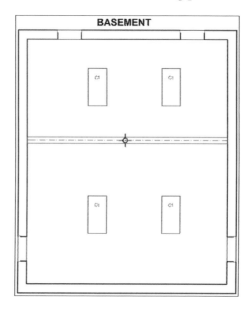

The following screenshot shows the reflected ceiling plan of the first floor:

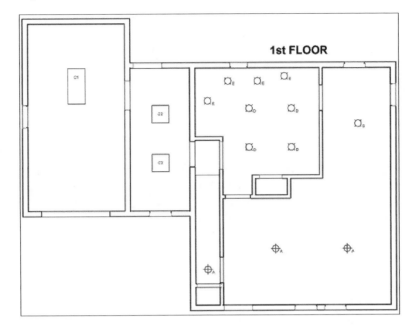

The following screenshot shows reflected ceiling plan of the second floor:

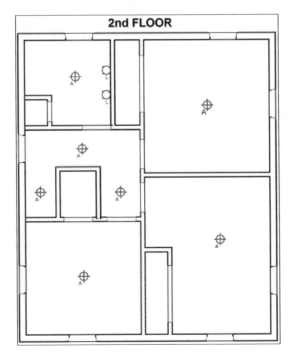

Light fixture schedule

To help us quantify the light fixtures to be installed in our house, we will create a very basic light fixture schedule, as follows:

1. Navigate to **Document menu | Schedules and Lists | Schedules | Scheme Settings**.

2. Then, the **Scheme Settings** window will appear. Click on the **New** button.

3. Enter LIGHT FIXTURE SCHEDULE in the **Name** box and leave the **ID** box empty.

4. Expand the **Criteria** panel and change the element type to **Lamp**.

5. Expand the **Fields** panel and click on the **Add...** button, the **Available Parameters** window will appear. Then, expand **General**, select **Library Part Name**, and click on the **Add** button. Then, select **Quantity** and click on the **Add** button.

6. You'll need a parameter that is not available by default the **Text** parameter:

   ○ Click on the delta symbol at the right of the **Add** button at the bottom of the **Scheme Settings** window and click on **Add Object Parameters**

   ○ Then, the **Additional Object Parameters** window will appear. Navigate to the **Ceiling Lamp 19.gsm** object under **ArchiCAD Library 19 | Object Library 19 26 Electrical 19 | 26 51 00 Interior Lighting 19**

   ○ Click on the txt variable in the **Available Parameters** pane, and click on the **Add** button to make it one of the selected parameters.

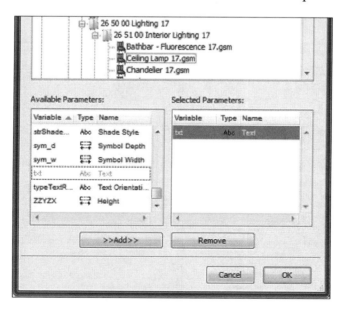

7. Under the **Fields** panel, sort the fields in the following order: **Text, Library Part Name**, and then **Quantity**, as shown in the following screenshot:

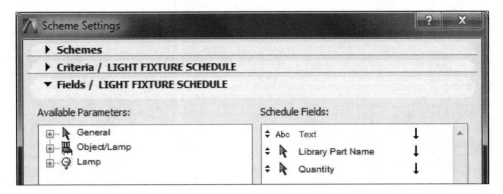

8. Click on **OK** and your schedule will appear. You can adjust the width of the columns by dragging the top of the column, just as with a spreadsheet program, as shown in the following screenshot:

LIGHT FIXTURE SCHEDULE		
Type	Library Part Name	Quantity
A	Ceiling Lamp 17	10
B	Chandelier 17	1
C1	Fluorescent Lamp 17	5
C2	Fluorescent Lamp 17	2
D	Halogen Recessed 17	4
E	Recessed Spot 17	4
L	Wall Lamp 17	2

Creating a schedule view

To create a view for the schedule, perform the following steps:

1. With the schedule still open, go to the view map and click on the **Save current view** button (if you have closed the schedule, open it from the project map under **Schedules | Element**).

2. The **Save View** window will appear. Change the scale to 1' = 1'-0". All the other settings can be kept as is. Your view is ready to be placed on a sheet.

Elevation views

Open one of the elevation views from **View Map** in the **CD Elevations** clone folder. You will see the basement level and mesh you created to represent the land. This would be fine if it were a section (except the mesh should be as deep as the basement), but we want the exterior elevation views to show what you would see if you were standing outside looking at the house. We will change the vertical setting on each of the elevations to remove the below ground view by performing the following steps:

1. Go to the View Map and open the CD Elevations clone folder. Right-click on the **EAST ELEVATION** view. Click on **Elevation Settings**. The **Elevation Selection Settings** window will appear.

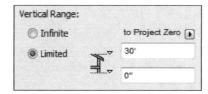

2. On the **General** panel, change the **Vertical Range** to **Limited**. In the top box, enter `30'` and click on **OK**.

3. Do the same for the other three elevation views in the `CD Elevations` clone folder.

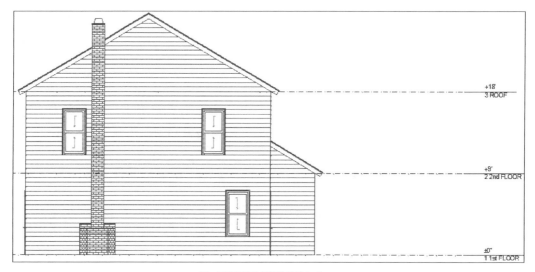

The EAST ELEVATION view

Elevation markers

Notice that on any of the plan views, the elevation markers are pretty far away from the exterior walls. Open the **1st Floor Plan** view and move each of the markers closer to the house. This will ensure that when you place the floor plan views on a sheet, the elevation tags will appear on the view without taking up too much space on the sheet and leaving too much white space on the view.

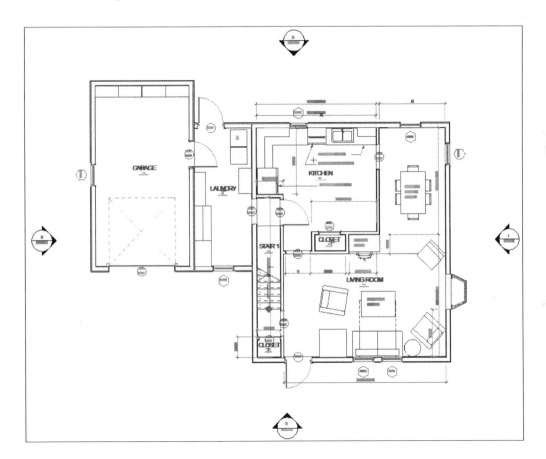

Enlarged plans

Some rooms in the house will require an enlarged scale drawing because there is too much stuff to fit in a one-fourth drawing. This is typical for rooms that have casework and plumbing fixtures. We will create enlarged plans for the kitchen and the bathroom.

The Detail tool

The **Detail** tool is what you use to draw the call-outs and markers on the plan. Each time you use it, it will create a new large-scale view under the `Details` folder in the project map. We will start our experience with the **Detail** tool by tweaking the detail default settings, as follows:

1. Double-click on the **Detail** tool icon in the **Toolbox** palette. This will open the **Detail Default Settings** window. Expand the **Marker** panel.

2. Go to the **Parameters** pane and expand **Marker Geometry**. Then, make the following changes:

    - **Editable Polygon Radius: On**
    - **Polygon Radius: 1'**
    - **Polygon Line Type: Dashed Long**

3. On the **Parameters** pane, expand **2D Representation**. Make the following changes to make the line weights a little bit bolder:

    - **Contour Pen: 7**
    - **Division Line Pen: 7**
    - **Marker Line Pen Color: 7**
    - **Marker Polygon Pen: 7**

The following screenshot shows some of the parameter settings for the **Detail** tool:

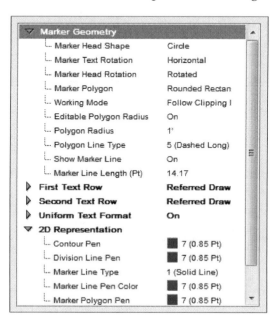

Enlarged plan views

We need to create new floor plan views of the areas that have many items in a small space and require more annotations. To do this effectively, we will use a scale that increases the size of the drawing elements. We will do this for three rooms: the kitchen, laundry room and bathroom.

The first thing you should do, however, is create a folder in the view map to put your new views into:

1. Go to the **View Map** and click on the **New Folder** button.
2. The **Create New Folder** dialog box will pop-up; enter `CD Enlarged Plans`.
3. Click on the **Create** button.
4. Drag the new folder into a position above **CD Elevations** and below **CD Demo Plans**.

Layer preparation for enlarged plans

The notes that you put onto the enlarged plans will need to be on their own layer, specifically for the enlarged plans, and the same is true for dimensions. Create a new layer called **A-ANNO-TEXT-024** and create another layer named **A-DIMS-024**. The number at the end of the name denotes the scale of the drawings that it will be used up on.

The layer combination for the enlarged plans will need to be modified in order to show casework, appliances, and plumbing fixtures, as follows:

1. First, open the **Layer Settings** manager (*Ctrl + L*).
2. Select the **Enlarged Plan** layer combination in the left pane.
3. Unhide the following layers in the left pane:
    ◦ **A-ANNO-TEXT-024**
    ◦ **A-DIMS-024**
    ◦ **A-CSWK**
    ◦ **A-EQMT**
    ◦ **A-FLOR-FIXT**
4. Hide the **A-ANNO-TEXT**, **A-MARK-SECT**, and **A-ROOF** layers.
5. Click on the **Update** button in the bottom-left corner. Then, click on **OK**. If you don't use the **Update** button, your changes will not be saved on layer combination.

Kitchen

There is an abundance of activity in the kitchen, so much so that we need a large-scale plan in order to legibly document it:

1. Open the **1st FLOOR PLAN** view from the `CD Floor Plans` clone folder in the view map. Then, zoom into the kitchen.

2. Start the **Detail** tool from the **Toolbox** palette. In the **Info Box** palette, change the ID to `P-101` and **Name** to `KITCHEN`.

3. You will be prompted (at the bottom of the screen) to enter the first corner of the rectangle detail polygon. Do that to define the boundary polygon of the enlarged plan view, as follows:

    a. Click on the top-left part outside the exterior wall of the kitchen.

    b. Click on the bottom-right corner of the kitchen, outside the kitchen wall.

4. Then, the hammer cursor will appear. Click on a blank area just outside the detail polygon that you created (to finish the command). The detail marker will be placed.

5. Open your new view, go to the project map, and open **P-101 KITCHEN** from under the **Details** folder; or open it by selecting the detail marker, right click on it, and select **Open Detail Drawing**.

6. After you open the view, click on the **Fit in the Window** button at the bottom of your view window.

7. Then, create a new view in the view map. From the **Navigator | View Map** palette, click the **Save current view** button and the **Save View** window will appear. Make the following changes:

    a. **Layer Combination: Enlarged Plan**.

    b. **Scale: 1/2" = 1'-0"**.

    c. **Model View Options: Construction Documents**.

    d. **Dimensions: Enlarged Scale**.

    e. Click on the **Create** button.

8. Drag your new view into the `CD Enlarged Plans` folder that you created.

9. Open the enlarged kitchen plan view, add notes and dimensions per the following screenshot, and use the **A-ANNO-TEXT-024** layer.

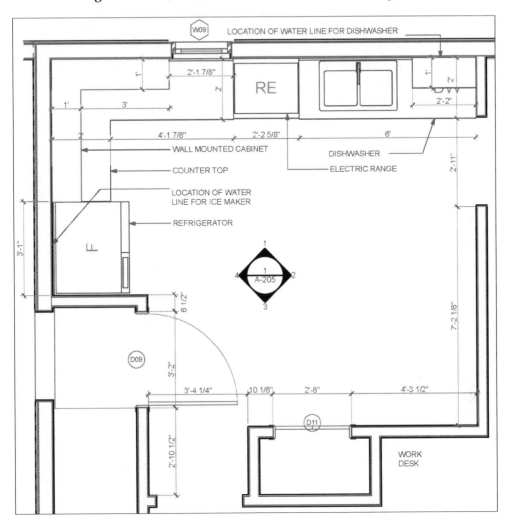

Laundry room

The laundry room contains casework and appliances. This room will also require an enlarged plan view, as follows:

1. Open the **1st FLOOR PLAN** view from the `CD Floor Plans` clone folder in the view map. Then, zoom into the kitchen.

2. Start the **Detail** tool from the **Toolbox** palette. In the **Info Box** palette, change the ID to `P-102` and **Name** to `LAUNDRY RM`.

3. Follow steps three through eight from the preceding kitchen exercise.

4. Open the enlarged laundry room view and add notes and dimensions as per the following screenshot; use layer **A-ANNO-TEXT-024**.

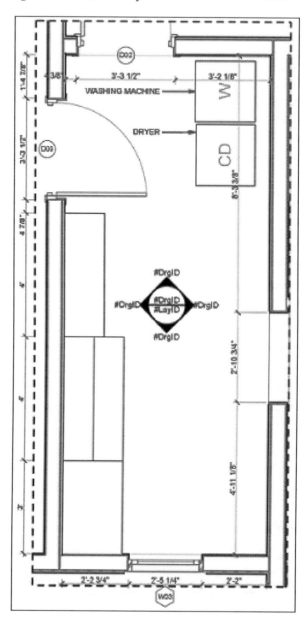

Bathroom

The bathroom is another room that requires a large-scale plan view to provide space for detailed documentation:

1. Open the **2nd FLOOR PLAN** view from the `CD Floor Plans` clone folder in the view map. Zoom into the bathroom.

2. Start the **Detail** tool from the **Toolbox** palette. In the **Info Box** palette, change the ID to `P-103` and **Name** to `BATH RM`.

3. Follow step three through eight from the kitchen exercise earlier.

4. Open the enlarged bath room plan view and add notes and dimensions as per the following screenshot; use layer **A-ANNO-TEXT-024**.

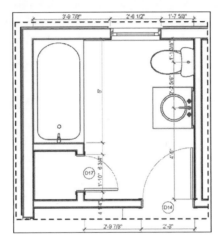

Sections

A section view shows a perpendicular view of something that has been cut vertically. When we speak of sections within construction documents, we usually mean building or wall sections. Building sections contain all the stories of a building, and a wall section is either just a single wall spanning all stories or one story.

Sections are created using the **Section** tool, placing the marker symbology on the plan view with two clicks. When you use the tool, it looks as if you are just creating a 2D symbol, but you are also creating a vertical slice view inside your model.

Layer preparation for sections

Open the **Layer Settings** window, select the **Sections** layer combination, and unhide the following layers:

- **A-CSWK**
- **A-ANNO-TEXT-024**

 Don't forget to click on the **Update** button!

Let's start by creating two building sections. These sections should be strategically located to show activity in your building that may not be described fully by a floor plan. Your first section will cut through the stair (north to south) and the second will cut through the center of the house at the kitchen pantry (east to west):

1. Go to **View Map** and click on the **1st FLOOR PLAN** view from under **CD Floor Plans**.

2. Double-click on the section tool icon to open the default settings. The **Section Default Settings** window will appear.

3. Make the following edits under the **General** panel and then click on **OK**:
    - **Reference ID**: S-101
    - **Name**: BUILDING SECTION – NORTH SOUTH

4. Enter the first node of your section line by clicking below the exterior wall below the front hall closest. Enter your second node above the kitchen (orthogonally) exterior wall. Then, the ArchiCAD **eyeball cursor** will appear. It will prompt you to click on one side of the section line to set the **view direction** and define the **horizontal range** (depth of view). Click on the right side of the section line past the dining room wall.

5. If the section line is not positioned well, you can move it to where it needs to go. You can change the length of the section line by dragging one of the hotspots on the section line at the marker. You can also change the reference ID and name of a section at any time via the Section Selection Settings (*Ctrl* + *T*) or from the **Info Box** palette.

6. Double-click on the section tool icon again to bring up the section default settings window. Make the following edits under the **General** panel and then click on **OK**:
    - **Reference ID**: S-102
    - **Name**: BUILDING SECTION – EAST WEST

7. Enter the first node of your section line to the left of the garage along with the kitchen pantry closet. Complete the section line by clicking on the opposite end of the house just outside the exterior wall. When the eyeball cursor appears, click anywhere above the section line and the north garage wall.

8. Select one of your new section lines. You should see where your horizontal range is (it is denoted by lines and a hotspot). You can drag that hotspot if you need to reposition the horizontal range. The following screenshot shows both section lines selected, showing their horizontal range and hotspots (many layers have been hidden for clarity).

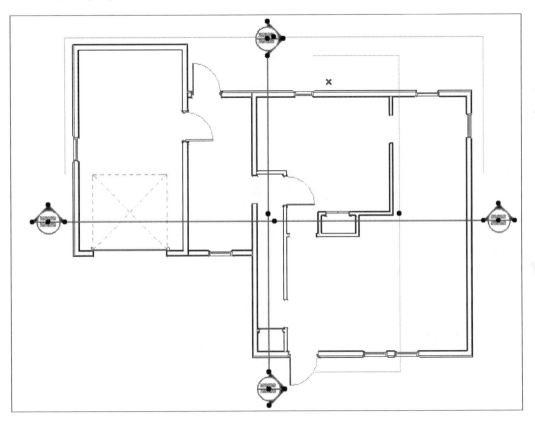

Notice that the information inside the markers is currently showing the values #DrgID and #LayID. As soon as the elevation views are placed on a layout, the marker values will change according to the layout they are placed on.

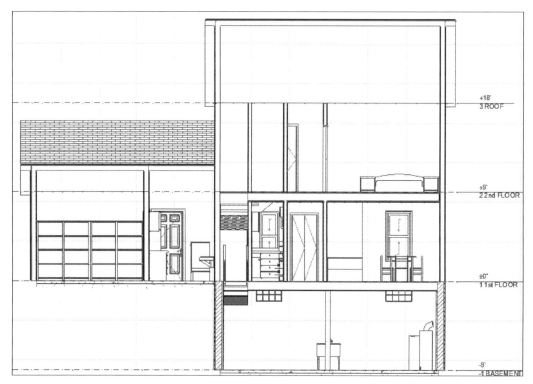

The building section looking North

Interior elevations

The **Interior Elevation** tool is different from the standard elevation tool because it is designed to recognize single story views. It is also designed to accommodate the multiple walls that any room may have. We will use it to create elevations of interior walls that have a significant amount of detail.

The next exercise will take you through the creation of interior elevations for the kitchen and laundry room because of all the casework in those rooms. In addition, you will create an elevation in the bathroom to sufficiently show the vanity and wall-mounted light fixtures.

The layer combination used for these views will be **Sections** by default. This is what we want, so we will keep it that way.

 The standard elevation markers and views were already created inside the project template we use to start this project with. Since this is a fairly simple building design, we will not need to create any additional standard elevations.

Kitchen

The abundance of vertical objects such as cabinets and appliances in the kitchen makes it a prime location for interior elevations. The following steps will show you how to easily create an interior elevation of each wall in the kitchen:

1. Go to **View Map**, open the **1st FLOOR PLAN** view from under **CD Floor Plans**, and zoom into the kitchen.

2. Click on the **Interior Elevation** tool icon. Then, go to the **Info Box** palette and check the following:
   ° Ensure that the construction method is set to **Rectangular**
   ° Change the interior elevation name in the **Name** box to **INTERIOR ELEVATION @ KITCHEN**
   ° Change the **Marker reference** to **The first placed drawing of the viewpoint**

3. The next step is to pick points in the plan view to define a rectangle along the extents of the room, to define the interior elevation limit line (depth of view). Then, a third point to define the standpoint distance (starting viewpoint), as follows:
   ° First, click on the rectangle, just beyond the walls of the kitchen, in the top-left corner; secondly, click on the opposite corner beyond the work desk.

○   Then, click inside the room so that the standpoint limit is well within the room. Refer to the following screenshot (some layers here have been hidden for clarity):

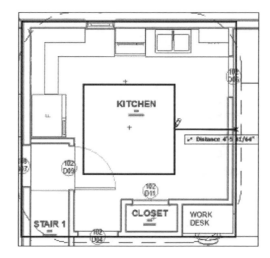

Go to the CD Interior Elevations folder in the view map and check out your four new interior elevations, as follows:

1. Select the **IE-01 INTERIOR ELEVATION @ KITCHEN** interior elevation group. Click on the **Settings** button at the bottom of the **View Map** palette.

2. Change the scale to 1/2" = 1'-0" (under the **General** panel).

3. Finally, open each interior elevation to see how it worked!

Adding kitchen annotations

Add notes and dimensions to each of your new kitchen elevations. Use the following diagram as a guide:

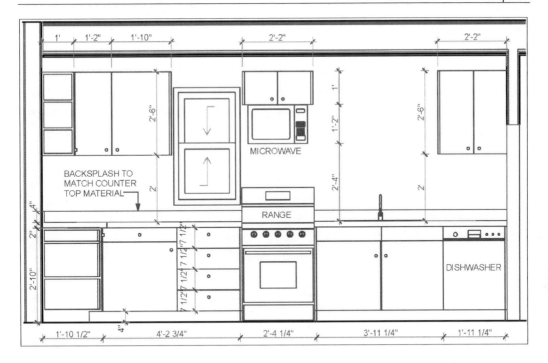

Laundry room

The laundry room will need interior elevations because it has casework and appliances. The following steps will help you create interior elevations for the laundry room:

1. Go to **View Map** and open the **1st FLOOR PLAN** view from under **CD Floor Plans**. Then, zoom into the laundry room.

2. Click on the **Interior Elevation** tool icon. Go to the **Info Box** palette and do the following:

    °   Change the interior elevation name in the **Name** box to INTERIOR ELEVATION @ LAUNDRY RM

    °   Change **Marker reference** to **The first placed drawing of the viewpoint**

3. Define the interior elevation limit line and standpoint distance. This time, we will use the magic wand to create the limit line, as follows:

   ° Hold your *Spacebar* down and click inside the laundry room.

   ° Then, click inside the room so that the standpoint limit is well within the room to clear the washer and dryer. Refer to the following image:

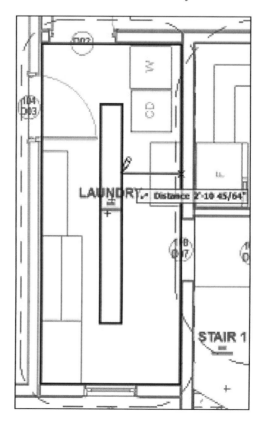

Go to the CD Interior Elevations folder in the view map elevations and then perform the following steps:

1. Select the **IE-02 INTERIOR ELEVATION @ LAUNDRY RM** interior elevation group and click on the **Settings** button at the bottom of the **View Map** palette.

2. Change the scale to 1/2" = 1'-0" (under the **General** panel).

Adding elevation annotations

Add notes and dimensions to each of your new laundry room elevations. Use the following image as a guide:

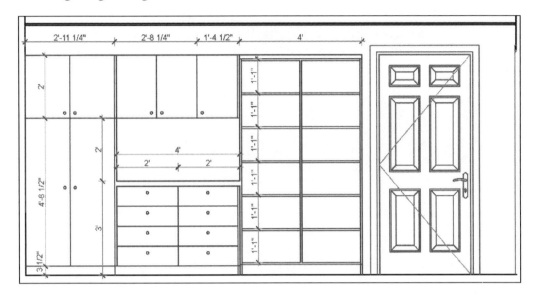

Bathroom

For the bathroom, we only need one elevation, so we will use the **Single** construction method:

1. Go to the view map and open the **2nd FLOOR PLAN** view from under **CD Floor Plans**. Then, zoom into the bathroom.

2. Click on the **Interior Elevation** tool icon. Go to the **Info Box** palette and do as follows:

    o   Set the construction method to **Single**

    o   Change the interior elevation name in the **Name** box to INTERIOR ELEVATION @ BATH RM

    o   Change the **Marker reference** to **The first placed drawing of the viewpoint**

3. Define the interior elevation limit line and the standpoint distance and then perform the following steps:

   ○ Click on the top-right corner of the room and then click on the bottom-right corner.

   ○ Then, click inside the room so that the standpoint limit is well within the room to clear the toilet and vanity. Refer to the following image:

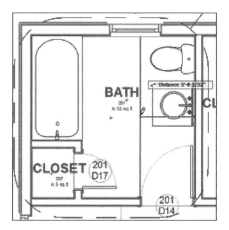

Go to the `CD Interior Elevations` folder in the view map elevations.

1. Select the **IE-03 INTERIOR ELEVATION @ KITCHEN** interior elevation group and click on the **Settings** button at the bottom of the **View Map** palette.

2. Change the scale to `1/2" = 1'-0"` (under the **General** panel).

Bathroom annotations

Add notes and dimensions to each of your new kitchen elevations. Use the following screenshot as a guide:

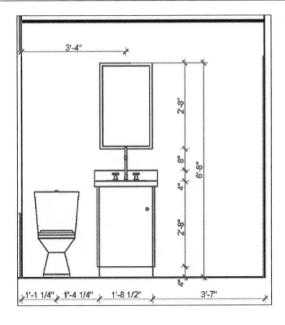

Layout Book

The **Layout Book** palette is where you create and manage your sheets. Before you begin creating sheets, you should be familiar with the features of the palette. Refer to the following list and legend:

- a. Settings
- b. New Layout
- c. New Master Layout
- d. New Subset
- e. Update
- f. Delete
- g. Layout ID (Sheet number) & Sheet Name of selected sheet
- h. Master Layout of selected sheet
- i. Size of selected sheet

Here is a screenshot of the **Layout Book** palette; refer to the preceding alphabetic list:

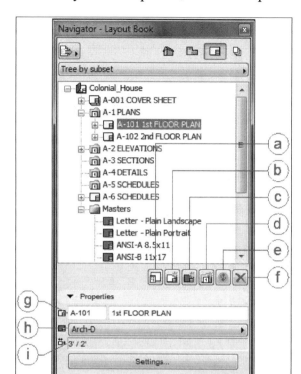

Master Layout

A **Master Layout** is a title block. A project can have multiple master layouts and they are managed via the **Layout Book** palette. Master layouts work similar to an Xref or block in AutoCAD. When you make a change to a master, it automatically updates all the instances of where that master is used. And master layouts are similar to how a title block family works in Revit but editing a master is easier than changing a family in Revit. Masters have their own view environment within the project, which allows you to edit just like a regular drawing view.

For our project, we will be using the Arch-D master. Arch-D is a 24" x 3" sheet and a standard size for small- to medium-size buildings.

 If you open a layout (sheet) and the title block lines and text do not appear, go to the **View** pull-down menu and then navigate to **On-Screen View Options | Master Items onto Layout**.

Drawings (views onto layouts)

A view placed on a layout is referred to as a drawing. Go to the **Toolbox** palette under **Document** and there, you will find the **Drawing** tool. Open the default settings window and look around to get familiar with what's there.

New layouts (sheets)

The template file that we used to create this project did not provide a sheet for the basement story views. We will start working in the layout book by creating a new sheet for the basement plans.

Floor plan sheets

The floor plan drawings are usually the main focus of any project, so we will start with the floor plans:

1. Go to the **Layout Book** palette and click on the **A-1 PLANS** subset icon. Click on the **New Layout** button. The **Create New Layout** window will appear and perform the following steps:

    a. Under **Layout Identification**, select the **Custom ID** radio button and enter A-100.

    b. In the **Name** box, enter BASEMENT PLAN.

    c. Click on the **Create** button.

2. The sheet will be placed under the **2nd FLOOR PLAN** sheet in the view map. Select your new basement plan sheet and drag it up above the **1st FLOOR PLAN** sheet, as shown in the following screenshot:

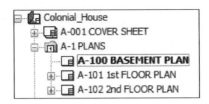

To place drawing views on your layouts, perform the following steps:

1. Open the layout that you created, **A-100 BASEMENT PLAN**, and change the **Navigator** palette to **View Map**. Go to **CD Floor Plans** and drag the **-1. BASEMENT** view on the sheet. Then, place it on the right-hand side.

2. Click on the **View Map** button on the **Navigator** palette, go to the CD Ceiling Plans clone folder, and drag the **-1. BASEMENT** view on the sheet. Place it to the left of the first plan that you placed.

3. Open the **A-101 1st FLOOR PLAN** layout (under **A-1 PLANS**). Select the floor plan view that is already on the layout and move it to the right to make room for the ceiling plan.

4. Change the **Navigator** palette to the view map and open the CD Ceiling Plans folder. Drag the **1. 1st FLOOR** view from that folder on to the sheet. Place it to the left of the floor plan already on the sheet.

5. Open the **A-102 2nd FLOOR PLAN** layout. Select the floor plan view that is already on the sheet and move it to the right to make room for the ceiling plan.

6. Change the **Navigator** palette to the view map. Open the CD Ceiling Plans folder. Drag the **2. 2nd FLOOR** view from that folder on the layout. Place it to the left of the floor plan, which is already there.

Creating sheets for sections

To create a sheet for your sections, perform the following steps:

1. Go to the **Layout Book** palette and click on the **A-3 SECTIONS** subset icon. Click on the **New Layout** button. The **Create New Layout** window will appear. Then perform the following steps:

    a. Under **Layout Identification**, select the **Custom ID** radio button and enter A-301.

    b. In the **Name** box, enter **SECTIONS**.

    c. Click on the **Create** button.

2. Open the **A-301 SECTIONS** layout.

3. Go to the view map and drag-and-drop the two section views under **CD Sections** onto the layout.

 If your new layout appears at the bottom of all the layouts instead of where you want it, then just drag it to the appropriate subset folder.

Creating a sheet for details

Create a sheet for your details (enlarged plans) by performing the following steps:

1. Go to the **Layout Book** palette and click on the **A-4 DETAILS** subset icon. Click on the **New Layout** button. The **Create New Layout** window will appear and then perform the following steps:

    a. Under **Layout Identification**, select the **Custom ID** radio button and enter A-401.

    b. In the **Name** box, enter DETAILS.

    c. Click on the **Create** button.

2. Then, open the **A-401 DETAILS** layout.

3. Go to the view map and drag and drop each of the detail views under **CD Enlarged Plans** onto the layout.

Creating a sheet for interior elevations

Here, we will create a sheet for the interior elevation views using the following steps:

1. Right click on the A-2 ELEVATIONS layout folder from the **Layout Book** palette. Select **Create New Layout** from the right-click menu.

2. Enter INTERIOR ELEVATIONS in the **Name** box.

3. Then, switch to the view map.

4. Drag-and-drop the first interior elevation group onto the layout (all four interior elevations should appear on the layout).

5. Drag-and-drop the second interior elevation group onto the layout.

6. Finally, drag-and-drop the single bathroom interior elevation onto the layout.

Schedules sheet

Let's create a sheet for your schedules using the following steps:

1. Go to the **Layout Book** palette and click on the **A-5 SCHEDULES** subset icon. Click on the **New Layout** button. The **Create New Layout** window will appear. Then perform the following steps:

    a. Under **Layout Identification**, select the **Custom ID** radio button and enter A-501.

    b. In the **Name** box, enter SCHEDULES.

    c. Click on the **Create** button.

2. Open the **A-501 SCHEDULES** layout from the **Layout Book** palette. Switch to the view map and drag-and-drop the **LIGHT FIXTURE SCHEDULE** you created onto the sheet.

3. Notice that the schedule drawing was given a title bar and scale. You do not need a title on a schedule because it already has a title built into it. So, we will turn off the title bar with the following steps:

   a. Select the schedule on the sheet and press *Ctrl + T* to open the **Drawing Selection Settings** window.

   b. Go to the **Title** panel at the bottom. Change the title from **NCS Drawing Title** to **No Title**, and click on **OK**.

4. Place the other two schedules in the view map, **Door Schedule**, and **Window Schedule** onto the **A-501 SCHEDULES** layout. Follow step 2 to turn off their title bars as well.

[You can change the drawing default settings to use no title before placing the schedules views on the layout. You just need to remember to set it back to your standard title when you are done.]

Printing

You will learn that printing in ArchiCAD offers you a robust array of features. There are three ways in which you can print something from ArchiCAD. You can use the Print command, Plot command, or Publisher using a preconfigured publisher set. The Print command is typically used for your small format printing, such as 1" x 17" and smaller. The Plot command is typically used for everything larger than 1" x 17".

You can print a view, single sheet, or multiple sheets at a time or just the area within a marquee in a view.

Setting up to print or plot

Before you plot anything on a large-format printer (known as a plotter), you need to configure the **plot setup** for your plotter type— the connection port/path, sheet size, and location of your spool folder, as follows:

1. Go to the **File** menu and select **Plot Setup....** The **Plot Setup** window will appear.

2. Select the manufacturer (make) of your plotter from the top drop-down list. Then, select the model number from the second drop-down list.

    If your plotter make and model does not appear in the list, use **Hewlett-Packard, HP Design Jet 650C**.

3. Set your paper size category and size designation.

4. Click on the **Setup** button under the **Connection** heading and set it to connect to your plotter.

5. Click on the **Select** button under the **Spool Folder** heading and set it to a location where you would want to save your plot files.

6. Click on **OK**.

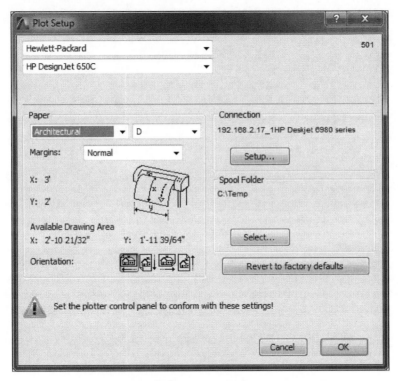

A plot setup example

Page setup

Setting up for printing using a small-format printer with the `Print` command is a bit simpler than the plot setup. It assigns the printer, paper size and orientation:

1. Go to the **File** menu and select **Page Setup**. The Page Setup window will appear.

2. Select your printer from the **Name** list. If the printer you want to use is not in the list, then click on the **Network** button and browse connect to a new printer.

3. Then, set your paper size and orientation.

4. Click on **OK**.

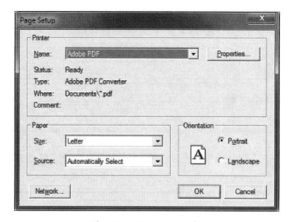

The page setup example

Plotting a layout

For our first printing task, let's plot a single full-size sheet with the `Plot` command, as follows:

1. Open the **A-101 1st FLOOR PLAN** layout from the **Layout Book** palette.

2. Go to the **File** menu and click on **Plot...** The **Plot Layout** window will open.

3. Under the **Destination** heading, select **Plotter**.

4. Under the **Source** heading, select **Active Layout**.

5. Under the **Resize** heading, select **Custom**. If the value is less than 100 percent, then don't worry; it is acceptable because there is a margin to accommodate.

6. Under **Margin Options**, select **Use Plotter Margin**.

7. Under **Plot with…** you can select whatever is appropriate for your plotter and needs, such as **Color**, **Grayscale**, or **Black and White**.

8. Under the **Arrangement** heading, you will see a blue rectangle representing the layout graphics inside a black rectangle that represents the paper's edge.

9. Finally, click on the **Plot** button.

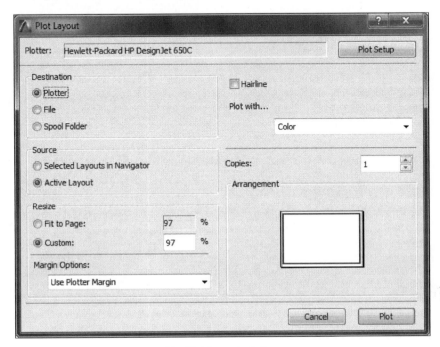

The Plot Layout window

Printing a layout (to fit)

Now, let's print that same layout to a small format printer, scaled to fit within a letter size print:

1. Keep the same layout open from the preceding exercise. Go to the **File** menu and select **Print** or press the key combination of *Ctrl + P*. The **Print Layout** window will open.

2. The printer will be identified at the top of the window. If it is incorrect, then click on the **Page Setup** button and assign the correct printer.

3. Under the **Source** heading, select **Entire Layout**.

4. Under the **Size** heading, select **Fit to Page**.

5. Under the **Arrangement** heading, the blue rectangle should fit inside the black rectangle (there should only be one black rectangle).

6. Compare the other settings to the following screenshot.

7. Finally, click on the **Print** button.

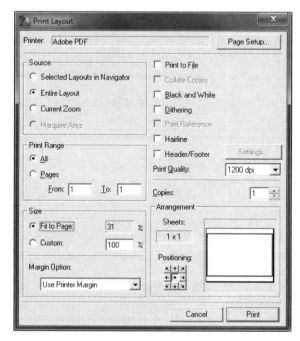

The Print Layout window

Printing multiple drawings

Printing multiple layouts or sets of drawings is best handled via the Publisher. Refer to *Chapter 8, Work Sharing with ArchiCAD*, to learn how to create a Publisher set.

Exporting files

ArchiCAD can export to a multitude of different file formats. The most commonly used formats are PDF and DWG. The simplest method is to use the **Save As** command from the **File** menu:

1. Open any layout or view.

2. Go to the **File** menu and select **Save as.**

3. At the bottom of the **Save as** window, click on the button next to the **Save as Type** option. You will see that there are seven types of ArchiCAD formats and 12 other file formats:

   ° The top four formats in the list will export the entire project file with views, layouts, and so on.

   ° The remaining formats in the list will save only the current view or layout. If you need to export to 3D, you will need to have a 3D view open when you export your file.

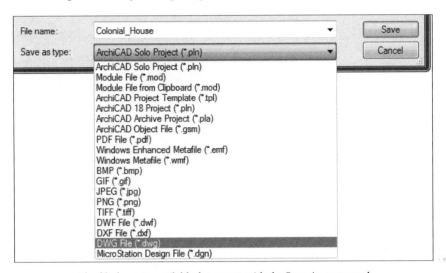

The file formats available for export with the Save As command

 In addition to the **Save As** method, PDF files can also be created via the Print command. You need to have a PDF printer installed on your computer, such as Adobe PDF or another PDF creation program.

Exporting multiple files

Exporting multiple files at a time is best handled by the Publisher. Refer to *Chapter 8, Work Sharing with ArchiCAD*, to learn how to export multiple files with a publisher set.

Summary

In this chapter, you learned about the project workflow of ArchiCAD as it relates to the documentation. You set up views with the view map and created sheets in the **Layout Book** palette. You also configured layer combinations and learned about schedules. All of this fits into the overall project workflow in ArchiCAD. The next phase in our workflow adventure takes us into the world of printing and collaboration. This is where the Publisher (a part of the **Navigator** palette) comes into play.

4
Project Setup and Modeling Part 1 – A Healthcare Building Project

Here we go; it is now time to start our healthcare building! Aside from being bigger than the residential project that we made, this project will have more views, sheets, and linked files. This chapter will cover the initial project setup and creation of the core and shell model elements. The following is a list of the main topics covered in this chapter:

- Project settings
- Hotlinks and Xrefs (abbreviation for external reference file)
- Columns and column grids
- Exterior walls
- Floors and roofs

Project setup

You will want to create a few file folders on your computer (or network server) to contain the multiple files used in your new project with the help of the following steps:

1. Find a good location for your top-level project folder and name the folder `Commercial_Project.`

2. Open the new folder and create the following sub folders for exporting PDF and DWG files and a folder for your custom objects and files to be used as Xrefs:

    ◦ **Export**
    ◦ **Library**
    ◦ **Xref**

Notice the underscore in the project folder name just outlined. It is always a good idea to avoid using spaces in folder names. This lends itself to avoiding broken hyperlinks when you or anyone else needs to send project folder paths to other users.

You will create your core and shell model with ArchiCAD's commercial project template. The template will have all the basic stuff you need to get started. Open ArchiCAD and then perform the following steps:

1. The **Start ArchiCAD** dialog box will appear. Select **Create a New Project** radio button at the top.

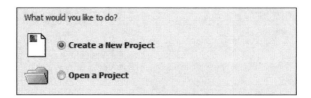

2. Select the **Use a Template** radio button under **Set up Project Settings.**
3. Then, select **ArchiCAD 19 Commercial Template.tpl** from the drop down list.

4. Next, click on **New**. This will open a blank project file.
5. Go to the **File** menu and click on **Save**.
6. Browse to your new project folder—Commercial_Project. Name your file Commercial_Bldg-Shell.
7. Finally, click on **Save**.

Project settings

We are going to create a building with eight stories, which includes a story for the roof, stair bulkhead, and basement. The template that we just opened only has two storeys so we need to add six more.

Stories

Perform the following steps to build stories:

1. On the **Navigator** palette, select the **Project Map** icon.

2. Right click on **Stories** and (**Navigator** palette) select **Story Settings**.

3. In the **Story Settings** window, click on **1st FLOOR**. Then, click on the **Insert Below** button. Enter the name **Ground** in the **Name** box. Enter 12' in the **Height to Next** box.

4. Click on **Ground**. Then, click on the **Insert Below** button. Enter the name BASEMENT in the **Name** box and then enter 10 in the **Height to Next** box.

5. Click on **2nd FLOOR**. Then, click on the **Insert Above** button. Enter the name 3rd Floor in the **Name** box and 12' in the **Height to Next** box.

6. Click on **3rd FLOOR**. Click on the **Insert Above** button. Enter the name 4th Floor in the **Name** box. Enter 12' into the **Height to Next** box.

7. Then, click on **4th FLOOR**. Click on the **Insert Above** button. Enter the name ROOF in the **Name** box and 10' in the **Height to Next** box.

8. Then, click on **ROOF**. Click on the **Insert Above** button. Enter the name STAIR BULKHEAD in the **Name** box and 10' in the **Height to Next** box.

9. Finally, click on **OK**.

Your list of stories should now look similar to the stories shown in the following **Story Settings** window:

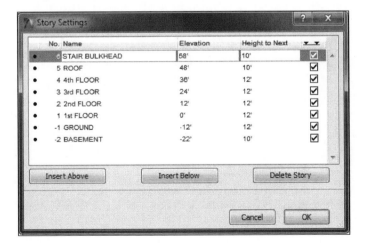

Units

On the menu bar, navigate to **Options | Project Preferences | Working Units** and then make sure that the following values are set for the parameters listed here:

- **Model Units** is **feet & fractional inches**
- **Fractions** is **1/64**
- **Layout Units** is **1/64**
- **Angle Unit** is **decimal degrees**
- **Decimals** is **2**

Hotlinks

The hotlink project will be comprised of multiple ArchiCAD model files. These files will be "hotlinked" into each other. These are also referred to as **hotlink modules**. This means that they will be embedded inside each other with a connection to the original file, which can be updated at any time.

When to split your project model and when not to

There is no exact formula for when you need to split your project models up. The answer lies within the combination of key factors such as building size and the number of ArchiCAD users that will be working in the models and your computer resources. Start with as few models that you feel necessary and then split when you see a strong need for it.

Here are some reasons as to why we split the project into multiple ArchiCAD files:

- **Size**: When model files get big in size (bytes), they start to slow down. I guess you could say that computer resources cannot keep up with the demands of a BIM project model of any significant size. One day, this may no longer be the case. But for now, BIM is still an untamed animal for computer resources.

- **Teamwork**: There is a limit to how many people can be in a single model without the workflow slowing down and experiencing delays. This could be visualized in the form of a traffic jam.

- **Crash protection**: If one model crashes or is corrupted, you will have a different model to work in while the other one gets fixed.

However, to be clear from a model management standpoint, the fewer models in a project, the better. Here are some reasons not to split your project models:

- **Attribute management**: Layers are model specific and if you are not careful, you will end up with way more layers than you will need. Composite structures can get out of whack. A composite can have the same name in two different models but can be totally different in structure. The same applies with profiles, line types, fill patterns, and materials. This only happens in big and long-running projects but it is something to always be aware of.

- **Jumping in and out of models to work in the same physical area of the building**: Each time you do this, you need to update the hotlinks. In other words, updating the model in one file; then going over to the other file, which has the first model linked; and then updating the link.

Importing and exporting attribute settings

You can export your attribute settings to a file (.aat) for importing it in another project file, or to use it as a backup for your current project.

To export your attribute settings, do as follows:

1. Go to the **Options** menu and navigate to **Element Attributes | Attribute Manager...**.
2. Select an attribute category.
3. Select the attributes in the left pane.
4. Click on the **Append** button to add to the left pane.
5. Finally, click on the **Save** button.

To import attribute settings, do as follows:

1. Open the attribute manager and click on the **Open** button.
2. Browse the attribute file and click on **Open**.

Xrefs

Xrefs originated in the Autodesk AutoCAD CAD program. They are AutoCAD DWG files externally referenced (linked) into each other without actually being embedded. We will use floor plan Xrefs as a guide to trace over for locating the exterior walls and columns.

You will need to download the DWG files that will be used as Xrefs in our project. Go to http://www.packtpub.com and create a new user account (if you have not already done so). Go to your Packt account, register this book, and download the files associated with this book.

Attaching Xrefs

The first thing to learn about Xrefs is how to attach them. If you are an AutoCAD user, this should be a familiar process. Let's attach the Xref for the first floor:

1. Open the **1st FLOOR** viewpoint from the project map.

2. Go to the **File** menu and navigate to **External Content | Attach Xref....**

3. After the Attach Xref window will opens, browse the file `Xref_Bldg-Shell-01.dwg`.

4. Set the reference type to **Overlay**.

5. Un-check the box for **Insertion Point, Scale**, and **Rotation**.

6. Set the **Anchor Point** to **Drawing's own origin**.

7. Place on **Story 1. 1st FLOOR**.

8. Then set **Translator** to **02 For editable import**.

9. Next, click on **Attach**.

10. Then, the **DWG/DXF Partial Open** window will appear. This gives you the opportunity to deselect any layer in the Xref that you do not want to import. In your case, you can keep them all and click on **OK**.

11. The Xref may take a few moments to appear. Zoom out to view the whole plan.

12. Open the other story viewpoints and repeat the preceding steps for each story. Be sure that the **Place on Story** setting matches the story you are attaching.

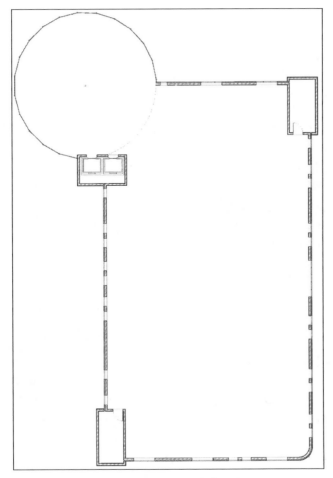

The attached Xref_Bldg-Shell-01.dwg

Xref layers

When you attach an Xref, your project file will gain the layers within Xref. Open the layer settings manager. Scroll to the bottom of the layer list and you will see that all the Xref layers are separated from the ArchiCAD layers. The Xref is not placed on a particular ArchiCAD layer but controlled via all the layers contained inside. In other words, you cannot assign an Xref to a specific layer.

If you wish, you can hide the Xref layers from being displayed in the **Layers** list. Go to the upper-right corner of the layer settings manager and click on the **Layer** filter button. Then, click on **Hide Xref layers** (this only hides the layers in the list view and not on your drawings).

Layer combinations

Your new Xref layers will not be shown in any of your existing layer combinations. You should unhide them in the layer combination you intend to use for drafting or modeling. Let's update the layer combination named **Drafting**:

1. Open the layer settings manager (*Ctrl + L*).

2. Click on the **Drafting** layer combination in the **Layer Combinations** pane.

3. Then, select all the Xref layers in the **Layers** pane.

4. Click on the big **Show** button (open eye) at the lower-right corner of the pane.

5. Finally, click on the **Update** button.

More about the ArchiCAD GUI

Working on a bigger project will mean that you will change settings and attributes more often than compared to a small project. It is recommended that you take advantage of some of ArchiCAD's palettes and toolbars to improve your production speed.

The Quick Options palette

To help make setting changes go quicker, you will want to have the **Quick Options** palette on your screen. This allows you to quickly change the current layer combination, view scale, model view options, pen set, and more.

Go to the **Window** menu and select **Palettes, Quick Options**. Place the palette where you like. Typically, it is placed under the **Navigator** palette.

The Attributes toolbar

In the early stages of any project, you will be modifying with various attribute settings. The **Attributes** toolbar will save you many clicks and it is highly recommended that you use it.

Right click on any toolbar already on your screen (or right clicking on a blank space in the toolbar area will work too). The right click menu for toolbars will appear. Click on **Attributes**. Then, the **Attributes** toolbar will appear. Move it to where you want it to stay.

Exterior walls

One of the main components of our shell and core model is the exterior walls. We will use the wall tool for the majority of the exterior walls and the **Curtain Wall** tool for the main entrance at the northwest corner of the building.

Elevation marks

The default exterior elevation markers need to be moved to accommodate for the size and location of our building, which can be done by performing the following steps:

1. Open the **1st FLOOR** viewpoint form the project map. Zoom out using the **Fit in Window** button at the bottom of the view window.

2. Select the North elevation marker and drag it up to the top of the floor plan just beyond the column grid. Stretch the endpoints of marker range line so that they extend beyond the extents of the building.

3. Do the same for the other three elevation markers. Move the east marker to the east side, extent the marker range, move the west marker to the west side, extend its marker range, and move the south marker to the south side and extend its marker range.

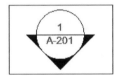

An example of the North elevation mark

The Wall tool

Model the external walls on each story using the attached Xrefs as a guide. The wall default settings will have the **Wall Top** set to the story mentioned previously and the **Home** story set to the current story.

Use the wall composite in the following list for each story:

- Basement:
    - All walls = Concrete Cast - Basement
- Ground:
    - Main exterior walls = Brick Mas. + Ins. "Block + Gyp.
    - Exterior stair walls = Metal Seam on " CMU
    - Interior stair walls = Gyp on " CMU

- First floor: Composite Place Holder
  - ° Main exterior walls = Brick Mas. + Ins. 8" Block + Gyp
  - ° Exterior stair walls = Metal Seam on 8" CMU
  - ° Interior stair walls = Gyp on " CMU

- Second floor: Composite Place Holder
  - ° Main exterior walls = Brick Mas. + Ins. "Block + Gyp
  - ° Exterior stair walls = Metal Seam on " CMU
  - ° Interior stair walls = Gyp on " CMU

- Third floor: Composite Place Holder
  - ° Main exterior walls = Brick Mas. + Ins. "Block + Gyp
  - ° Exterior stair walls = Metal Seam on 8" CMU
  - ° Interior stair walls = Gyp on 8" CMU

- Fourth floor: Composite Place Holder
  - ° Main exterior walls = Brick Mas. + Ins. 8" Block + Gyp
  - ° Exterior stair walls = Metal Seam on " CMU
  - ° Interior stair walls = Gyp on " CMU

- Roof: Composite Place Holder
  - ° Main exterior walls = Brick Mas. +Ins. 8" Block + Gyp. - 4' high
  - ° Exterior stair walls = Metal Seam on 8" CMU — 8' above Stair Bulkhead level (to be trimmed to roof)
  - ° Mechanical equipment protection walls = Metal Seam on " CMU — 8' above Roof (not linked) — *Do not create these walls until you are finished with the roof. Refer to the Roof exercise later in this chapter.*

When you finish, switch to a 3D view. Your walls should look similar to the following screenshot:

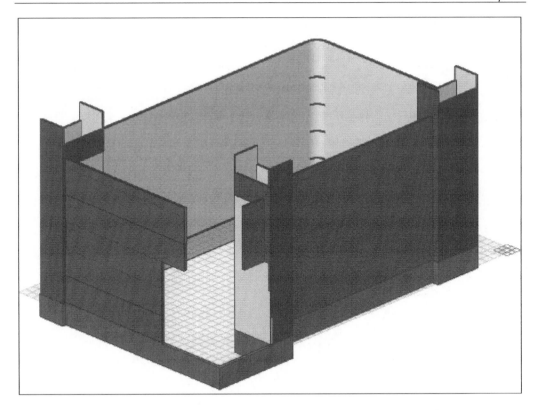

The Curtain Wall tool

The curtain wall is a wall object that contains a frame, panel, accessory, and junction components. These components are arranged on a base surface according to a curtain wall **scheme**. The scheme is a grid of vertical lines and horizontal lines with dimensions for spacing.

Curtain wall #1

Create a curtain wall for the curved external walls at the northwest corner of the Xref plans. Use Xref as a template. This curtain wall will span from the bottom of the ground floor story to the top of the second floor, as follows:

1. Open the **Ground** story viewpoint and zoom in on the upper-left corner of the building.

2. Double click on the **Curtain Wall** tool icon in the **Toolbox** palette to open the **Curtain Wall Default Settings** window.

3. Under the **Curtain Wall System** settings, ensure that **-1. Ground** story is the **Home Story**.

4. Click on **Scheme** in the pane at the left.

   a. Under **Primary Grid Lines**, click on the minus button multiple times until there is only one grid line. Set the size of the grid line to 8'.

   b. Under **Secondary Grid Lines**, click on the plus button multiple times until there are seven grid lines. Change the size of grid ID #1 to 2', #2 to 10', #3 to 2', #4 to 10', #5 to 2', #6 to 10', and #7 to 2'.

   c. In the **Preview** pane, you will see a graphic representation of the scheme; click inside each of the 2' panels. You will see the panel turn to a dark gray color. It signifies that it is a **distinct panel**. The non-gray panels are **main panels** (see the following image).

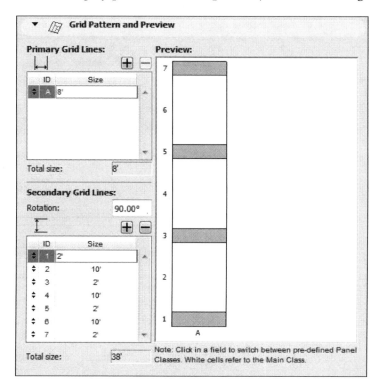

5. Click on **Boundary** under **Frames** in the pane at the left. and change the **Frame Type** to **Generic**.

6. Click on **Mullion** under **Frames** in the pane at the left and change the **Frame Type** to **Generic**.

7. Then, click on **Transom** under **Frames** in the pane at the left and change the **Frame Type** to **Generic**.

8. Next, click on **Main** under **Panels** in the pane at the left and change the **Frame Type** to **CW Window 19**.

9. Click on **Distinct** under **Panels** in the pane at the left and change the **Frame Type** to **CW Panel 19**.

10. Set the layer to **A-WALL-EXTR** and click on **OK**.

11. Go to the **Info Box** palette and set the geometry method to **Curved**.

12. You will be prompted at the lower left to **Enter Curtain Wall Centerpoint**. Then, click on the center of the atrium (the Xref has a cross to mark the center).

13. Enter the curtain wall startpoint and click on the outside edge of the bottom left of the round atrium wall.

14. Click to complete curtain wall. Then, click on the upper-right part of the curved atrium wall where it intersects the horizontal north wall.

15. Then, the **Sun Cursor** will appear and you will be prompted (at lower left) to determine the external side. Click outside the building.

16. The **Place Curtain Wall** dialog box will appear. Click on the third button at the right to use the bottom of the curtain wall as an anchor point and measure the curtain wall length from there. Change the height in the top box to 38'. The bottom box should be 0''. (See the following image). Finally, click on the **Place** button.

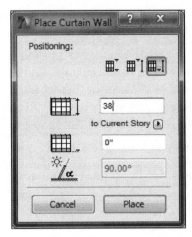

The Place Curtain Wall dialog box ready to place the curtain wall

Curtain Wall #2

Your second curtain wall will span from the third floor to the top of the fourth floor. The scheme will be similar to Curtain Wall #1, as follows:

1. Open the **3rd Floor** viewpoint and zoom into the atrium at the upper-left part of the building. Note that it has a much smaller radius than the Curtain Wall #1.

2. Double-click on the Curtain Wall tool in the **Toolbox** palette to open the curtain wall default settings window.

3. Under the **Curtain Wall System** settings, ensure that **3. 3rd Floor** story is the **Home Story**.

4. Click on **Scheme** in the pane at the left. Use the same grid pattern as Curtain Wall #1 but change the size of the **Primary Grid** to 4' and remove **Secondary Grid** ID's **6** and **7**.

5. Keep the same layer, frame, and panel settings used for Curtain Wall #1 and click on **OK**.

6. You will be prompted at the lower left of **Enter Curtain Wall Centerpoint**. Then, click on the center of the atrium (the Xref has a cross to mark the center).

7. Enter the curtain wall startpoint and click on the outside edge at the bottom-left part of the round atrium wall.

8. Click to complete curtain wall and click on the upper-right part of the curved atrium wall where it intersects the horizontal north wall.

9. The **Sun Cursor** will appear and you will be prompted (at lower-left) to determine the external side. Click outside the building.

10. Then, the **Place Curtain Wall** window will appear. Click on the third button at the right to use the bottom of the curtain wall as an anchor point and measure the curtain wall length from there. Change the height in the top box to 26'. The bottom box should be 0". Finally, click on the **Place** button.

Floors

Floors need to be created for each story with the **Slab** tool. Use the following list to determine what kind of slab needs to be built on each story. Model the edge of each slab to the inside edge of each exterior wall. For the upper floors of the atrium, use the lines drawn on the Xref as a guide.

All floor slabs will be on **A-FLOR** layer.

Use the floor composite in the following list for each story:

- **Basement: Conc. Slab—4" on Gravel**
- **Ground: Conc.Top. o/ Stl Deck**
- **First floor: Conc.Top. o/ Stl Deck**
- **Second floor: Conc.Top. o/ Stl Deck**—To the outside edge of upper atrium and walls (see line on Xref)
- **Third floor: Conc.Top. o/ Stl Deck**—To the outside edge of the upper atrium (see the line on Xref)
- **Fourth floor: Conc.Top. o/ Stl Deck**—To the outside edge of the atrium (see the line on Xref)

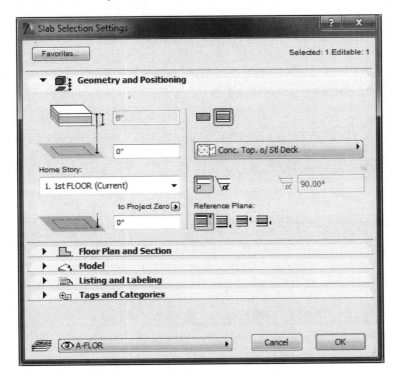

Use the magic wand in the center of each plan to create a quick slab. Then, select the slab and stretch and create new points to bring the slab edges in the stair shafts. See the following screenshot to look at the new points being created:

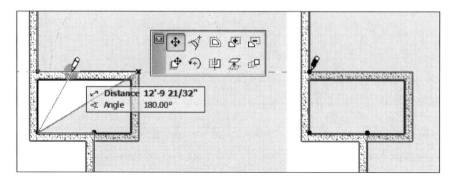

After the slab points are changed as shown higher up, your completed slab will look as in following screenshot:

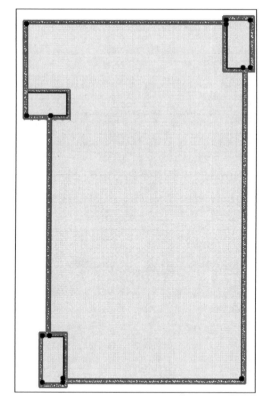

A completed slab

Another quick way to add/extend the slab where required, is to select the slab, click on the edge to activate the pet palette, and click on the **Add to Polygon** button. Refer to the following screenshot of the pet palette:

Roofs

There are multiple roofs on our building: one over the atrium, one at the roof story, and a small roof over all of the stair bulkheads. Each of these roofs will use a different composite structure. However, we will create our roofs with the **Mesh** and **Shell** tool instead of the **Roof** tool.

The Mesh tool

You will create the main roof with the Mesh tool. Using the line pattern shown on the Xref for the **Roof** story, you will create multiple mesh elements inside each of the shapes defined by the pattern. Then, you will assign a height to some of the points to create a slope, as follows:

1. Open the **5. Roof** viewpoint and ensure that the criss-cross line pattern on the Xref is shown.

2. Open the **Mesh Default Settings** and double-click on the **Mesh** icon on the **Toolbox** palette (see the following screenshot).

    a. Change the height to 1'-4".

    b. Change the **Structure** type to **Solid Body** (third button).

    c. Change the **Building Material** to **22-05 40 | Steel Deck**.

    d. Set the layer to **A-ROOF**.

e. Finally, click on **OK**.

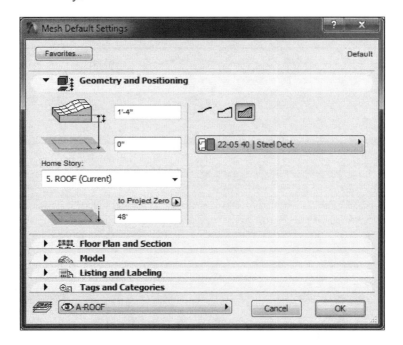

3. Use the Magic Wand (*Spacebar*) to create a mesh inside each of the shapes of the line pattern.

 Do not create a mesh inside the stair shafts or the atrium.

4. There are five criss-cross intersections on the pattern. The roof drains will be placed at these five locations. You need to set the heights of all the points at those locations to -1'-0" (negative 1').

5. Select a mesh that touches one of the roof drain locations. The mesh will be highlighted and points will appear. Click on the point at the roof drain location. The pet palette will appear and then click on the **Elevate Mesh Point** button. Change the height to -1'.

6. Do this for every mesh that touches a roof drain intersection.

7. Now you should have a multi-faceted sloped roof. There will be more ridges than what is shown on the Xref pattern. This is okay. See the following screenshot of the roof story:

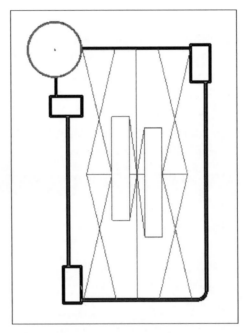

The top view of the Roof mesh

After you have created your mesh elements with the Magic Wand, some of your points and ridges may be imperfect. You will see this only after you select a mesh. You can manually drag points into the proper location or create new meshes with the **Polygonal Geometry** ,method to ensure the points and boundaries are exact.

Now you can model the walls for the roof top equipment inside the two long rectangles at the center of the roof story (refer to the *Exterior Walls* exercise).

The Shell tool

The **Shell** tool creates 3D elements that the other typical modeling tools cannot. There are three different shell construction methods: **Extrusion, Revolve,** and **Ruled**. We will use the extrusion method to create the roofs over the stair shafts and the Revolve to create the roof over the atrium and entry at northeast wing of our building.

Shell type #1

The Extrusion method with the Simple construction method will create a half-pipe shape with three clicks. The first two clicks define the length of the pipe and the third defines the width and size of the half circle:

1. Open the **6. Stair Bulkhead** viewpoint. Turn on the **Trace** feature (*Alt + F2*) and choose the reference to be **Below Current Story**. Zoom in on the stair shaft at the northeast corner.

2. Double-click on the **Shell** tool icon in the **Tool Box** palette to open the **Shell Default Settings** window and set the layer to **A-ROOF**.

3. Change to building material to **Standing Seam Mtl Roof**. Set the geometry method to **Extruded** and click on **OK**.

The shell Default Settings window

4. Go to the **Info Box** palette and ensure the **Construction Method** is set to **Simple**. This will use a simple arc as the profile.

5. Make your first click on the upper-left exterior corner of the northeast stair wall.

6. Then second click on the upper-right exterior corner of the stair wall.

7. Place the third and final click on the lower right corner. Wait for a couple seconds and your shell will appear.

8. Switch to a 3D view and look at your first shell!

9. Repeat the preceding steps for the other two stair shafts.

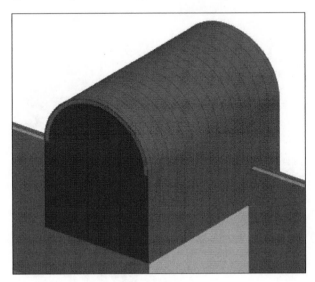

The shell type #1

Shell type #2

The **Revolve** method with the **Simple** construction method will create a dome shape with three clicks. The first click sets the center, second defines the radius of the dome, and third defines the circumference; similar to how the **Arc/Circle** tool works.

1. Open the **5. Roof** viewpoint and zoom in on the atrium at the northeast corner. There will be a center point drawn in the Xref at the center of the atrium that you will use as a guide.

2. Start the **Shell** tool. Go to the **Info Box** palette and set the **Geometry Method** to **Revolved** and the **Construction Method** to **Simple**. The layer should be **A-ROOF**.

3. Make your first click on the center point symbol in the Xref.

4. Your second click should be at the right edge where the north exterior wall meets the curtain wall.

5. Your third and final click should come all the way around to form a complete circle.

The shell type #2

6. Switch to a 3D view and your building will look as in the following image:

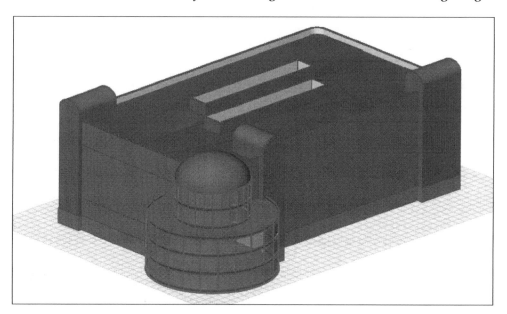

Columns and Grids

Our building requires a grid of columns and grid lines. You will learn how to create an array of horizontal and vertical column lines form the column grid with the **Grid** tool and **Grid System** tool.

We will use two column sizes: 12" x 12" and 8" x 8". However, one of the column types we need to use requires a profile that is not currently in our project file. Therefore, we will need to create it. We need to do a little prep work that involves the creation of a new profile and some custom composites.

Using profiles

A profile in ArchiCAD is a 2D line drawing that defines a simple shape, which can be used as walls, beams, or columns. It is the cross-section outline. See the example profiles in the following image:

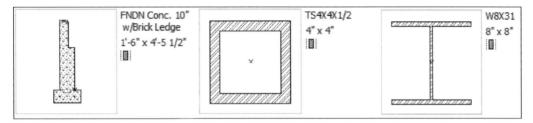

The three profile examples

We will begin by duplicating an existing profile and changing it to create the new profile that we need, as follows:

1. Go to the **Options** menu and navigate to **Element Attributes | Attribute Manager**. The **Attribute Manager** window will appear.

2. Click on the **Profile** tab (it looks like the cross-section of an I-beam). Then, click on the profile named **W8X31**. Next, click on the **Duplicate** button. This will create a new profile named **W8X31 (2)**. Select the new profile and from the **Name** box below the list, change the name to W12X31.

3. Click on **OK**. The **Confirm Changes** window will appear. Then, click on the **Create** button.

4. The new profile definition has been created but it is just a duplicate of the **W8X31** profile. You need to open the profile manager and change its size. To do this, go to the **Options** menu and select **Element Attributes**. Click on **Profile Manager**. The **Profile Manager** window will appear.

5. From the **Choose Profile** list, select the profile you that created—**W12X31** (if the profile you created is still named **W8X31 (2)**, then open the **Attribute Manager**, select the profile, rename it, click on the **Apply** button, and click on **OK**).

6. Click on the **Edit Profile** button and the **Profile Editor** window will open; it will contain the fill used for the W8X31 profile. You need to change the fill outline to be `12"` high by `12"` wide. Use the marquee tool to stretch the top up 2" and the bottom down 2".

7. When finished editing the fill, click the **Store Profile** button, and close the **Profile Editor** window. See the following screenshot of the **Profile Manager**:

The Profile Manager window

Composites

A **composite** is a sandwich of materials that make up the building structure elements, such as walls, floors, or roofs. For instance, a typical interior wall will have a composite, containing a layer of gypsum board on top of a layer of wood framing and a layer of gypsum board at the bottom.

We need to create new composites for three exterior wall types and one for the stair bulkhead roofs with the help of the following steps:

Custom Composite #1

1. Click on the **Composites** button on the **Attributes** toolbar or go to the **Options** menu and navigate to **Element Attributes | Composites...**. The **Composite Structures** window will open.

2. Click on the big drop-down bar at the top and select the composite named **EIFS on 8" CMU**. Click on the **Duplicate** button. The **Duplicate Composite Structure** window will open.

3. Change the name to **Metal Seam on 8" CMU** and click on **OK**.

4. In the **Edit Skin and Line Structure** panel, change the top skin layer from **22-07 24 | EFIS** to **22-07 61 | Standing Seam Metal Wall**. Take a look at the following screenshot of the **Composite Structures** window:

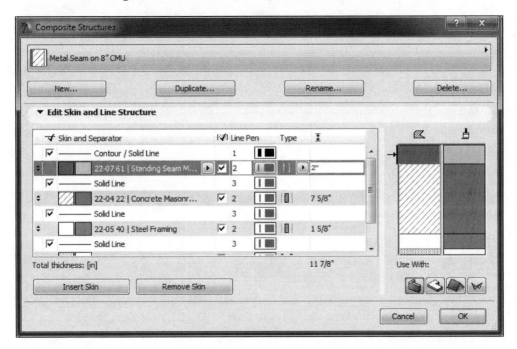

Custom Composite #2

1. With the **Composite Structures** window still open, click on the big drop-down bar at the top and select the composite named **EIFS on 8" CMU**. Then, click on the **Duplicate** button and the **Duplicate Composite Structure** window will open.

2. Change the name to `Concrete Cast - Basement` and click on **OK**.

3. In the **Edit Skin** and **Line Structure** panel, navigate to the **22-07 24 | EFIS** skin and click on the **Remove Skin** button. Change the skin named **22-04 22 | Concrete Masonry Unit** to **22-03 31 | Structural Concrete** and change the thickness to 1"-4".

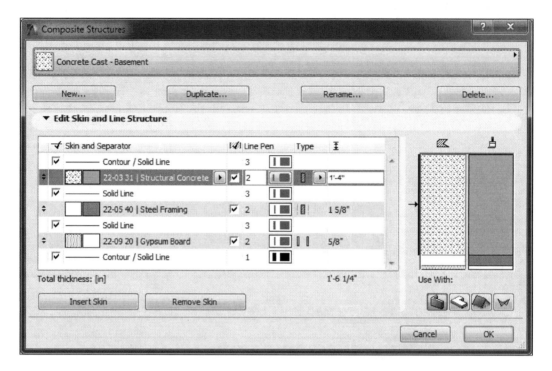

Custom Composite #3

1. With the Composite Structures window still open, click on the big drop-down bar at the top and select the composite named **EIFS on 8" CMU**. Click on the **Duplicate** button and the **Duplicate Composite Structure** window will open.

2. Change the name to Gyp on 8" CMU and click on **OK**.

3. In the **Edit Skin** and **Line Structure** panel, navigate to the **22-07 24 | EFIS** skin and change the skin to **22-09 20 | Gypsum Board**. Change the thickness to 5/8".

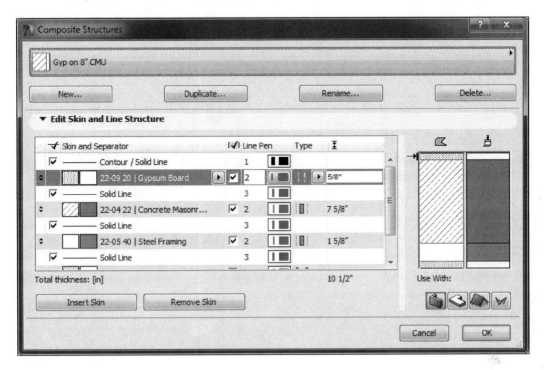

Custom Composite #4

1. With the **Composite Structures** window still open, click on the big-drop down bar at the top and select the composite named **Standing Seam Mtl Roof**. Click on the **Duplicate** button and the **Duplicate Composite Structure** window will open.

2. Change the name to Standing Seam Mtl Roof on Steel Frame and click on **OK**.

3. In the **Edit Skin** and **Line Structure** panel, change the bottom skin layer from **22-07 61 | Underlayment** to **22-05 40 | Steel Frame + Insulation** and change the thickness to 3 5/8".

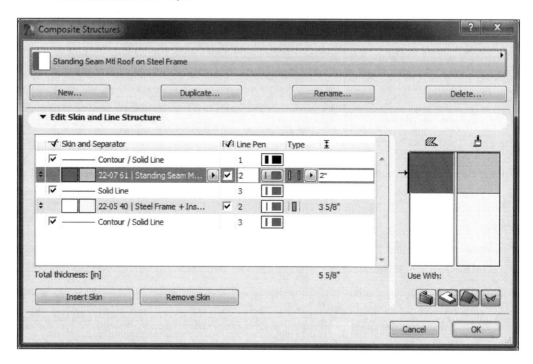

The Grid tool

The **Grid** tool is what you can use to create the column line grid (one grid at a time). Each grid element is composed of a grid line and grid marker (commonly referred to as a grid bubble). Grid elements that are typically placed on floor plan views will appear vertically in sections and elevations. Grid elements can also be placed within the 3D views. We will use the **Grid** tool after we use the **Grid System** tool.

Using the Grid System tool

Your building needs to have a matrix of columns in place to hold up all the floors. These columns will be arranged in a standard rectangular pattern and organized by grid lines. You can place grid lines and columns, one at a time, or create them in one action with the **Grid System** tool. We will use the **Grid System** tool to create six horizontal and four vertical grid lines and columns at each grid intersection. To do this, perform the following steps:

1. Open the Shell model and a ground floor view and zoom in on the lower-left corner. We need to create a snap point to place the grid system. To do this, we will use the **Guide Line** tool,

2. Click on the **Guide Lines** button on the **Standard** toolbar. See the following screenshot:

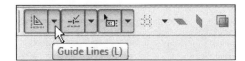

3. Click the drop-down button attached to the **Guide Lines** button and select **Create Guide Line Segment**. See the following screenshot:

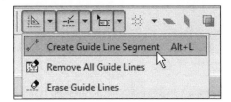

4. Draw a guide line from the top inside edge of the main southern exterior wall to the left, past the end point of the west wall above.

5. Draw a guide line from the bottom inside edge of the west exterior wall down past the southern exterior wall. This will create the intersection we need to place to be the insertion point for the grid system, as shown in the following screenshot:

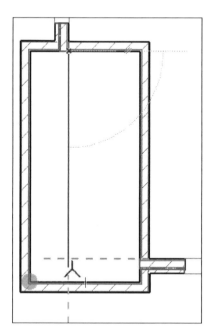

6. Go to the **Design** menu and click on **Grid System**. The **Grid System Settings** window will open.

7. In the **General Settings** panel, check the boxes for **Elements at Grid line intersections**, **Dimension lines**, and **Total Dimension**.

8. For the **Elements at Grid line** intersections option, set it to **Column** and click on the **Settings** button directly to the right. The **Column Default Settings** window will open.

9. Set the column structure to **Complex Profile** and profile from the drop-down button to **W12X31**, as shown in the following screenshot:

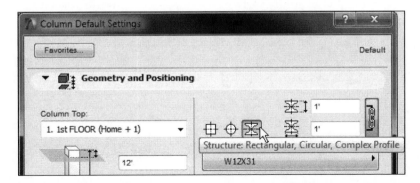

10. Under the **Grid Elements** panel in the **Extension** panel, set the **Anchor** position to the lower right corner. Then, check the boxes under **Markers** to show on the north and east.

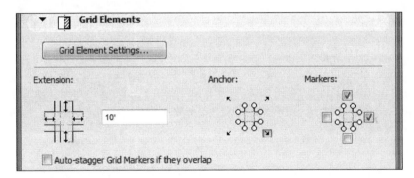

11. In the **Naming rules** panel, ensure that the radio button is on to generate names automatically. The horizontal grids start at **A**, while the vertical grids start at **1**.

12. In the **Grid positions** panel under horizontal grid lines, select one of the distance dimensions and click on the plus button to add a grid line. You should have the horizontal grid lines **A** through **F**.

13. Under the **Vertical grid lines** pane, click on the bottom grid number and click on the minus button until you have four vertical grid lines. Use the screenshot below to set the correct distances for both the horizontal and vertical instances:

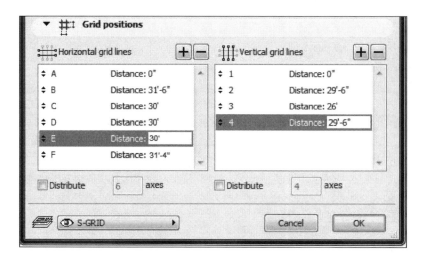

14. Ensure that the layer is set to **S-GRID** and press the **OK** button.

15. Place the grid system at the intersection of the guide lines that you created. When prompted for a rotation angle, click off to the right at an angle of **0.00** and see the following zoomed-in screenshot the grid system intersection point.

Remember, you can hold the *Shift* key down to ensure an orthogonal angle.

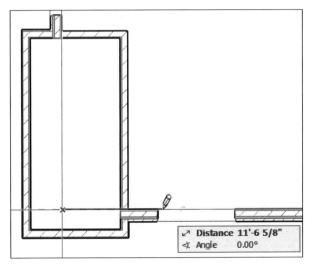

The grid system insertion point

Adjusting the column grid

After you place the column grid system, you will notice that some of the columns are partially inside walls. Therefore, you will need to adjust the location of some of the columns and grid lines with the help of the following points:

1. Zoom in to the bottom of the building at column line **A**. Select grid line **A** and the four columns on it. Move them up so that the bottom of the two middle columns are on the inside edge of the wall.

2. Move the column at grid intersection **A-1** to the lower-left corner of the stair shaft. See the following screenshot:

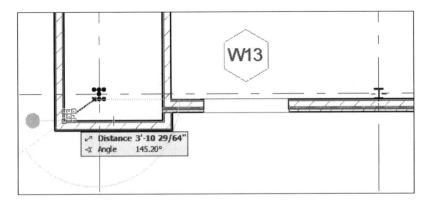

3. Move the column at grid intersection **A-4** to the inside edge of the curved wall at an angle of 135 degrees. See the following screenshot:

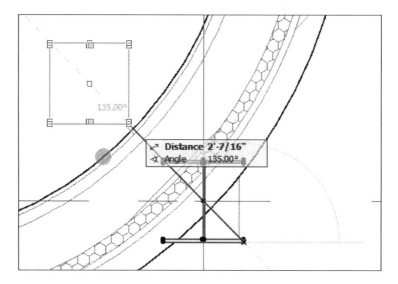

4. Then, zoom out and delete the column at grid intersection of **F-1**.

5. Select grid line 1 and the remaining columns along grid line 1 and move them to the inside edge of the west exterior wall.

6. Zoom in on the elevator shaft and move the column inside the shaft, down to the inside edge of the shaft wall at the bottom.

7. Zoom in on the upper-right corner of the building and move the column at grid intersection F-4 to the inside edge of the top right corner of the stair shaft.

8. Next, go to the other stories and delete or move the same columns as directed next.

See the screenshot image of the column grid system (so far):

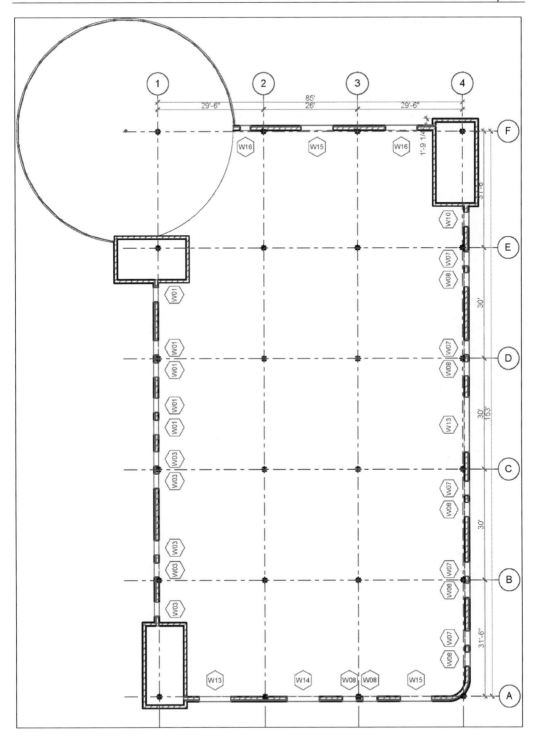

Creating additional grid lines

For each column that we moved away from a grid line, we need to create a new grid line or two since the columns we moved are no longer conforming to our original grid. This is a pretty common occurrence in a commercial project. You can have 90 percent of your columns conform to a basic grid but additional grid lines will need to be created to accommodate the design of the building. To create these additional grid lines, perform the following steps:

1. Hover your cursor over one of the grids, hold the *Alt* key down, and click (the eye dropper cursor will appear). This will activate the **Grid Element** tool and set all the properties to match the grid you clicked on. See the following screenshot:

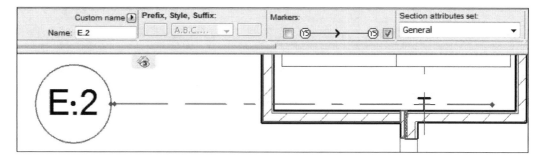

2. Start the **Grid Element** tool from the **Toolbox** palette (under **More**) and draw a short horizontal grid line for the column in the elevator shaft.

3. Select the grid line you just created, go to the **Info Box** palette, and change the value of **Name** to E.2. Then, in the **Markers** panel, check only one box to display the bubble on the left endpoint, as shown in the following screenshot:

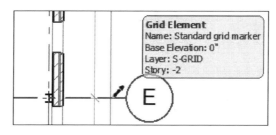

4. Do the same for the column in the southwest stair shaft. Since this column line will be below column line A, make the name for the new grid line **A**, and change the original A grid to **A.1**.

5. Create a vertical grid element for the column in the southwest stair shaft. Name it `0.1` and show the bubble at the bottom endpoint only.

6. Go to the southeast corner of the building and create a new vertical and horizontal grid element for the column there. Align with the other column line above. Name the vertical element `3.9` and horizontal element `A.2`.

7. The horizontal grid element will overlap the A.1 grid so we will need to **stagger** the grid line. Select grid line A.2 and zoom in close to the bubble where you will see two magenta grips. Click on one of the farthest from the bubble and drag the grip up about 5' and over to the left about 2'. See the following screenshot:

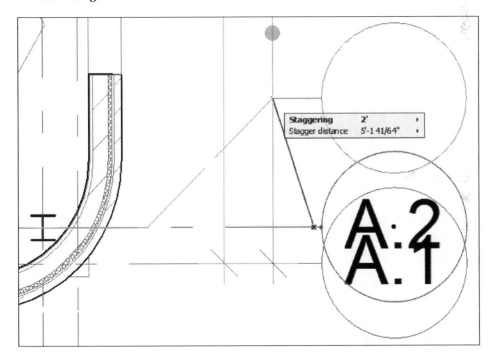

8. Go to the column in the northeast stair shaft and create a vertical grid element named 4.1 and horizontal grid element named F.1. Stagger them both.

9. Zoom out and your grids should look similar to the following screenshot:

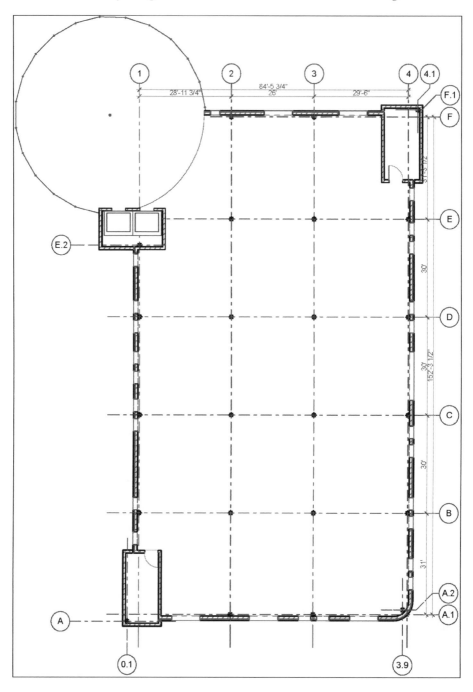

Summary

In this chapter, we set up the project environment settings for our new building. We created the exteriors walls, floors, and roofs for our shell and core model file. During those exercises, we created new composite structures for our walls and roof shells. The shell & core model will be the first of the three ArchiCAD model files that makeup our commercial project. In the next chapter, we will create the interior model file.

5
Project Setup and Modeling Part 2 – A Healthcare Building Project

In this chapter, we will create our architectural interior model. You will again need to perform some of the setup that we did for the shell model in *Chapter 4, Project Setup and Modeling Part 1 – A Healthcare Building Project*. We will hotlink the shell model into the interior model and attach some Xrefs. In this chapter, we will create and manage views and layers and there will be plenty of modeling to be done. The following is a list of the main topics in this chapter:

- Stories and units
- Hotlinks and Xrefs
- Modeling
- Creating views and view management
- Layer management

Project configuration and file linking

The first step in this chapter is to start ArchiCAD and create a new project with the ArchiCAD 19 commercial template. To do this, perform the following steps:

1. When the **Start ArchiCAD** dialog box appears, select **Create a New Project** radio button at the top.

2. Select the **Use a Template** radio button under **Set up Project Settings**.

3. Then, select **ArchiCAD 19 Commercial Template.tpl** from the drop-down list.

4. Click on **New** and this will open a blank project file.

Saving the project

Let's save our new project model file and give it a name. Then, we will be ready to quickly save our work at any time we work. It is always good to save your file after you have completed a task. To save your file perform the following steps:

1. Go up to the **File** menu and click on **Save**.

2. Browse your project folder, Commercial_Project and name your file Commercial_Bldg-Interior.

3. Lastly, click on **Save**.

Creating stories

The story settings in the interior model will need to match the shell model's story settings exactly. Follow these steps to create your stories:

1. On the **Navigator** palette, select the **Project Map** icon.

2. Right click on **Stories** (in the **Navigator** palette) and select **Story Settings**.

3. In the **Story Settings** window, click on **1st FLOOR** and then click on the **Insert Below** button. Enter Ground in the **Name** box and 12' in the **Height to Next** box.

4. Click on **Ground**. Then, click on the **Insert Below** button. Enter BASEMENT in the **Name** box and 10' in the **Height to Next** box.

5. Click on **2nd FLOOR**. Next, click on the **Insert Above** button. Enter 3rd Floor in the **Name** box and 12' in the **Height to Next** box.

6. Click on **3rd FLOOR**. Then, click on the **Insert Above** button. Enter **4th Floor** in the **Name** box and 12' into the **Height to Next** box.

7. Click on **4th FLOOR** and click on the **Insert Above** button. Enter ROOF in the **Name** box and 10' in the **Height to Next** box.

8. Click on **ROOF**. Next, click on the **Insert Above** button. Enter the name STAIR BULKHEAD in the **Name** box and 10' in the **Height to Next** box.

9. Finally, click on **OK**.

Your list of stories will now look similar to this:

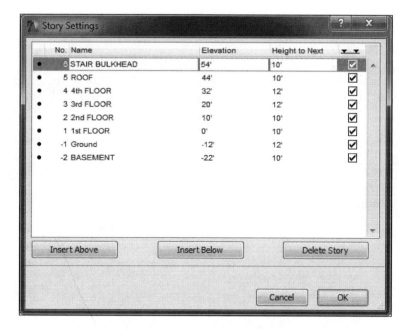

Units

The next task will be to configure the unit type and dimension accuracy for this project model file.

On the menu bar, navigate to **Options | Project Preferences | Working Units** and then perform the following tasks:

- Ensure **Model Unit** is set to **feet & fractional inches**
- Set **Fractions** to **1/64**
- Ensure that **Layout Unit** is **feet & fractional inches**
- Ensure that **Angle Unit** is set to **decimal degrees**
- See to it that **Decimals** is set to **2**
- Make sure that **Angle & Font Size Decimals in Dialog Boxes** is set to **2**

Hotlinking

A hotlink is an embedded copy of an ArchiCAD model file that is linked to the original model file. Whenever the original file is changed, the embedded hotlinked copy can be updated.

If you are an AutoCAD user, you can think of a hotlink as a block inside your drawing that is linked to an external file. Unlike external reference files (Xrefs) in AutoCAD, you don't need the original model file after it is hotlinked.

You can also use hotlinked modules for pieces and parts of your building that repeat and are in multiple locations, such as office furniture layouts, and hospital exam rooms.

 [Only ArchiCAD files can be hotlinks.   ]

This lesson will walk you through the process of linking the core and shell ArchiCAD model.

Layer preparation for hotlinks

It is a good practice to have a layer for each hotlink in your project. To do so, do the following:

1. First, open the **Layer Settings Manager** window (*Ctrl + L*).
2. Then, click on the **New** button.
3. Enter A-HTLK-SHEL as the name.
4. Show the new layer in every layer combination at the left. With **A-HTLK-SHEL** selected on the right, go to the layer and click on the eye icon next to every layer combination.

Hotlink the core and shell model

With the following steps, you will hotlink the model you created in the previous chapter:

1. Go to the project map and open the **1st FLOOR** viewpoint.
2. Go to the **File** menu and navigate to **External Content | Place Hotlinked Module...**.

3. Then, the **Place Module** window will open. At the top of the window, change the **Master Layer** to **A-HTLK-SHEL**.

4. At the bottom of the window, click on the **Choose Hotlink...** button.

5. The **Choose Hotlink** window will open. Click on the **New Hotlink...** button and then click on **From file**.

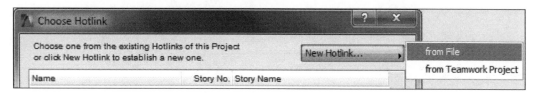

 The other **Choose Hotlink** option from **Teamwork Project**, will not be used for our project, since we are not utilizing the **Teamwork** work sharing feature.

6. Browse to the `Commercial_Bldg-Shell.pln` file and click on the **Select** button.

7. The **Choose Story** window will open. Push the radio button next to **All Stories** and click on **OK**.

8. Click on the **OK** button on the **Choose Hotlink** window.

9. Next, click on the **Place Module** button on the **Place Module** window.

10. The **Match Stories** window will appear. Ensure the story in the drop-down list is set to **1. 1st FLOOR (0')**. Then, click on **OK**.

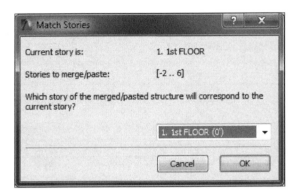

11. Next, the **Paste Options** window will appear. Set the **Where to Paste:** option to **Original Location** and **Zoom:** to **Zoom to Pasted Elements**.

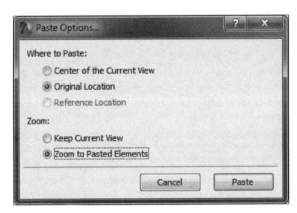

12. The shell model will appear on the screen with an active marquee running around it. Click anywhere outside of the marquee to finish the placement.

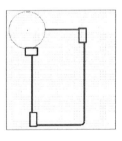

Your shell model is now hotlinked into your interior model. You can open other storeys and see that they match what you would see in the shell model.

Moving the elevation marks

In *Chapter 4, Project Setup and Modeling Part 1 – A Healthcare Building Project*, the elevation marks need to be moved in order to properly show the outside of the building. Right now they are on the southwest part of the building and need to be individually placed into an appropriate location; to do so, perform the following steps:

1. Open the **1st FLOOR** viewpoint and zoom all the way out by clicking on the **Fit in Window** button at the bottom of your view. You can also just zoom out by using the scroll wheel on your mouse.

2. Drag the north elevation mark so that it is above the north end of the building; drag the east elevation mark to the east of the building and so on until they are all placed around the building.

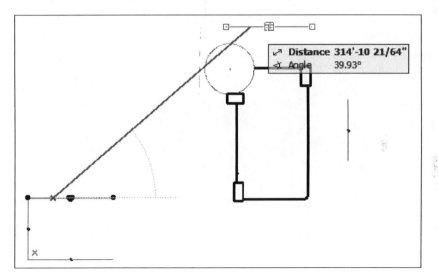

3. After they are placed at their appropriate locations, select each elevation mark and stretch their view widths to correspond with the width of the building.

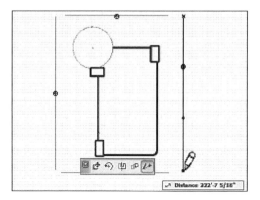

4. Finally, open one of the elevation viewpoints and the whole building will appear.

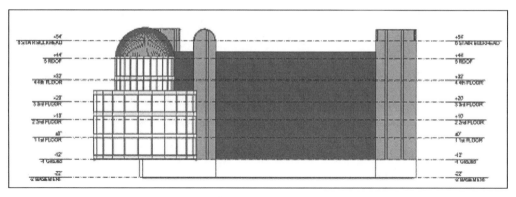

The West elevation

Attaching Xrefs

We will use Xrefs again as a guide for drawing our walls. We will start with the first floor:

1. Open the **1st FLOOR** viewpoint from the project map.

2. Go to the **File** menu and click on **External Content**. Then, attach the Xref.

3. The **Attach Xref** window will open. Browse to the `Xref_Bldg-Intr-01.dwg` file.

4. Set the reference type to **Overlay**.

5. Uncheck the box for **Insertion Point, Scale**, and **Rotation**.

6. Next, set the **Anchor Point** to **Drawing's own origin**.

7. Place on Story **1. 1st FLOOR**.

8. Then, set the value for **Translator** to **02 For editable import**.

9. The **DWG/DXF Partial Open** window will appear. This gives you the opportunity to deselect any layer in the Xref that you do not want to import. In your case, you can keep them all and click on **OK**.

10. The Xref may take a few moments to appear. Zoom out to view the whole plan.

The following image shows the first floor Xref and `Xref_Bldg-Intr-01.dwg`:

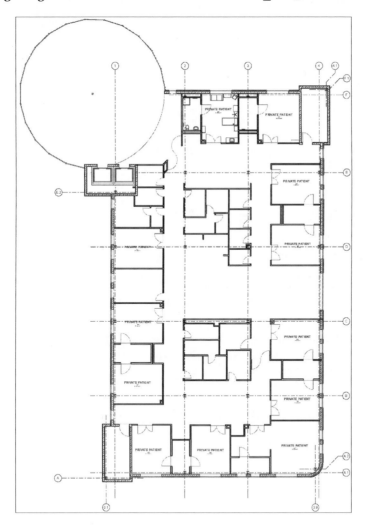

Open the other story viewpoints and repeat the previous steps for each story. Be sure that the **Place on Story** setting matches the story that you are attaching.

Hotlinking the interior model

Our next task is to hotlink the interior model into the shell model. We need to place windows on the exterior walls. This needs to be done inside the shell model.

Open the interior model and follow the previous steps that you used for linking the shell model into the interior model.

Modeling tools

The interior model will consist mainly of walls (partitions) and objects (doors, casework). We will start with modeling the walls. There are two wall composite types in our project template that are designed for commercial interior walls. These composite types are:

- Wall Stl 2x4 – 1hr UL W403
- Wall Stl 2x4 – 2hr UL W403

These composite types are named according to their fire safety ratings; hence, the 1hr and 2hr designations.

Creating new composites

Most of the walls that we need do not need to be fire rated so we will make copies of the preceding composites and create a couple of nonrated composite types, as follows:

1. Open the **Composite Structures Attribute Management** window **Options | Element Attributes | Composites…**.
2. Click on the big **Composite Structure** drop-down button at the top and change it to **Wall Stl 2x4 - 1hr UL W403**.
3. Click on the **Duplicate** button and enter the name Wall Stl 4-7/8". Then, click on **OK**.
4. Next, change the composite structure to **Wall Stl 2x4 - 2hr UL W403**.
5. Click on the **Duplicate** button and enter the name Wall Stl 7-1/8" and click on **OK**.

6. Look at the list of skins in the **Edit Skin** and **Line Structure** panel. Change the thickness of the steel framing skin from `3-5/8"` to `4-5/8"`. See the following screenshot. Then, click on **OK**.

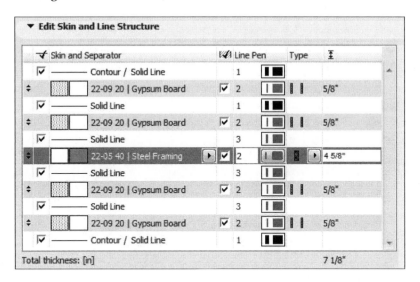

Adjusting layer combinations

You should unhide the Xref layers in the layer combination that you intend to use for drafting or modeling. Let's update the layer combination named **Drafting** with the help of the following steps:

1. Open the layer settings manager (*Ctrl + L*).
2. Click on the **Drafting** layer combination in the **Layer Combinations** pane.
3. Then, select all the Xref layers in the **Layers** pane.
4. Finally, click on the **Update** button.

Modeling the interior walls

Now, you are all set to begin modeling your interior walls. The Xrefs are linked for tracing over, and you have the composite types for each wall type you will need. You will set the wall height, composite, and the layer:

1. Open the first floor viewpoint from the project map and set the active layer combination to **Drafting**.

2. Double-click on the **Wall** tool to open the wall default settings and expand the **Geometry and Positioning** panel.

   ° Change the top offset setting from 0" to -6" (negative 6"). This will bring the wall up to the underside of the floor slab above.

   ° Set the composite to **Wall Stl 4-7/8"** and select **OK**.

3. Go to the **Info Box** palette and ensure the layer is set to **A-WALL-INTR**.

4. Set the reference line location to **Outside Face** or **Inside Face**. This way you can snap your wall endpoints to the edges and the endpoints of the walls in the Xref.

5. Set your geometry method to the **Single** or **Chained** method and begin drawing in your walls.

   ° The **Single** method concludes the wall after your second click

   ° The **Chained** method keeps the wall tool active after every click until you decide to double click on your final click to terminate the tool

The following screenshot shows where to enter the top offset dimension:

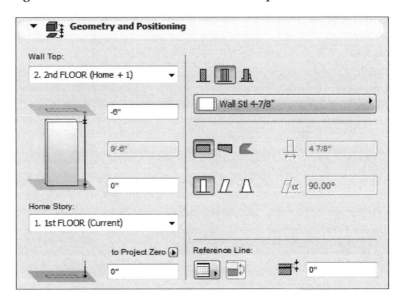

 When you are drawing walls, you can change the reference line location on the fly from the **Info Box** palette after you have already started drawing.

Creating objects

After you have modeled the interior walls in the interior model, you are ready to place the interior doors. When you are finished with that, create the exterior windows in the shell model. Place the doors on the interior model walls. Use the following doors for the specific sizes:

- Single swing doors will be **D1 Commercial Door 19**
- Uneven double doors will be **D2 Commercial Door 19**
- Double egress doors will be **D2 Double Egress Metal 19**

The panels on the double egress door will not automatically be of equal length. You will need to set the door panel parameter named `Main Door Panel Width` to a value that is half of the door width. The following screenshot shows the setting for a 7'-6" double egress door:

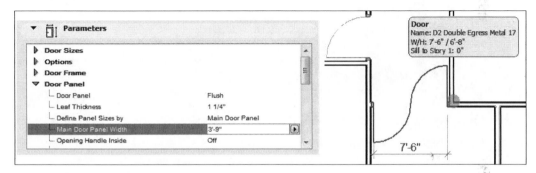

Creating windows

You will create windows for the exterior of the building. Therefore, we need to open the shell model since that is where the exterior walls are. Your first windows that you create will be pretty simple and will coordinate with the other features of the building. In this case, we will align the bottom of the windows with the curtain wall mullions at the entry atrium:

1. Open the shell model, go to **level 1** and set the layer combination to **Drafting**.

2. Double-click on the window tool icon in the **Toolbox** palette. At the upper-left of the **Window Selection Settings** window, click on the green chair icon to turn on the sub type view (see the following screenshot):

3. Open the GS Storefront Window folder and select **Storefront Window 19**.

4. Go to the **Preview and Positioning** panel and set the window width to 4'-0", the height to 5'-2", and set the **Header to Story height** to 7'-2".

5. Go to the **Parameters** panel and match the following **Frame** and **Panel** settings:
    - **Frame Thickness** = 2"
    - **Frame Width** = 2"
    - **Bottom Rail Width** = 2"
    - **Horizontal Div. Number** = 1
    - **Middle Vert. Div. Number** = 1

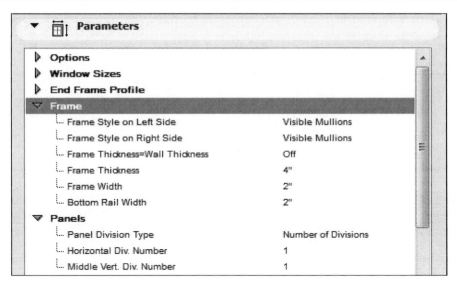

The parameter settings for the storefront window

6. Place this window at the single pane window locations on every floor except for the north side.

7. The single pane window locations on the north wall will be the same window as previous, except you will change the width to be 3'0".

There are two other versions of our window that we need to create. There are triple pane windows that go on the north and south exterior walls. And we need to create a window with five panes for the east exterior wall:

1. Insert one of the single pane windows onto the north exterior wall and open the selection settings for the new copy of that window:

    ° Change the width of the window to 9'-0".

    ° Go to the **Storefront Settings** panel and change panel horizontal division number to **3**. Keep the vertical division number as **1**.

2. Place this window at all of the triple pane window locations on the north and south exterior walls.

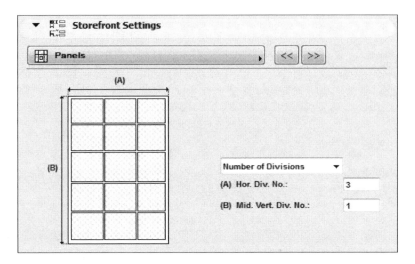

3. Insert one of your new triple pane windows onto the east exterior wall and open the selection settings for the copied window:

    ° Change the width of the window to 15'-0".

    ° Go to the **Storefront Settings** panel and change panel horizontal division number to **5**. Keep the vertical division number as **1**.

4. Place this window at all of the 5-pane window locations on the east exterior wall.

When you are finished placing all the exterior windows, your elevation views will look like the following screenshots:

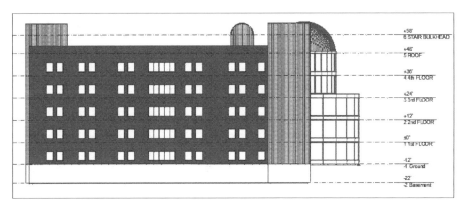

The East elevation

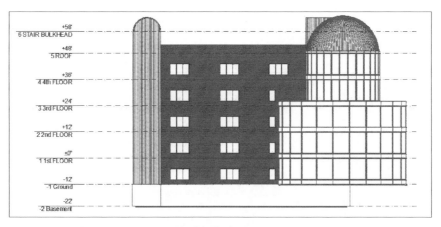

The North elevation

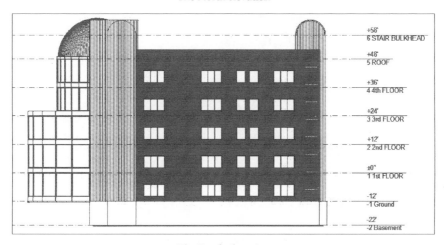

The South elevation

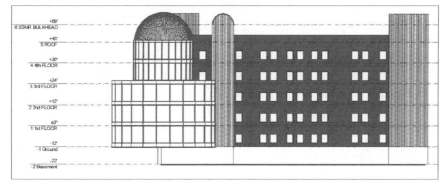

The West elevation

Remember, windows and doors do not have their own layer setting because they assume the layer of the wall they are placed in.

Views

The types of views we need for this project will be similar to the first project that we created. We will just need more views and we will need to be diligent with our organization.

The types of views will be as follows:

- Floor plans — 1/8" scale and 1/4" scale
- Ceiling plans — 1/8" scale and 1/4" scale
- Exterior elevations and interior elevations
- Building and wall sections
- Stair plans, stair sections, and details
- Ceiling details
- Roof details
- Exterior plan details
- Exterior section details
- Casework details

Creating layers

You will need to create the following layers to help build the layer combinations needed for our view types. These new layers use a convention designed to designate the drawing scale:

- **A-ANNO-CLNG-048**
- **A-ANNO-CLNG-DETL**
- **A-ANNO-NOTE-024**
- **A-ANNO-NOTE-048**
- **A-ANNO-NOTE-192**
- **A-DIMS-048**
- **A-DIMS-192**

Renaming layers

Some of the layers should be renamed in order to conform to the new convention used in the new layers you created:

- Rename **A-ANNO-CEIL** to A-ANNO-CLNG-096
- Rename **A-ANNO-ENLG** to A-ANNO-NOTE-048
- Rename **A-ANNO-NOTE** to A-ANNO-NOTE-096
- Rename **A-DIMS** to A-DIMS-096
- Rename **A-DIMS-ENLG** to A-DIMS-048

Creating and modifying layer combinations

The main driver behind your different view types are the custom layer combinations you will assign. You will need to have a layer combination for each view type. The following section will show you what layers to hide and show for each layer combination that you will need.

Enlarged floor plans (1/4"=1'-0")

Open the **Layer Settings Manager** (*Ctrl + L*) and select the **Enlarged Plan** layer combination. In the **Enlarged Floor Plan** layer combination, we want to hide the annotation layers of scales that do not match ¼"=1'-0 (or 048).

Now, hide the following layers:

- **A-ANNO-CLNG-048**
- **A-ANNO-CLNG-096**
- **A-ANNO-NOTE-024**
- **A-ANNO-NOTE-096**
- **A-ANNO-NOTE-192**
- **A-DIMS-DETL**
- **A-DIMS-192**

Show the following layers:

- **A-ANNO-NOTE-048**
- **A-DIMS-048**

Reflected ceiling plans (1/8"=1'-0")

Open the **Layer Settings Manager** (*Ctrl + L*) and select the **Reflected Ceiling Plan** layer combination. We will hide the annotation layers created for scales that do not match 1/8"=1'0" (096).

Now, hide the following layers:

- **A-ANNO-CLNG-048**
- **A-ANNO-NOTE-024**
- **A-ANNO-NOTE-048**
- **A-ANNO-NOTE-096**
- **A-ANNO-NOTE-192**
- **A-DIMS-024**
- **A-DIMS-048**
- **A-DIMS-096**
- **A-DIMS-192**

Show the following layers:

- **A-ANNO-CLNG-096**

Enlarged ceiling plans (1/8"=1'-0")

Open the **Layer Settings Manager** (*Ctrl + L*), click on the **Reflected Ceiling Plan** layer combination, and click on the **New** button to create a new layer combination. Now, enter Enlarged Ceiling Plan.

Next, hide the following layers:

- **A-ANNO-CLNG-048**
- **A-ANNO-NOTE-024**
- **A-ANNO-NOTE-048**
- **A-ANNO-NOTE-096**
- **A-ANNO-NOTE-192**
- **A-DIMS-024**
- **A-DIMS-048**
- **A-DIMS-096**
- **A-DIMS-192**

Show the following layers:

- **A-ANNO-CLNG-096**

Sections & Elevations

Open the **Layer Settings Manager** (*Ctrl* + *L*), select the **Sections** layer combination, and rename it to `Sections & Elevations`. Then, hide the following layers:

- **A-ANNO-CLNG-048**
- **A-ANNO-CLNG-096**
- **A-ANNO-NOTE-192**
- **A-DIMS-192**

Show the following layers:

- **A-DIMS-024**
- **A-DIMS-048**
- **A-DIMS-096**

Go to the view map and click on the `Interior Elevations` clone folder. Then, push the **Settings** button and set the layer combination to **Sections & Elevations**.

Plan details

Open the **Layer Settings Manager** (*Ctrl* + *L*) and select the **Enlarged Plan** layer combination. Hide the following layers:

- **A-ANNO-CLNG-048**
- **A-ANNO-CLNG-096**
- **A-ANNO-NOTE-048**
- **A-ANNO-NOTE-096**
- **A-ANNO-NOTE-192**
- **A-DIMS-096**
- **A-DIMS-192**

Show the following layers:

- **A-ANNO-NOTE-024**
- **A-DIMS-024**

Deleting layer combinations

The following layer combinations are not necessary for our project. Therefore, they should be deleted:

- **HVAC Model**
- **Plumbing Plan**
- **Structural Plan**

Maintaining layer combinations

As the project progresses, you will either encounter the need for new layers or that you don't need certain layers. New layers are hidden by default in all your layer combinations. So when you add layers, make sure you set that layer to show in the layer combinations you want it to show in.

The layer combination named **All visible and unlocked**, which comes with the project template, needs to be updated every time you add a new layer. It is not a magic layer combination. It is just as static as all the others.

Compiled layer matrix

See the following table for a complete layer matrix that shows the suggested layer state for each layer in each layer combination:

name	All visible and unlocked	Drafting	Enlarged Floor Plan	Enlarged Reflected Ceiling Plan	Floor Plan	Plan Detail	Presentation Plan	Reflected Ceiling Detail	Reflected Ceiling Plan	Sections & Elevations	Sections Detail	Site Plan
A-ANNO-CLNG-048	●		●									
A-ANNO-CLNG-096	●								●			
A-ANNO-CLNG-DETL	●							●				
A-ANNO-NOTE-048	●		●									
A-ANNO-NOTE-096	●	●					●			●		
A-ANNO-NOTE-192	●											●
A-ANNO-REFR	●	●			●							
A-ANNO-REVC	●	●	●	●	●	●	●	●	●	●	●	●
A-ANNO-TEXT	●	●	●	●	●	●	●	●	●	●	●	●
A-AREA-IDEN	●		●	●	●		●					
A-AREA-PATT	●		●	●	●		●					●
A-BEAM	●				●				●	●		
A-CLNG	●					●	●		●	●		
A-COLS	●	●	●	●	●	●	●	●	●	●	●	●
A-DEMO	●											
A-DETL-IDEN	●	●	●	●	●	●	●	●	●	●	●	●
A-DIMS-048	●		●	●								
A-DIMS-096	●	●			●		●			●	●	
A-DIMS-DETL	●	●				●		●				●
A-DIMS-LEVL	●	●								●	●	
A-EQMT	●	●	●		●	●	●			●	●	
A-FLOR	●	●	●	●	●	●	●	●	●	●	●	
A-FLOR-FIXT	●	●	●	●	●	●	●	●	●	●	●	
A-FLOR-RISR	●	●	●	●		●	●	●	●	●	●	
A-FLOR-STRS	●	●	●	●	●	●	●	●	●	●	●	
A-FLOR-WDWK	●	●	●				●			●	●	
A-FURN	●	●	●		●	●	●			●	●	
A-GLAZ-FULL	●	●	●	●	●	●	●	●	●	●	●	●

name	All visible and unlocked	Drafting	Enlarged Floor Plan	Enlarged Reflected Ceiling Plan	Floor Plan	Plan Detail	Presentation Plan	Reflected Ceiling Detail	Reflected Ceiling Plan	Sections & Elevations	Sections Detail	Site Plan
A-HTLK-SHEL	●	●	●	●	●	●	●	●	●	●	●	●
A-LITE	●			●					●	●	●	●
A-MARK-DETL	●	●	●	●	●	●	●			●	●	●
A-MARK-ELEV	●	●	●	●	●	●	●			●	●	●
A-MARK-SECT	●	●	●	●	●	●	●			●	●	●
A-NPLT	●											
A-NPLT-HTSP	●	●										
A-NPLT-SEO	●	●										
A-PICT	●	●	●	●	●	●	●	●	●	●		
ArchiCAD Layer	●	●	●	●	●	●	●	●	●	●	●	●
A-ROOF	●	●	●	●	●	●	●			●	●	●
A-WALL-EXTR	●	●	●	●	●	●	●	●	●	●	●	●
A-WALL-INTR	●	●	●	●	●	●	●	●	●	●	●	●
C-TOPO	●											●
C-TOPO-02FT	●											●
C-TOPO-10FT	●											●
C-TOPO-TEXT	●											●
E-POWR	●		●							●	●	
L-PLNT	●											●
L-SITE	●											●
M-EXHS	●			●		●		●	●			
M-HVAC	●			●		●		●	●			●
P-ANNO	●	●	●	●	●	●	●	●	●	●		
S-ANNO	●											
S-FNDN	●				●					●	●	
S-GRID	●	●	●	●	●	●	●			●	●	
S-METL	●									●	●	
S-SLAB	●				●					●	●	

Cloning folders

We have many different view types to create and manage. For most of these view types, we should create clone folders. Using clone folders allows you to control multiple views with the settings inside one clone folder.

The following is a list of clone folders to be created:

- Enlarged floor plans
- Enlarged ceiling plans
- Ceiling details
- Exterior plan details

The following steps will take you through the process of creating a clone folder. To prepare for these steps, open the view map on the **Navigator** palette and then perform the following steps:

1. From the view map, click on the **Clone a Folder** button. The **Clone a Folder** configuration window will appear.

2. In the **Identification** panel, click on **Stories**; change the **Name** setting to `Custom` and enter `Enlarged Floor Plans` in the text box.

3. In the **General** panel:
    - Change the value for **Layer Combination** to **Enlarged Floor Plan**
    - Set the Scale to `1/4" = 1'-0"`
    - Set the value for **Model View Options** to **Construction Documents**
    - Set the value for **Renovation Filter** to **04 New Construction**

4. In the **2D/3D Documents** panel, change the **Zooming** setting to **Fit in window**.

5. Then, click on the **Clone** button.

6. Find the new folder in **View Map**, select it, and drag it up to the position just below **Floor Plans**.

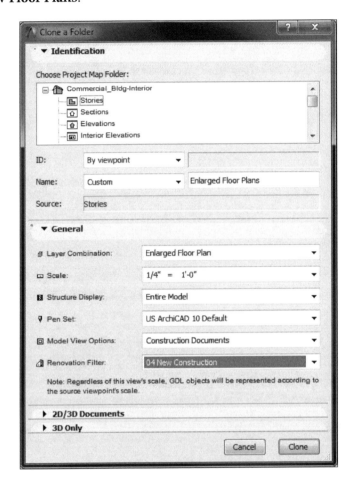

For the remaining clone folder types, follow the preceding steps and use the following matrix as a guide for setting the layer combination, scale, and model view options for each clone folder.

clone folder	Layer Combination	Scale	Model View Options
Enlarged Floor Plans	Enlarged Floor Plan	1/4"=1'-0"	Construction Documents
Enlarged Ceiling Plans	Enlarged Reflected Ceiling Plan	1/4"=1'-0"	Reflected Ceiling Plan
Interior elevations	Sections & Elevations	1/2"=1'-0"	Construction Documents
Ceiling details	Reflected Ceiling Detail	3"=1'-0"	Reflected Ceiling Plan
Exterior plan details	Plan Detail	3"=1'-0"	Construction Documents

Deleting clone folders

Some of the clone folders that come with the project template are not needed for our project. Delete the following existing clone folders:

- `Structural Plans`
- `HVAC Plans`

Click on the clone folder and press the *Delete* key on your keyboard. You will get a warning stating that deleting views is undoable. Click on the **Delete anyway** button.

Creating new view map folders

Not all of our view map folders need to be clone folders; but we will want regular view folders to keep things well organized. You will have to create new view folders for each of the following types of views:

- Casework details
- Exterior section details
- Roof details
- Stair plans
- Stair sections
- Stair details

Use the following steps for each of the view types listed higher up:

1. Open the view map on the **Navigator** palette and click on the **New Folder** button.

2. The **Create New Folder** dialog box will open. Enter `Casework Details` and click on the **Create** button.

Your project folder structure is complete and ready for the production of the views required to produce a construction document set.

Summary

In this chapter, we created a second model and interior model and hotlinked the interior and shell models into each other. We attached Xrefs and created new composite types for our interior walls. We added doors to the interior walls and created three different window types for the exterior walls. Also, we set up the main structure of our layer combinations and majority of the views to be placed on sheets. In the next chapter, we will create our first custom object from the scratch and populate the model with various other objects.

6
Objects, Drafting, and Annotation – A Healthcare Building Project

In this chapter, we will add more content to our building such as casework and plumbing fixtures. We will create a custom new object, insert configure zones (rooms), and create annotation for our views. The following is the list of the major topics included in this chapter:

- Zones
- Adding objects to a patient room
- Surface material creation
- Modeling a custom reception desk
- Creating a custom object
- Attributes
- Drafting tools

Creating zones

Creating all the zones in our building is a big and important task. The zones will represent the rooms in your building. Each zone contains the identity data that defines a room. You could think of them as room objects. The Xref files that we attached in *Chapter 5, Project Setup and Modeling Part 2 – A Healthcare Building Project*, have the room names in them to help you identify specific room types.

Be sure that all your walls are cleanly connected and that there are no gaps. We are going to use the Magic Wand tool to automatically create the zone boundaries. Otherwise, we could manually draw a boundary for each room, but that would take too much time. To do this, perform the following steps:

1. Open the **Renovation** palette and make sure that **Default elements** is set to **04 New Construction**. To open the **Renovation** palette, navigate to **Window | Palettes | Renovation**.

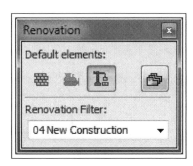

2. Open the **1st FLOOR PLAN** from the view map under **Construction Documentation\Floor Plans**. Then, zoom in on the upper-left corner of the building near the entrance.

3. Double-click on the **Zone** tool icon in the **Toolbox** palette.

4. Set the **Category** to **2.1 Conditioned Space**.

5. Next, change the value for **Name** to **PRIVATE PATIENT**.

6. Then, change the room number to 1001.

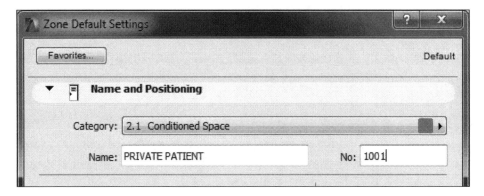

7. Ensure that the layer is set to **A-AREA-IDEN**.

8. Next, click on **OK**.

9. On the **Info Box** palette, set the **Construction Method** to **Inner Edge**.

10. Then, click inside the first patient room (with double doors and a window). The hammer icon will appear. Click inside the room again to place the zone tag.

11. Next, click inside the next patient room to the right and click again to place the zone tag. Notice that the room number automatically increases to **1002**.

12. Do this for all the patient rooms on this floor.

This process will probably cause zones to overlap. If you get the **You have clicked into an existing Zone. Do it anyway?** warning, then click on the **No** button.

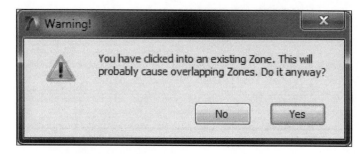

You will most likely find that one of your zones is bleeding into the rest of the building (probably the last one that you placed). Make sure your walls are cleanly connected and that there are no gaps. Also check that your renovation status is correct.

Updating zones

If you need to fix a gap in a wall in an effort to resolve a bleeding zone, you will need to use the **Update Zones** tool to get the zone to regenerate its boundary. Or if you have moved the walls in your zone (room), you can use the **Update Zones** tool to make the zone element conform to the new wall configuration. This can be performed on multiple zones at once or just one at a time. To do so, do as follows:

1. Select the zone(s) that you want to update.

2. Go to the **Design** menu and click on **Update Zones...**.

3. The **Update Zones** window will appear. Check the **Keep Zone Stamp position if updated** box.

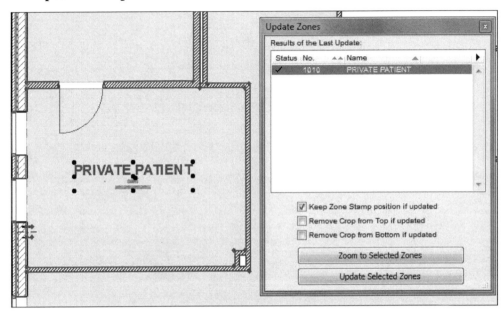

Zone bleeding into other rooms

4. Then, click on the **Update Selected Zones** button.

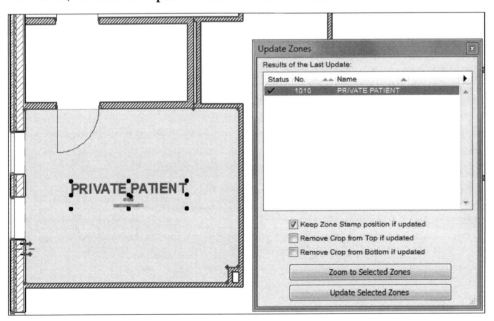

The zone shown after gaps is filled and updated

5. Close the **Update Zones** window when you are finished (click on the **X** icon in the upper-right corner).

Adding casework and plumbing fixtures

We will start adding casework and fixtures to the private patient rooms and adjoining shower room. Each patient room will have the following objects inserted from the ArchiCAD library with the specified parameter settings:

- **Armchair**: 01 19
- **Basin**: 19
- **Bedside cabinet**: 19
- **Cabinet base triple door**: 19
- **Grab bar**: 01 19
- **Hospital bed**: 19
- **Infusion stand**: 19
- **Medical cart**: 19
- **Office table**: 19 (3'0" x 1'-6")
- **Plasma TV**: 19
- **Shower cabin**: 19
- **Sofa**: 19
- **Towel bar**: 01 19
- **Wall mount table**: 19
- **WC**: 19

The following screenshot shows the typical layout of the above furniture and casework, from the preceding list:

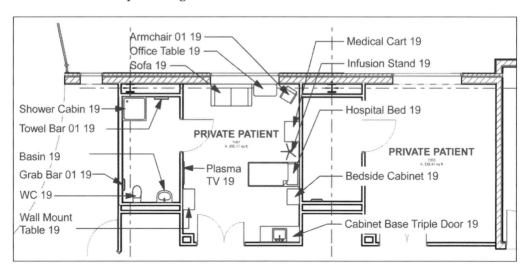

Creating a new surface material

Our next task will be to create a new surface material. The exercise will give you the necessary skill to create a surface material you may need for rendering any specific object. We will do that by duplicating an existing surface, giving it a new name, and changing its color. To do so, perform the following steps:

1. Click on the **Surfaces** icon on the **Attributes** toolbar (or navigate to **Options | Element Attributes… | Surfaces…**).

2. Change the surface to **06 | P Laminate**.

3. Then, press the **New** button.

4. Name the surface 06 | P Laminate Black.

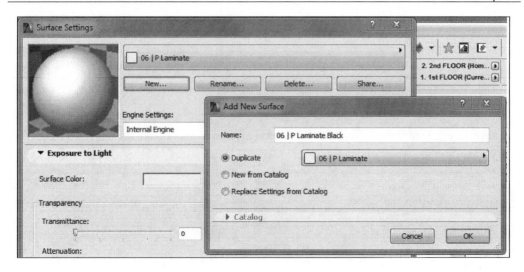

5. Change the surface color setting to black and double-click on the beige color swatch to the right of **Surface Color:**. The **Edit Color** window will appear. Click on the black color in the lower left under **Basic colors:** and then click **OK**.

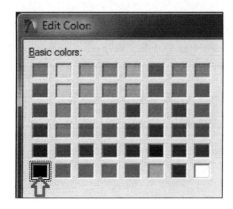

6.   Change the **Specular color** to light gray. Double-click on the color swatch under **Glowing** next to **Specular Color.** See the following screenshot:

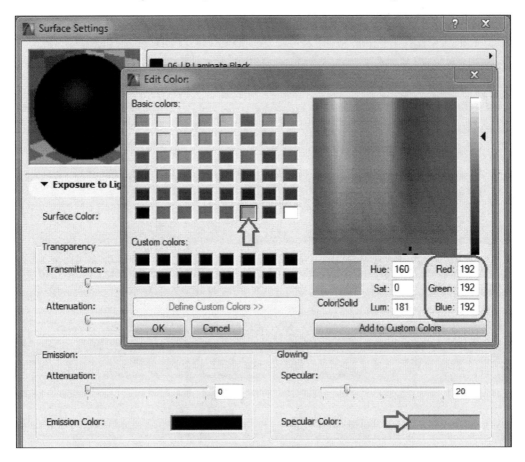

7.   Click on **OK** and again click on **OK** to close **Surface Settings**.

Creating a reception desk

We are going to create the reception desk (greeter's desk) at the ground floor entry (vestibule). This process will involve using the wall, slab, and some of the 2D drafting tools. The table top will be an unusual and free-form shape that you will create with the slab tool. You will learn how to use 2D lines to define the boundary of the table shape.

The main entrance of our building is on the ground floor, so that is what we will work on in the next exercise.

Drawing the desktop outline

We want the shape of the table to relate to shapes of the surrounding elements, so it will have a symmetrical arc. The following will walk you through the process:

1. Go to the view map and open the **Ground** view. Zoom in on the upper-left area of the building where the atrium meets the rectangular shape of the main building.

2. Go to the **Standard** toolbar and set the **Special Snap** points to **Half**.

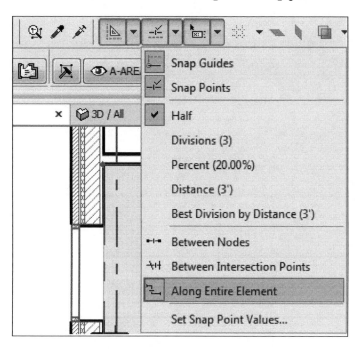

3. Then, start the **Arc/Circle** tool and use the **Centerpoint** and **Radius** geometry method.

4. Enter the arc center point; make your first click (**Centerpoint**) on the midpoint of the wall on the right.

5. Enter the arc start point and click on the intersection where the curtain wall meets the north exterior wall. See the following screenshot:

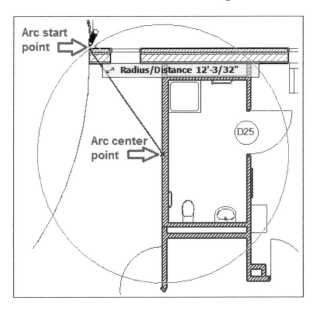

6. Draw your arc down to the left to form a quarter circle; as you move your cursor down, type the letter A to activate the angle entry box. Type in the number 90 and press the *Enter* key. You will have a perfect quarter circle arc.

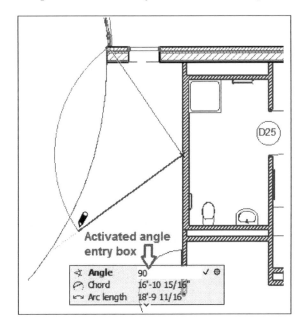

7. Draw another arc with the same center point and make the start point of the arc at the bottom-right corner of the small window on the exterior wall. Draw the arc down, parallel to the first arc, and click on the bottom endpoint of the first arc. See the following screenshot:

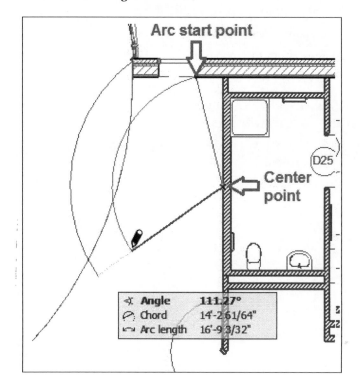

8. Draw a line to connect the bottom ends of the two arcs.

9. Then, draw two lines to connect the top arc endpoints to wrap the table outline around the wall at the top.

Creating the desk top

Our next task will be to create the top surface for the desk. We will do this with the **Slab** tool:

1. First, hide the **A-FLOR** layer. This will hide the arc of the floor slab in the shell model below the table, which would otherwise interfere with our slab creation. If this does not hide the arc, open the shell model and see what layer it is really on.

2. Start the **Slab** tool and open the **Slab Selection Settings** window to do the following:

    ◦ Set the layer to **A-FURN**

    ◦ Set the composite to **41-30 30 | Cherry**

    ◦ Set the slab thickness to 1"

    ◦ Set the **Offset to Home Story** to 2'-6"

    ◦ Finally, click on **OK**

3. Hold the *Spacebar* down to activate the Magic Wand tool and click inside the desktop outline. This will create the slab.

4. Hold your *Shift* key down and select the new slab to confirm its creation. See the following screenshot:

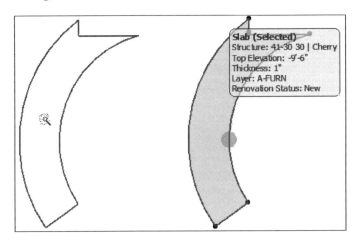

Creating the desktop support walls

The walls that support the desktop will be made of the same material as the desktop and will be inset from the desktop edge:

1. Start the **Wall** tool and open the **Wall Selection Settings** window. Then, make the following configurations:

    ◦ **Wall height**: 2'-5"

    ◦ **Bottom offset**: 0'-0"

    ◦ **Composite: 41-30 30 | Cherry**

- ○ **Wall thickness: 2"**
- ○ **Layer: A-FURN**

2. Set the geometry method to **Curved Centerpoint and Radius**. Enter the **Arc Wall** Centerpoint by clicking on the midpoint of the wall you used to create the desktop arc.

3. Enter the **Arc Wall** Centerpoint by zooming in on the upper-left of the desktop. Then, click just inside the desktop. See the following screenshot:

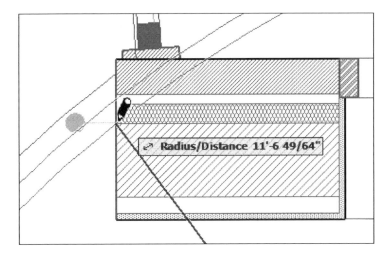

4. Zoom out and draw the wall down to the bottom of the desktop arc edge.

5. Zoom in on the bottom of the desktop and create a straight wall along the bottom edge of the desktop. Then, drag that wall in to match the inset distance of the curved wall.

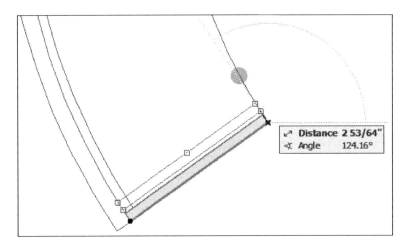

6. Select the two new walls and click on the **Intersect** button.

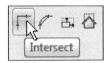

Viewing your desk in 3D

It is always a good idea to check your work in a 3D view. Let's do that now:

1. Select the walls and desktop that you created and press the *F5* key. This will show your selection in a 3D window and nothing else. See the following screenshot:

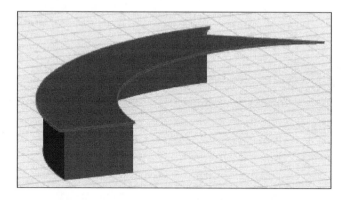

   Or use a single floor marquee.

2. Turn the **A-FLOR** layer back on.

3. Start the **Marquee** tool from the **Toolbox** palette. Go to the **Info Box** palette and ensure the selection method is set to **Single Floor** (AKA the Skinny Marquee).

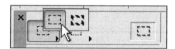

4. Draw a rectangle around the desk, nearby walls, and double doors below the desk with the marquee. Then, press the *F5* key. See the following screenshot:

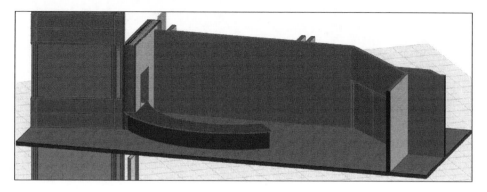

Creating a new object

This next exercise is more advanced than previous object lessons in this book. We will delve into some of the code used to define objects and also see how to manipulate the parameters visible to the end user.

For this lesson, we are going to create another desk by using what we created in the previous lesson. Then we will save it as an object. You will modify the slab and walls to fit into a different location in the building. Then, you will learn how to turn the desk into an object that can be easily copied to multiple places in the building model:

1. Select the slab and walls that made up the desk in the previous lesson and make a copy (*Ctrl* + *Shift* + *D*). Then, place it in the pantry area on the ground level between column grid intersections D-2 & C-3.

2. Rotate it approximately 55 degrees counter clockwise so that the short edge of the table is straight up and down and move it up against the column. See the following screenshot:

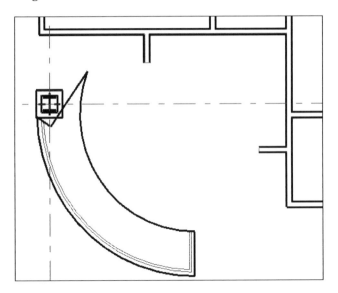

3. Select the walls and change their height to **2'-11"**.

4. Change the **Reference Plane Offset** to **Home Story height** on the slab to **2'-11"**.

5. Zoom in on the jagged edge of the desk and select the slab. Click on the inside corner hotspot of the slab and the pet palette will appear. Then, click on the **Move Node** button to drag the node over the bottom right corner of the furring wall. (This is similar to using grips in AutoCAD).

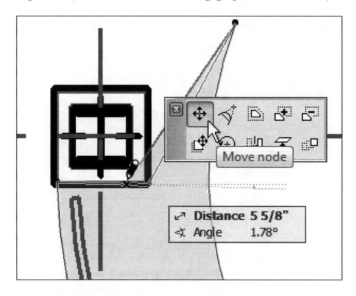

6. Click on the long edge of the top pointed piece and push the **Insert New Node** button on the pet palette. Then, drag the new node over to the top-right corner.

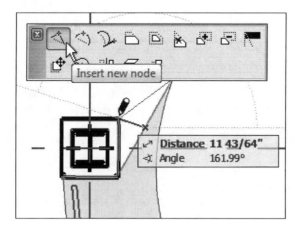

7. Click on the node to bring up the pet palette; then click on the **Subtract from Polygon** button. With this method, you will use your cursor to draw a shape that will trim the slab. You could think of it as trimming with a polygonal shape.

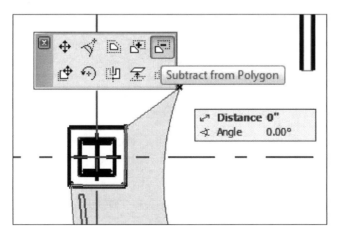

8. Draw a straight line from the top of the column-furring wall to the right, which is just past the slab edge. Then, draw a line straight up past the slab point; then, over to the left and back down to your first click.

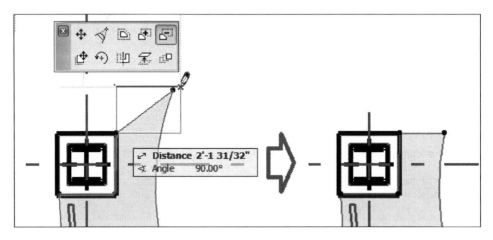

9. With the slab selected, click on the top-right node to bring up the pet palette and click on the **Fillet/Chamfer** button.

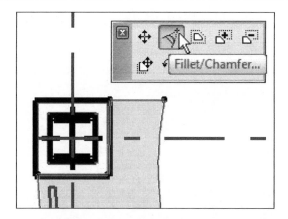

10. The **Fillet/Chamfer** dialog box will appear. Click on the **Fillet** radio button, enter 1', and click on **OK**.

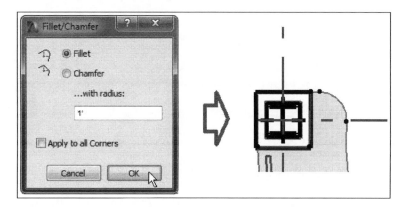

11. Select the slab and walls that support the desktop. Then, go to the **File** menu and navigate to **Libraries and Objects | Save Selection as... | Object**.

12. Then, the **Save Object** window will appear. Enter the **Pantry Counter** name in the **Name** box at the top and press the **Save** button.

13. The **Change Object's Basic Settings** window will appear. It will create and assign parameters based on the different elements in your new object. Finally, press **OK**.

Refer to the following screenshot of a 3D view of the desk:

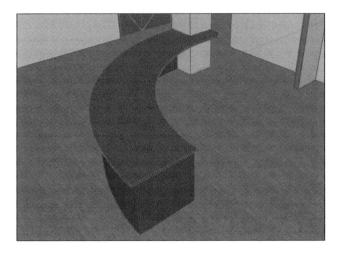

Using your new object

The elements you used to create the object are still independent elements (and remain where you left them). And now your new object is ready to use:

1. Open the **Object Default Settings** window.

2. Go to the browser pane and click on **Embedded Library**. Your new object will appear in the folder contents pane.

3. Select **Pantry Counter** and place it anywhere in a plan view.

After you place it, you will find it difficult to select, unless you grab the lower right corner of the desktop. This demonstrates the need to add hotspots to your new object.

Adding hotspots to an object

A hotspot is a node (or point) that can be used to define selection points. We are going to add hotspots to the object to provide easier selection. We will do this by reusing the original slab and walls and then recreating (overwriting) the object:

1. Before we begin, hide the layer **A-WALL-INTR**. This will make it easier to work with our object's elements.

2. Go to the **More** panel on the **Toolbox** palette and click on the **Hotspot** tool.

3. Zoom in on the desktop slab and click on each endpoint on the slab to insert the hotspots. Also, put a hotspot on the midpoint of each arc slab edge. See the following screenshot example:

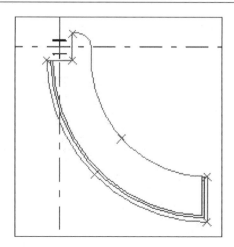

4. Select the hotspots, walls, and slab and save them as **Pantry Counter** again. Then navigate to the **File | Libraries and Objects | Save Selection as… | Object**.

5. Then, the **Change Object's Basic Settings** window will open. We will take this opportunity to rename the attributes that were automatically created. Rename the attributes according to the next image:

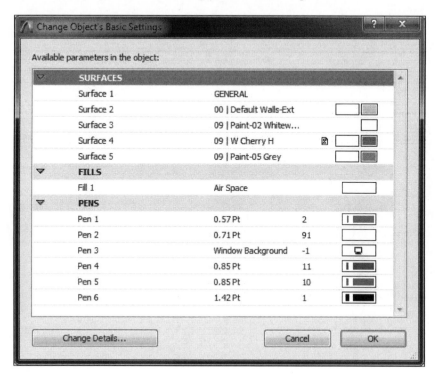

6.   Start the **Object** tool and place the **Pantry Counter** object. You will have a much easier time selecting it now.

Looking at the code inside an object

The walls that we used to create the object are shown in plan view, but this is not what we want to see. We will open the object and remove the 2D plan geometry that represents the walls. We will also dig into the code to control the surfaces in 3D.

The 2D and 3D geometry of an object is actually defined by a code after the object is created. You can select any object in your model and open the object editor to see all the code that defines that object:

1.   Select the **Pantry Counter** object you just created and press the key combination of *Ctrl + Shift + O*. This will open the object editor (or the long way to get there is via **File | Libraries and Objects | Open Object**).

2.   Go to the left side of the object editor window and click on the **Parameters** button. There is an extra parameter that we will not need. Find the attribute named **Surface 5**, click on the name, and then click on the **Delete** button at the top. See the following screenshot image:

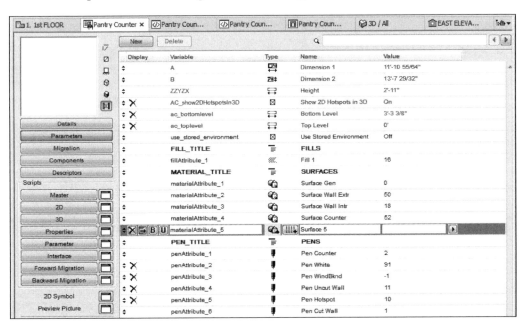

3. Take note of the parameter named **Pen Uncut Wall**. This is the pen used to represent the wall elements in 2D plan views that we want to remove. Each parameter has a variable assigned to it. The assigned variable will be used in the 2D script to define the uncut wall. Click on the variable box for **Pen Uncut Wall** and copy the variable name (**penAttribute_4**).

4. Now let's look at the code that defines 2D geometry. Click on the **2D** button in the **Scripts** panel to the left. At the top, you will see a text that identifies the object, the date the file was created, and the ArchiCAD version. This is the script that defines 2D geometry:

```
!    Name      : Pantry Counter.gsm
!    Date      : Monday, June 09, 2015
!    Version   : 19.00
!    Written by ArchiCAD
!

mul2     A/3.628602, B/4.163374
add2     -275'-2.1467", -141'-5.7685"
pen      penAttribute_1
poly2_b{5}      14,        1,        0,        3,        1,        0,
         0'-0.0000", 0'-0.0000", 3'-3.3701", 0'-0.0000", 0'-0.0000",
         277'-1.0499", 153'-2.0413",        1,
         275'-2.1467", 153'-2.0413",        1,
         287'-1.0051", 153'-4.6507",      900,
         0'-0.0000", 291'-10.1088",     4001,
```

Here is a description of the code in the preceding screenshot:

  ○ The first line of code starts with `mul2`. This is used to establish scale transformations.

  ○ The second line starts with `add2`. This prepares positioning.

  ○ The third line begins with `pen`. This defines the pen to be used in the following geometry code.

  ○ The fourth line is where geometry creation begins with `poly2_b`, which creates a poly line. It is followed by coordinates for the poly line to follow. The coordinates for a drawing command such as `poly2_b` end where the next geometry routine begins. The next geometry routine will begin with the `pen` command or another geometry command.

5. We want to remove all the instances where the uncut wall pen is used. However, for the sake of preserving code and demonstrating a feature, we will "comment" the code out. In other words, we will make the software ignore the code:

   ○ Press the key combination of *Ctrl + F* to bring up the **Text Window Find** tool.

   ○ Paste in the variable name for the uncut wall and press the **Find** button. Then you will be taken to the first instance of the variable being used.

   ○ With your cursor, select the line of code beginning with Pen down to the line before the next instance of Pen. See the following example where the variable name for the uncut wall is penAttribute_4:

```
        0'-0.0000", -284'-0.3739",   4001,
        275'-7.6824", 153'-1.3084",     1,
        275'-5.6818", 153'-1.3084",     1
pen       penAttribute_4
line_property       0
arc2      287'-1.0051", 153'-4.6507", 11'-7.3634", 181.3742522546, 268.8174366047
arc2      287'-1.0051", 153'-4.6507", 11'-5.3634", 181.3942651836, 267.9669629038
pen       penAttribute_2
fill fillAttribute_1
poly2_b{5}        5,       2,       2,       3, penAttribute_2, penAttribute_3,
```

6. In this case, the four lines of code selected define the two arcs in the uncut wall. With the four lines of code selected, press the exclamation point button at the upper-left of the 2D script window. This will add an exclamation point to the beginning of each line of code, which will tell ArchiCAD to ignore it. You can add in the exclamation points manually if you wish, but this way is faster:

7. Find the other location(s) where the uncut wall pen is used and comment out those lines as well.

8. Press the **Check Script** button at the top of the script editor window. If your script is good, you will get a popup stating that **The GDL script is OK**. If not, you will get a warning pop-up stating the problem and the line on which the error has occurred. Since you are not adding code or changing routines, you will be pretty safe here.

9. Close the object editor from the icon/drop-down menu at the upper-left corner or click on the upper right **X** icon. You will be prompted to save changes to the library part. Then click on the **Save** button.

10. The uncut wall lines will disappear. See the next image:

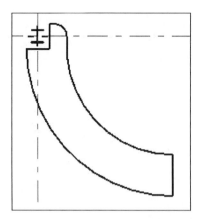

11. There is specifically a help menu for creating and modifying objects. It is called the **GDL** Reference Guide. The acronym GDL refers to the programming language used within the objects.

 Another way to achieve clean 2D lines is to draft inside the Symbol Window in the object editor. However, this method is primarily used for devices that are too small to show to scale.

Hiding the unused parameter

We removed the instances where a certain parameter was used in the 2D script so that it would not be shown. However, the parameter is still shown in the **Object Selection Settings** window under **Parameters**. The following steps will show you how to hide the parameter from the user:

1. Open the **Pantry Counter** object again. (Select it by pressing *Ctrl + Shift + O*).

2. Click on the **Parameters** button to display the parameter list. Select **Pen Uncut Wall** from the list and click at the far left in the **Display** column on the **X** button. This will hide the parameter from the user.

3. While you are in there, do the same for the following pen parameters:

   ○ **Pen White** (not useful)

   ○ **Pen WindBknd** (used by ArchiCAD to fill the inside of the walls and not useful)

   ○ **Pen Hotspot** (not useful)

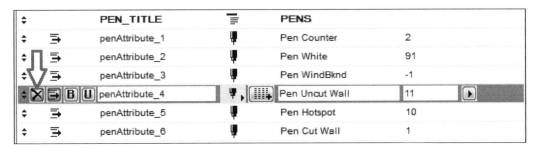

4. Next, close and save the object editor and click on the main **Pantry Counter** tab at the top of the drawing window to close the object editor. Then click on **Save** when prompted.

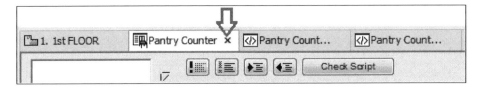

5. Select the object and bring up its selection settings (*Ctrl + T*) and you will see that those parameters are no longer shown.

Changing the display of the parameter list

When you open the **Selection Settings** window to change a parameter, you will notice that the **FILLS**, **SURFACES**, and **PENS** parameters are collapsed and indented. To change one, you need to click on the heading first to expand the list and then select the parameter you want to change. This is great when you have an object that has a large amount of parameters to manage. But in our case, we don't have that many objects and the expanding heading feature is not helpful. We will remove it so that our parameters are immediately accessible:

1. Select the **Pantry Counter** object and open the library part editor (*Ctrl + Shift + O*).

2. Open the **Parameters** list. Notice that all the parameters that are directly under **FILLS**, **SURFACES**, and **PENS** headings have the indent icon present. Turn off the indent for each of the parameters under the aforementioned headings by clicking on the indent icon. See the following screenshot:

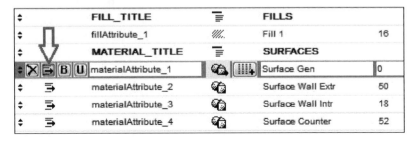

3. Save and close.

4. Open the object's selection settings window (*Ctrl + T*) and you will now see all the parameters without needing to expand the headings. See the next screenshot:

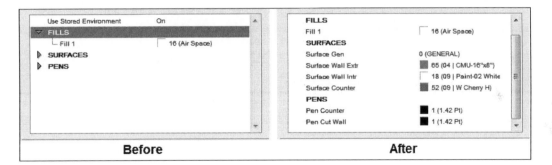

Before	After

Understanding attributes

The dictionary definition of an attribute is "something attributed as belonging to a person, thing, group, etc.; a quality, character, characteristic, or property: Sensitivity is one of his attributes." But within ArchiCAD, an attribute can be defined as a characteristic or property, such as color, shape, or texture.

For you to be successful in using ArchiCAD, is it essential that you understand what attributes are and how to manage them. The management of attributes can be a full-time job on very large projects. Following is a list of all the attribute types in ArchiCAD, with a brief explanation. The order of the list is based on the order used in the drop-down menu under **Options | Element Attributes**:

Layer Settings

The **Layer Settings** option is used to create, delete, and manage layers and layer combinations. You can use the keyboard shortcut *Ctrl + L* to open the layer settings manager window.

Line Types

The **Line Types** option is used to create, delete, and manage line types. New line types are created with dashes and symbols.

Fill Types

The **Fill Types** option is used to create, delete, and manage fill types, such as **Solid**, **Vectorial**, **Symbols**, and **Image** fills. It is also used to specify if a fill should be used as a drafting, cover, or cut fill. You can set the scale behavior to scale with plan (model size) or scale independent (paper size).

Building Materials

The **Building Materials** option is used to create, delete, and manage building materials to be used by composite structures such as **Precast Concrete**, **Steel Deck**, or **Heavy Timber**.

Composites

The **Composites** option is used to create, delete, and manage composites that use building materials for walls, slabs, shells, and roofs.

Pens & Colors

The **Pens & Colors** option is used to create, delete, and manage pen sets. It is also used to define color and line thickness for individual pens within each pen set.

Surfaces

The **Surfaces** option is used to create, delete, and manage surfaces such as a specific metal, wood, or plastic that can be used by any element.

Zone Categories

The **Zone Categories** option is used to create, delete, and manage zone categories. It also assigns the color, fill color, and zone tags that are to be used by each zone category.

Mark-Up Styles

The **Mark-Up Styles** option is used to create, delete, and manage mark-up styles. They assign the color used for the correction elements and highlighted elements for each style.

Profile Manager

The **Profile Manager** is used to create, delete, and manage the profile shapes used for columns, beams, and walls.

Renovation Override Styles

The **Renovation Override Styles** option is used to assign and manage the attributes used in renovation override styles. The attributes include pens, line types, and fill patterns.

Operation Profiles

The **Operation Profiles** option is used to create, delete, and manage operation profiles, which are the part of the energy evaluation features in ArchiCAD; configure the occupancy type, such as residential or non-residential; define the values for human heat gain, humidity, and water consumption; and set up daily schedules to gauge energy consumption.

Managing attributes

All the different attributes can be managed from one tool—the attribute manager. Tasks such as renaming, deleting, duplicating, and purging unused attributes can be performed with the help of the attribute manager. With very large projects, it is good practice to purge unused attributes. If you need to rename multiple layers, use the attribute manager as it will be faster:

1. Go to the **Options** menu and navigate to **Element Attributes | Attribute Manager**.

2. You will see that there is a tab for each attribute type and a list of all attributes. Most attributes have a **Purge Unused** button. The following screenshot shows the **Fill Types** page. Note that you can set whether the fill is available as a drafting, cover, or cut fill at the bottom of the left-hand pane.

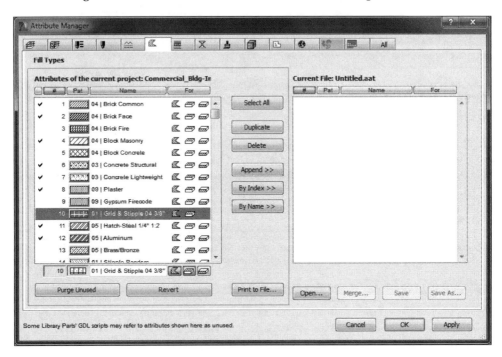

Drafting tools

Even though most of what we create in the model is three-dimensional, we still need to do some embellishing with the 2D line work. This task can be referred to as drafting. Drawing lines, arcs, and polylines is a pretty easy thing to do. Just remember that in ArchiCAD, you have the feature to add an arrow, dot, or tick mark at the beginning or end of your line or arc:

1. First, open the default settings for the line, arc, or polyline tool and you will see the arrowhead icon.

2. Click on it and see the different symbol options you have to place at either one or both ends of our line. See the next screenshot:

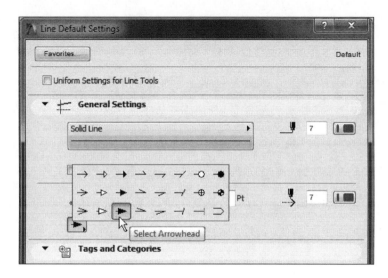

Modifying fills

Creating fills is easy. You just select the fill pattern you want and then draw the boundary to define that fill. However, oftentimes, you will need to change the shape of a fill that has already been drawn. The following exercise demonstrates many different ways in which you can modify a fill:

1. Double-click on the **Fill** tool and set the **Fill Type** to **Drafting Fill**.

2. Then change the **Fill Pattern** to **01 | Grid 02" D**.

3. Next, set the layer to **A-AREA-PATT**.

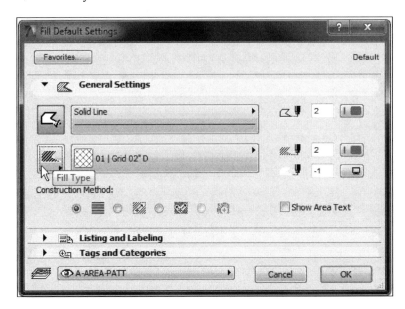

4. Click on **OK** and draw a small polygon, as shown in the following the example:

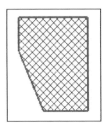

5. Then select the polygon. Hover your cursor over an edge and click the left mouse button and hold it. This will bring up the pet palette for editing edges. Click on the **Insert New Node** icon and pull the cursor away from the polygon, as shown in the following screenshot:

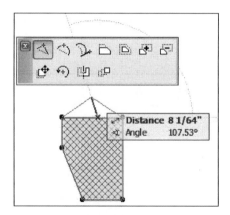

6. Do the same to a different edge and then press the **Curve edge** button on the pet palette. Then pull the cursor away from the polygon. See the following screenshot:

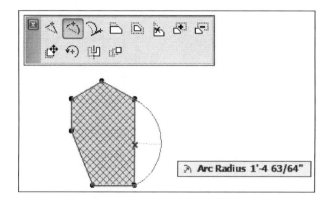

7. Bring up the pet palette on another edge and press the **Subtract from Polygon** button. Then draw a polygon inside the polygon. See the following screenshot:

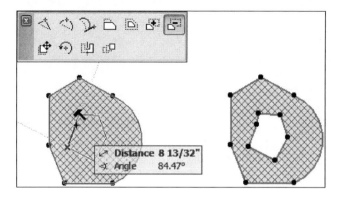

8. Experiment with all the editing commands on the pet palette. When you are finished, you will have a good understanding of how you can modify drafting elements.

Editing text

After you place the text in your project, there is a good chance that you may need to go back and change its contents. The trick to editing text is to have the **Text** tool active. Otherwise, it is more difficult to select text and initiate the editing mode. To do this, do as follows:

1. Start the **Text** tool and type in a text string.

2. With the **Text** tool still active, select the new text string. Notice that when you hover your cursor over the text string, the cursor changes to the straight text box edit cursor, as shown in the following screenshot:

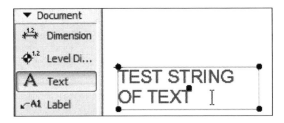

3. Click inside the text string and the text editing palettes will appear. As you can see, this is where you can change font and size and make text italic or bold. Select part or all of the text string and press the **B** icon to make the text bold, as shown in the following screenshot:

 If you try to edit a text string when the text tool is not active, you will have a harder time getting the text into edit mode.

Editing dimensions

After you have created a dimension, you may need to either delete or add a segment. The following steps will show you how to do just that:

1. Open the **1st FLOOR PLAN** view in the interior model, under the `Construction Documents` folder, and zoom in on the rooms at the bottom of the plan.

2. Start the **Dimension** tool and dimension the inside and outside edges of three walls. See the dimensions in the following screenshot:

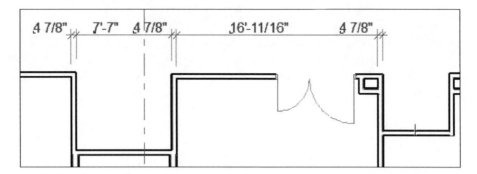

3. With the **Dimension** tool active, hold the *Shift* key down and select the tick mark of a witness line, of an inside wall edge, as shown in the next screenshot:

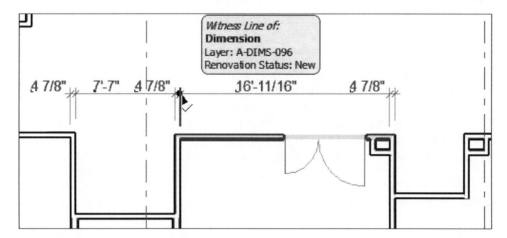

4. With the witness line selected, press the *Delete* key. This will remove a segment of the dimension and automatically adjust the adjoining segments.

5. This time, select the whole dimension (*Shift*). Hold the *Ctrl* key down and click on a different wall, off to the right.

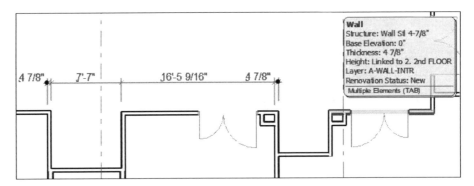

6. Now, you will have a new segment to the dimension string. See the finished example here:

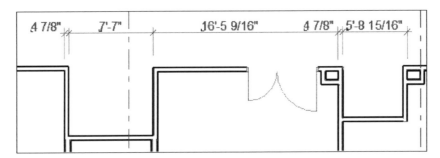

Summary

In this chapter, we worked with zones and zone categories and learned how to create a new surface material. We also got a brief overview of all the different attributes in ArchiCAD and the attribute manager. We learned how to create an object and edit the attributes and code inside an object. We learned how to add and subtract segments from dimensions and the basics about working with text.

In the next chapter, we will get into advanced view management, sheets, and mastering graphic control to produce great drawings.

7
Documentation – A Commercial Project

In this chapter, we will prepare views on our project for printing. We will learn how to manage and organize layouts. Now that you are more familiar with ArchiCAD, we will dive deeper into understanding the concepts and settings related to the documentation workflow.

The basic techniques are similar to the ones described in *Chapter 3, Documentation – A Residential Project*. Read it again if you feel that you need to refresh your memory of them or just refer to it as you read this chapter.

The following map illustrates the complexity and connections of the documentation workflow. You can see the hierarchy of how modeling and documentation is structured in ArchiCAD and how the settings and the different areas of the **Navigator** palette are connected to each other.

Review this map frequently as we go through the concepts of this chapter:

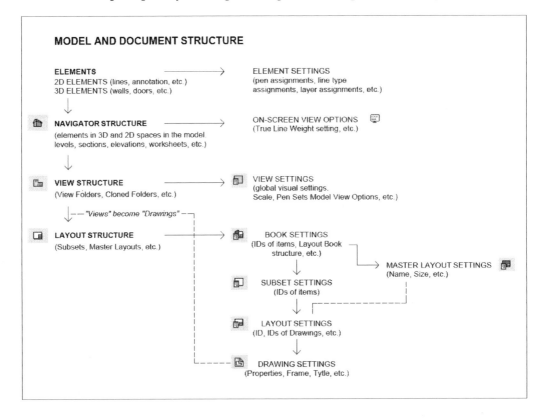

The topics we will cover in this chapter are as follows:

- View setup
- The organizer
- Documentation workflow
- Master layout setup
- Autotext
- Layout setup
- The drawing manager
- Printing technique

View setup

The first thing we need to make sure of is that our view settings are correct. This will define the look of our printout as well as help us keep a clean and organized set. You can access the **View Settings** dialog box by selecting a view in the **Navigator** palette and clicking on the **Settings** button at the bottom of **Navigator**. You can also right-click on a view in **Navigator** and select **View Settings** from the drop-down menu.

The **View Settings** dialog box consists of several areas, which are covered in the following sections.

Identification

Here, you can set the **ID** and **Name** of the view and also see the **Source** of the view. The **ID** and **Name** fields are the same as the first two fields in the **Properties** panel, at the bottom of the **Navigator** palette, once a view is selected; but here, we can adjust the ID and the name more specifically.

You can choose the ID and name to be based on the project map, which will follow them automatically as they are established in the project map. You can also specify custom values for these fields. This means that you will have a different ID and/or name for the view than the original **Source** in the project map. You can adjust the name and ID in the **Navigator** palette, which will make the values custom.

In certain cases, this might be useful but in general it is not recommended because it creates an added level of complexity, which will have to be managed manually. ArchiCAD is great at providing a high level of customization but this needs to be treated carefully. More custom settings will also mean that you will have to make more adjustments or changes manually in the future.

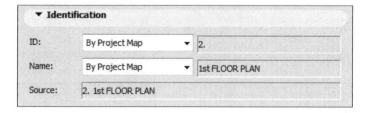

General – automate all!

This section has some of the most important settings that determine how the view will look when printed. You can select the **Layer Combination**, **Scale**, **Structure Display**, **Pen Set**, **Model View Options**, and **Renovation Filter** in this area. After making sure that the correct layer combination (which determines the visible content of our view) and scale is selected from the drop-down menu, we will focus on the **Pen Set** and **Model View Options**. These two settings have a big impact on the look of the printed view:

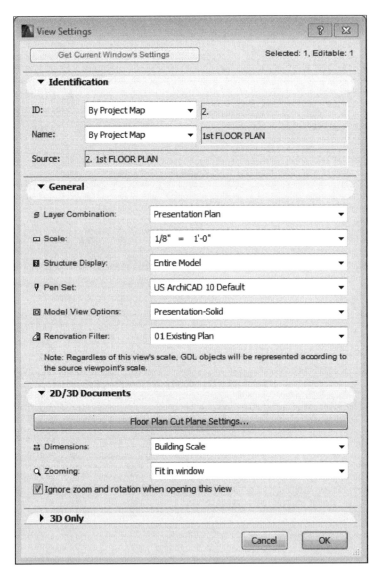

Pen Set

You can set up different pen sets for different presentation options by navigating to
Options | Element Attributes | Pens and Colors.

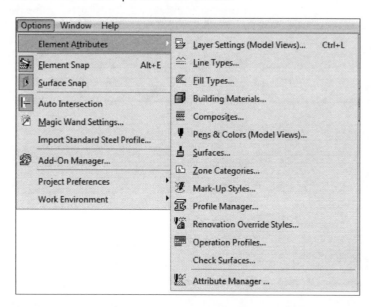

In the **View Settings** dialog box, you can select the appropriate pen set from the
General area | **Pen Set** drop-down list from the available options established
by going to **Options | Element Attributes | Pens and Colors**. Pen weights are
important to generate proper looking printouts.

The general recommendation is to use not more than five different pen weights that
have distinguishable differences between them. If your pen set includes more than
that, it will be hard for you to manage the look of your drawings. It is also good
practice to have the same pen set in colors and in black only. You can quickly assess
on the screen what the drawing will look like on paper with the black version of
the pen, while the colored versions of your pens are useful to differentiate elements
while your are working on your model.

Model View Options

The model view options are perhaps the second most important settings that you need to consider to create proper looking printouts. You can set up different model view options for different presentation options by navigating to **Document | Set Model View | Model View Options**.

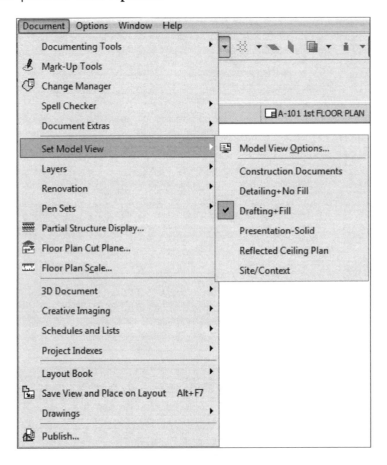

The **Model View Options** control the display intelligence of the model elements; unlike the visibility of whole model elements, which can be controlled with layer combinations. Model view options specify whether the parts of the model elements are visible in a specific view (for example, the door and window markers) or how the parts of the model elements are displayed (for example, the cut fills of the wall composites).

In combination with the view scale, these settings will ultimately define what your drawings will look like once printed.

Here, we need to mention a feature of the **View Settings** dialog that is easy to miss. The **Get Current Window's Settings** button at the top of the dialog box enables you to capture the as-is settings of your current window. For example, if you activated the **First Floor Enlarged Floor** plan, went to the **Layers Settings** dialog, and turned off a couple of layers manually, then clicking on the **Get Current Window's Settings** button will capture the current state of your custom layer visibility regardless of the previously set layer combination. You can also capture the current window's settings by right clicking on the view in the **Navigator** palette and choosing **Get Current Window's Settings**.

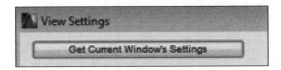

If you do either of the options mentioned, **Custom** will be specified in the **General / Layer Combination** field of the **View Settings** dialog. Adjusting visibility on the screen and not having to go through the effort of setting up and assigning all the aspects of the **General** area of the view settings seems like an easy shortcut. We will not use that, because it will make it very hard to manage our views that way.

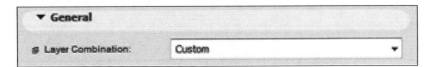

Our goal is to set all the aspects of the visibility of our views by the preset standards and automate all parts of the **General** area of **View Settings**. This practice will pay off in the long run because making changes centrally to any of the settings will be much quicker than readjusting every view one by one.

Another good management practice is to save pen sets in the attribute manager as an .aat file, and export **Model View Options** in the **Model View Options** dialog box as .xml files. Especially when you need to manage mutiple files and make sure that their settings are identical, you can easily import the pen sets and model view options into other files in this way. The Attribute Manager allows you to import pen sets from template (.tpl), plan (.pln), and archive (.pla) files as well as .aat and .xml files.

2D/3D Documents

The **2D/3D Documents** area allows you to set **Floor Plan Cut Plane Settings**, the **Dimensions** style, and **Zooming** of the view. The **Floor Plan Cut Plane Settings** are particularly important for displaying windows properly.

The **Floor Plan Cut Plane Settings** can also be accessed by navigating to **Document | Floor Plan Cut Plane**. For example, clerestory windows might not be displayed in floor plans properly unless we adjust the floor plan cut plane to the right height that intersects the clerestory windows. This is why you can adjust the floor plan cut plane per view in this area.

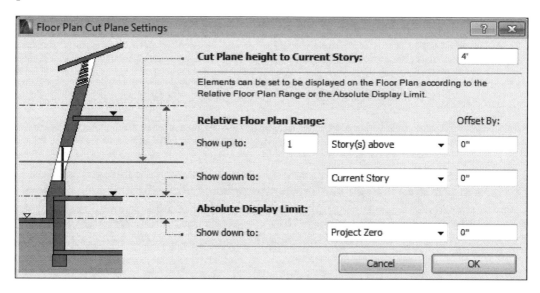

The **Zooming** controls the zoomed area once the view is activated (for example, by double-clicking on the view name in the **Navigator**). Some users prefer the views to ignore the zoom when activated. If you would like to set the views in the project to be independent of zoom factors, you can check the **Ignore zoom and rotation when opening this view** box. On the other hand, this option can be useful when dealing with an enlarged floor plan view where a specific area of the floor needs focus.

3D Only

As the name suggests, the **3D Only** area of the **View Settings** dialog controls the 3D view settings. You can select whether you'd like to generate the 3D view in the 3D window or as a rendering with the **Generate in** drop-down menu. You can also select a preset rendering style with the **Rendering Scene** drop-down menu.

For more information on view settings, refer to *Chapter 3, Documentation – A Residential Project*.

The organizer – how to access it and why it is important

The project organizer is one of the main tools that you can utilize while setting up your documentation. You can access it by clicking on the top-left button of the **Navigator** panel and selecting **Show Organizer**.

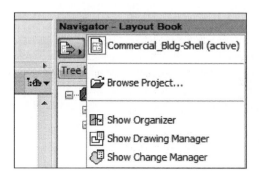

The organizer gives you a comprehensive view of your document set and allows you to set up and arrange your views, layouts, and publisher sets. We will use the organizer for many of the tasks that are required to set up our layouts, so we need to get familiar with it first.

Relationship between parts of the organizer

The organizer has two main panels, each of which can display the view map, layout book and publisher sets. Since the idea behind the organizer is to reference information from the left panel to the right, only the left panel shows the project map, which is the most rudimentary level of our model organization. You can right-click on each item in each panel, get more information and adjustment options of the item's settings, and pull over the items from one panel to the other populating the destination panel. The following diagram shows the concept of the documentation setup in ArchiCAD, starting with the project map on the left, followed by the view map, layout book, and publisher sets in the correct order:

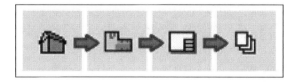

Let's set up the sides of the organizer by choosing the project map on the left and the view map on the right.

There are functional buttons in the lower-right corner of the organizer that can be helpful in creating a folder structure at each level of the document organization. Clicking on the **New Folder** button creates a new folder at the selected position and clicking on the yellow button on the lower-right next to **New Folder** can access the *Clone a folder* feature of ArchiCAD. We will focus on the *Clone a folder* feature because it allows us to generate an automated document structure.

Cloning a folder means that you are automatically referencing the content of a folder in another level of the document organization. For example, cloning the **Stories** category of the project map in the **View Map** panel will create a **View** folder that automatically follows any changes made to **Stories** in the project map. This means that a floor plan view will be automatically generated if you add a new story to your project. You can create multiple clones of the same project map category with different default view settings.

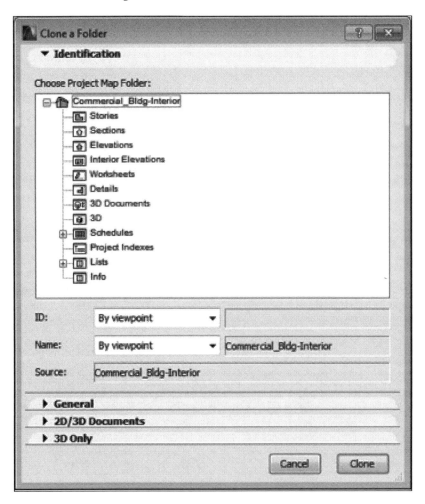

Documentation workflow

The documentation workflow is a subset of the project workflow (see *Chapter 3, Documentation – A Residential Project*, for more information). Our goal is to set up a part of our document properly and take advantage of the automated documentation system.

The documentation workflow in ArchiCAD can be divided into three steps:

- **View adjustment**: This is used to review the established views in our model and consider them as drawings that will be placed on sheets
- **Sheet setup**: This is used to create and review the layouts that will be needed to properly document our project
- **Drawing placement**: This is used to place the views on sheets and adjust the miscellaneous annotation

It is recommended to keep the whole workflow in mind from the beginning. You should create your model and place the 2D elements and annotations thinking about what they will look like on a printed page and how you will organize your document set.

Creating and adjusting layouts is performed in the layout book. We can work in the layout book either in the **Navigator** palette or by selecting the layout book as one of the panels of the organizer.

Let's switch the organizer to show the view map on the left and the layout book the right.

Layout Book (sheets)

The **Layout Book** palette is a collection of layouts, which are digital representations of our printed sheets. This is the final setting stage in our documentation workflow before we publish (print or save files) our documents.

Let's review the parts of the **Layout Book** palette before we go into further details. The following screenshot shows an example of the **Layout Book** palette from *Chapter 3, Documentation – A Residential Project*:

a. Settings
b. New layout
c. New master layout
d. New subset

   e. Update

   f. Delete

   g. Layout ID (sheet number) and the sheet name of the selected sheet

   h. Master layout of the selected sheet

   i. Size of the selected sheet

   j. Current revision of the selected sheet

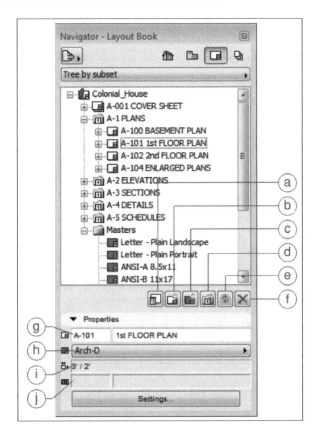

Layout Book settings

Let's right-click on the green **Layout Book** icon on the top of the list and select **Book Settings**. This will bring up the **Book Settings** dialog box, which will allow you to define how the IDs (that is, the numbering) of the items of the **Layout Book** palette will behave. You can also create a new issue and set up how numbering will behave in revisions. We will discuss the last two areas in detail in *Chapter 8, Work Sharing with ArchiCAD*.

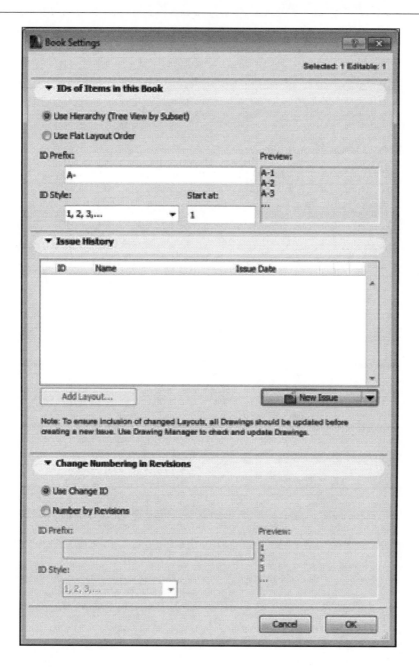

The layouts (building blocks of the **Layout Book**) have a specific editing environment where you can adjust several aspects of the look of the sheets and the placed drawings. The basis of every Layout is the Master Layout. Let's discuss the Master Layout's settings now (see *Chapter 3, Documentation – A Residential Project*, for more information).

Master Layout

Master Layouts drive the size and repeated elements of our layouts. Parts of the Master Layout can assume values automatically. We will discuss this feature in detail in the following sections. In general, we want to set up the Master Layout in a way that will require the least amount of manual adjustment on each sheet.

You can create and access the Master Layouts under the grey **Masters** portion of the **Layout Book** palette. To create a new Master Layout, you can either right-click on the grey **Masters** folder icon and select **New Master Layout**, or click on the third button at the lower part of the palette.

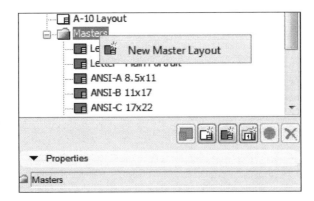

The **Create New Master Layout** dialog will allow you to name your new Master Layout and set its size, orientation, and margins. You can also define whether it will appear below or above the content of your layout. Typically, we will use the **Below Layout** option. The **Drawing Placement** area of this dialog box needs some attention. This is a useful feature when you need to place multiple views on the same sheet. For example, detail sheets usually have multiple details on them. You can add multiple views at the same time and let ArchiCAD either arrange them automatically or align them to a grid. You can also specify the details of the two arrangement styles by clicking on the button at the right.

Finally, you can set the newly created Master Layout as the default for new layouts.

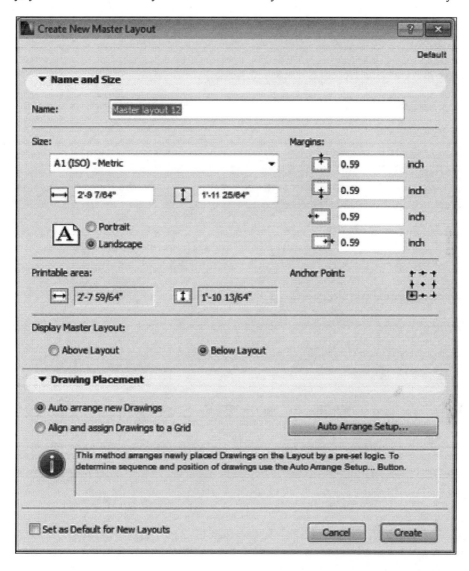

To work on a Master Layout, you can double-click on a specific layout in the list. You can add 2D elements (for example, borders and text) to the Master Layout. These elements will be repeated on every layout (sheet) that the specific Master Layout is assigned to. Master Layouts in ArchiCAD work in a similar way to Master Pages in Adobe InDesign. The elements of the Master Layout will appear in red to help us differentiate them from the other parts of the layout.

Autotext

It is the best practice to set up the Master Layout with as much intelligence as possible. The Autotext feature in ArchiCAD is very helpful in doing so. We can start adding Autotext by activating the **Text** tool and clicking on the second button at the top-left corner of the **Text** tool dialog.

This will create a code that will reference pre-established text values. Some Autotext values are actively assuming other referenced parameters. For example, we can insert an Autotext at the bottom-right corner of our Master Layout that will reference the sheet number. The actual sheet number will automatically change from layout to layout, referencing the sheet number parameter of the actual layout.

Another example of an Autotext is related to the project information. We can insert an Autotext as a repeating text element of our Master Layout, referring to the project name. We can do that by selecting the **Project Details Category** and **Project Name** Autotext item.

While we are in the Master Layout editing environment, we will see the code `#Project Name` appearing as text, but once we assign the Master Layout to a specific sheet, it will display the actual project name instead. We can then set and change the project name globally, affecting all of the sheets where the Autotext is inserted by navigating to **File | Info | Project Info**. We can also use this Master Layout in other projects with different project names without having to recreate it.

The source of the Autotext can be the project info as described earlier, or we can choose an Autotext Reference Drawing by right-clicking on a drawing in **Navigator** or **Organizer**, under a layout and selecting **Set as Autotext Reference**. When you select a drawing as an Autotext reference, it will appear in the **Category** list of the Autotext dialog box.

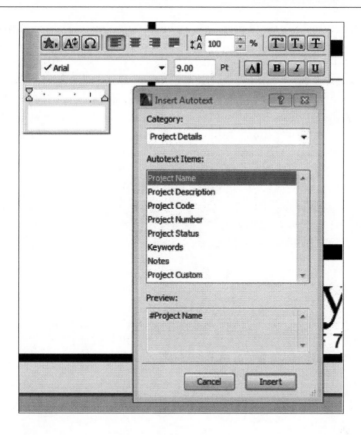

Creating a Master Layout

Let's see how creating a Master Layout works in action:

1. First, open **Layout Book** in the **Navigator**.

2. Second, click on the **New Master Layout** button.

3. Then, enter Simple Master 11 x 17 in the **Name** field.

4. Next, select **B (ANSI) - Engineering** from the drop-down list, under **Size** and select the **Landscape** orientation.

5. You can leave the **Margins** as they are for now. If you would like to adjust the margin of the sheet, you can do so by changing the values under **Margins**.

6. You can also leave the **Anchor Point** as it is.

7. Under **Display Master Layout**, select **Below Layout**. This will ensure that the graphic elements of the Master Layout will appear under the drawings that are placed on the Layout that this Master Layout is assigned to.

8. The **Drawing Placement** area allows you to set up a system, which is used to place multiple drawings at once. For example, this is useful when placing multiple detail drawings on a layout. ArchiCAD can automatically arrange them based on their distance from each other or align them based on a grid. You can keep the **Auto Arrange new Drawings** setting. The following screenshot shows the **Auto Arrange new Drawings** settings, which can be accessed by clicking on the **Auto Arrange Setup** button:

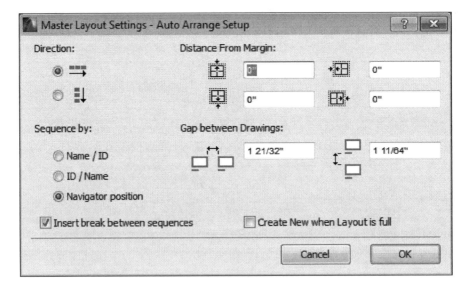

9. Finally, we will not check the **Set as Default for New Layouts** because we will not use this Master Layout for most layouts.

10. Click on **Create** to finish the process.

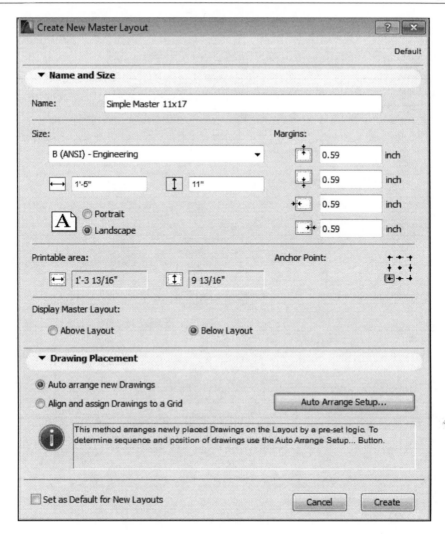

The new Master Layout will appear under the **Masters** icon and now, you can assign it to any Layout.

Layouts

Now that we are familiar with setting up a Master Layout, we are ready to move on to the next step, which is creating and setting up the layouts themselves. We have the ability to create a folder structure to keep our layout list organized. Folders in the **Layout Book** palette are called **subsets**.

To create a subset, you can right-click on the green **Layout Book** icon on the top of the list and select **Create New Subset**. Otherwise, you can click on the fourth, yellow button at the lower part of the palette. Subsets of subsets can also be created in this way. For example, you can create a subset called `Floor Plans` and then create different subsets of the `Floor Plans` subset for different floor plan scales.

When you click on the **New Subset** button, the **Create New Subset** dialog box will appear, allowing you to assign an ID and name to the subset as well as define how the IDs (that is numbering) of the items of the subset will behave.

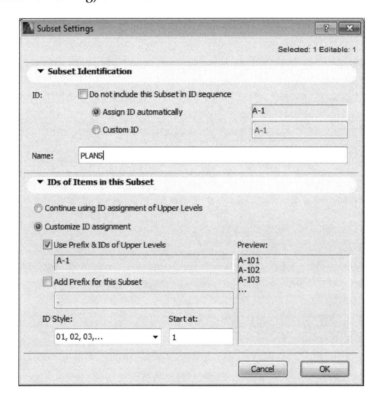

To create a new layout, you can either right-click on the green **Layout Book** icon on the top of the list and select **New Layout** or click on the second, white button at the lower part of the palette.

When you click on the **New Layout** button, the **New Layout** dialog box will appear, allowing you to assign an ID, name, and assign a Master Layout to the layout as well as define how the IDs (that is numbering) of the drawings placed on the layout will behave.

One level higher than the layout is the subset and one level higher than the subset is the Layout Book. You can choose whether you would like to automatically assign IDs based on the subset and the Layout Book or specify a custom ID for the layout.

 It is worth taking the time to set up the ID management at the Layout Book level and let ArchiCAD manage the IDs of the layouts.

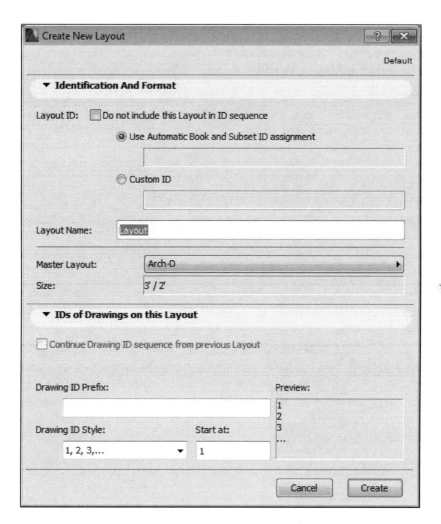

Creating a layout

Let's create a layout to see the previous theory in action:

1. Open **Layout Book** in the **Navigator** palette.

2. Click on the plus sign next to the **A-1 PLANS** subset if the tree structure is not unfolded.

3. Then, select the **A-1 PLANS** subset.

4. Next, click on the **New Layout** button.

5. Enter 2nd FLOOR PLAN in the **Layout Name** field and leave the ID setting to use the automatic assignment.

6. Finally, select **Arch-D** from the **Master Layout** drop-down list.

You will notice that the new layout assumed the next sequential ID to be **A-102** and it will appear under the **A-101 1st FLOOR PLAN** layout.

Adding views to layouts

Adding views to the layouts can be done in several different ways. We will discuss three of these options. We actually add **drawings** to layouts, which are **linked** to views, because at this point, we are dealing with a digital representation of a printout:

*   You can edit a layout by double-clicking on it in the Layout Book. In an active layout, you can right-click anywhere and select **Place Drawing**. You can also activate the **Drawing** tool and click anywhere within the layout to do the same. These two methods will bring up the **Place Drawing** dialog box Here, you can link the drawing to the view that you would like to use from a list.

- You can select an external source or an external Teamwork Project as the source of the view list. In these cases, we can browse an external file and review the available views in them. You can also select an internal view from the view map of the current file. After selecting the view, you can click on **Place** to place the drawing that is linked to the view on the layout.

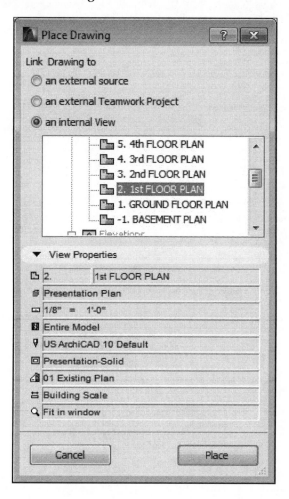

- The third and perhaps, the most intuitive option is to select a view in the organizer and drag it on top of a layout. After dropping the view on the layout, you can see the drawing with a white icon referencing the selected view listed under the layout.

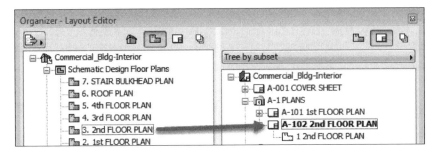

There are several ways to adjust the settings of a placed drawing. Right-clicking on the drawing will bring up a menu of options. Select **Drawing Selection Settings**, which will bring up the corresponding dialog box, allowing you to assign an ID and name to the drawing. It also defines whether the content of the drawing will be updated manually or automatically.

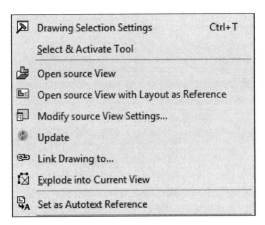

You can also adjust the properties of the drawing and turn on its frame and title. A pen set can be assigned under **Properties** and you can choose whether the drawing will be printed in its original colors, grayscale, or black and white.

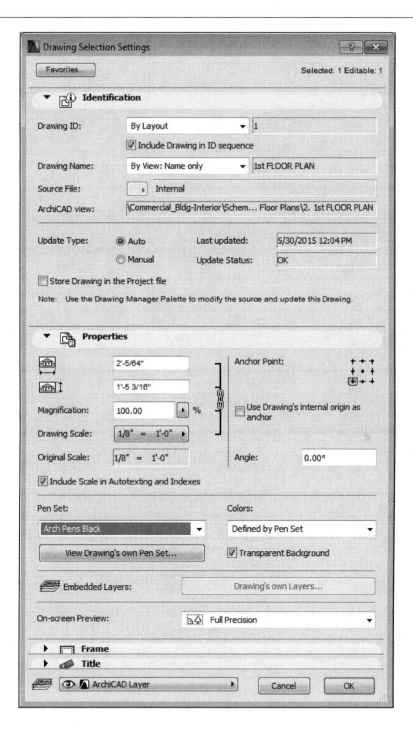

Titles are annotation library parts that can be assigned to drawings. Several titles are available in the basic template and each with different graphic appearances and options to display additional annotation elements (for example, drawing scale and graphic scale). If you do not want to show a title under your drawing, this is where you need to turn it off by selecting **No Title** from the drop-down menu that lists the different title types.

You can directly draw with a limited number of 2D tools on the layout in addition to placing drawings. However it is not recommended as manually created 2D elements are difficult to update and maintain.

Placing drawings on layouts

We will place a drawing on a layout and change its title to practice the concepts that were described earlier:

1. Open the organizer and set **View Map** on the left and **Layout Book** on the right.

2. Unfold the tree of the `Schematic Design Floor Plans` view folder by clicking on the plus sign next to it if it is not unfolded yet.

3. Click on the plus sign next to the **A-1 PLANS** subset if the tree structure is not unfolded.

4. Select the **2nd FLOOR PLAN** view and drag it on the top of the **A-102 2nd FLOOR PLAN** layout.

5. You will notice that the drawing will appear under the layout.

6. Double-click on the **A-102 2nd FLOOR PLAN** layout and close the organizer.

7. Right-click on the placed **2nd FLOOR PLAN** drawing and select **Drawing Selection Settings**.

8. Under **Title**, select **Simple Title** from the drop-down menu.

You will notice that the drawing's title has changed to only display the drawing name and scale.

Changes and adjustments

The **Drawing Manager** is a helpful tool to organize and track our drawings. You can activate it by clicking on the top-left button in the **Navigator** palette and selecting **Show Drawing Manager**.

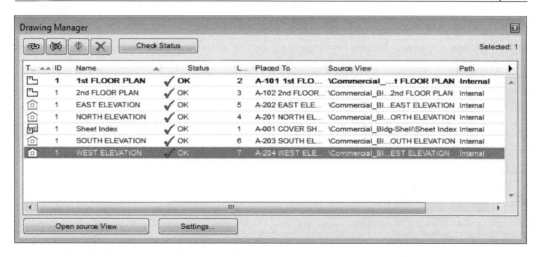

When you have a layout open with drawings placed on it, the Drawing Manager will highlight the drawings on the active layout in bold letters. This is helpful when you want to identify which drawings you are working with on the current layout. The Drawing Manager allows you to relink a drawing to a different view by clicking on the top-left button and selecting a view from the **Link to** list. You can also do this by right-clicking on the drawing itself and selecting **Link Drawing to** from the menu. We will make use of this feature shortly.

If you want to freeze a drawing's state on a layout, you can click on the second button on the top-left part of the panel. This will break the link between the drawing and the referenced view. This is not recommended because you will create a disconnected object in your documentation workflow that you will have to manage manually. You can also refresh and delete drawings with the remaining buttons.

You will find two buttons at the bottom of the Drawing Manager that will allow you to open the source view of the drawing and access its settings.

The Drawing Manager gives you a comprehensive overview of the drawings that are placed on your layouts. The drawing list has two columns that we need to mention here:

- The **Source View** column describes the position of the linked view of the internal view map or the view map of an external file.

- The **Path** column specifies the file path of the external file itself. This is very useful because, if you have several external drawings placed on your layouts, this is the only place where you can find the original file's path. If the linked view is in the current document, then **Path** will be set to **Internal**.

Setting up multiple layouts

Next, we will explore a layout technique that will help you set up multiple layouts quickly:

1. Open **Layout Book** in the organizer and set **View Map** on the left and **Layout Book** on the right.

2. Click on the plus sign next to the **A-1 PLANS** if the tree structure is not unfolded and select the **A-1 PLANS** subset.

3. Create a new layout by selecting the **A-102 2nd FLOOR PLAN** and holding down the *Ctrl* key. Then, drag the new layout on top of the **A-1 PLANS** subset.

4. Repeat Step 3 and create another layout.

5. You will notice that the IDs of the layouts will assume the next available number (**A-103** and **A-104**) but the names of the layouts will remain **A-102 2nd FLOOR PLAN**.

6. Rename the new layouts to **A-103 3rd FLOOR PLAN** and **A-104 4th FLOOR PLAN**.

7. Click on the plus button next to the layouts to see the drawings placed on them. Since we duplicated the **A-102 2nd FLOOR PLAN**, the new layouts will both have **2nd FLOOR PLAN** drawing on them.

8. Right click on the drawing, under the **A-103 3rd FLOOR PLAN** and select **Link Drawing to**.

9. Select **3rd FLOOR PLAN** from the **Link to** list of the internal views.

10. Repeat Steps 8 and 9 and relink the drawing under **A-104 4th FLOOR PLAN** to the **4th FLOOR PLAN** view.

You can create similar layouts of similar drawings rapidly, dragging-and-dropping while keeping the *Ctrl* key pressed technique that was previously described by only using the organizer. One of the benefits of this technique is that the drawings will be perfectly aligned on multiple layouts, since we created them by duplicating a carefully placed original to start with.

Printing

We will use a technique to quickly print a few selected pages for review. This is useful when you want to have a discussion with your project team and do not have a lot of time to spend on setting up a printing or publishing process:

1. First, open **Layout Book** in the **Navigator** palette.

2. Then, click on the plus sign next to **A-1 PLANS** and **A-2 ELEVATIONS**.

3. Select the following layouts by holding down the *Ctrl* key:

   ° **A-101 1st FLOOR PLAN**

   ° **A-102 2nd FLOOR PLAN**

   ° **A-201 NORTH ELEVATION**

   ° **A-202 EAST ELEVATION**

   ° **A-203 SOUTH ELEVATION**

   ° **A-204 WEST ELEVATION**

4. Go to the **File** menu and select **Print**. Otherwise, press the key combination of *Ctrl + P* and the **Print Layout** window will open.

5. The printer will be identified at the top of the window. If it is incorrect, click on the **Page Setup** button and assign the correct printer.

6. Under the **Source** heading, select **Selected Layouts in the Navigator**.

7. Under the **Size** heading, select **Fit to Page**.

8. Under the **Arrangement** heading, the blue rectangle should fit inside the black rectangle (there should only be one black rectangle).

9. Finally, click on the **Print** button.

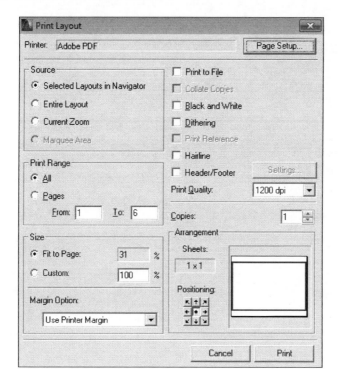

Summary

In this chapter, you learned about the project workflow of ArchiCAD as it relates to the documentation. You also learned the details of setting up views in **View Map** and creating sheets in the **Layout Book**. You also learned about Autotext and layout techniques and how the document set is organized. This all fits into the overall project workflow in ArchiCAD. The next phase in our workflow adventure will take us into the world of multiple layout exports and collaboration. This is where the Publisher (part of the **Navigator** palette) comes into play.

8

Work Sharing with ArchiCAD

Graphisoft has been focusing its efforts around the Open BIM concept for several years. The Open BIM concept is based on the idea of members of an extended design team collaborating and sharing content using various types of software and file formats.

In this chapter, we will:

- Review how the Publisher can automate the file export and printing process
- Learn how ArchiCAD can import and export different file formats that are important for successful collaboration
- Explore how the Teamwork environment enables multiple users to work on the same project
- Review some considerations that will help you when you want to collaborate with your co-workers in the same or different offices

Publisher

The Publisher is ArchiCAD's automation system that serves two main purposes. You can either print multiple layouts or drawings with it or export multiple files in various formats with literally the click of a button. Before you get to the stage of simply clicking on the **Publish** button, you need to set up your publisher sets.

Clicking on the top-right **Publisher Sets** button of the **Navigator** palette activates the publisher sets. The **Publisher Sets** window consists of two main areas, which are the list of **Publisher Sets** and **Publishing Properties**. You can reveal the content of a specific publisher set by either double-clicking its name in the list or by clicking on the **Publisher Sets** button and selecting it from the drop-down list.

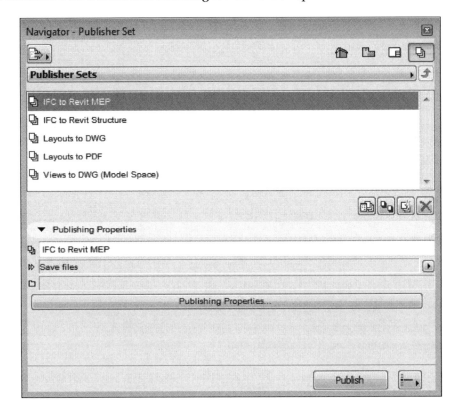

If you want to create a new publisher set, you will need to bring up the *Organizer* first, because you need the additional source field to populate your new set from. To look at this in action, open **Organizer** and set **Publisher Sets** on the right.

You will notice that publisher sets can be populated from **View Map**, **Layout Book**, and other publisher sets. You cannot add an item directly from the project map as none of the view settings are yet established at that level.

 You can drag and drop items from the left into the publisher set but you can also use the **Add Shortcut** button, which will appear under **View Map** or **Layout Book**, when you select an item in them. The **Add Shortcut** feature is similar to cloning a folder (see *Chapter 3, Documentation – A Residential Project*, for more information on that subject).

Publishing properties

Once you have created a publisher set, you can close **Organizer** and view and interact with the publishing set's elements in **Navigator**. The **Publishing Properties** area of the **Publishing Sets** window includes the **Publishing Properties** button, which we will discuss next.

Clicking on the **Publishing Properties** button in the lower part of the window will bring up the **Publisher Set Properties** dialog. You can select the **Publishing Method** in this dialog along with other related options. There are four publishing methods to choose from the top of the dialog:

- The first option is **Print**, which allows you to print a set of layouts or drawings at once. When you select this option, the rest of the dialog goes blank. The specific print settings are in a different area, which we will review later.

- The second option is **Save files**. Selecting this option allows you to choose the destination path and folder structure of the exported files. The **Create single file** method combines multiple layouts and drawings into a single file, which is only applicable to the PDF or BIMx Hyper-model formats. This is why the dialog allows you to choose one of these two formats at this step. The **Create a real folder structure** or **Create flat file structure** option will either mirror the folder organization of the publisher set or export the individual files into a single destination folder. You can choose the **Include Project Reviewer web environment** with these two options. The Include **Project Reviewer web environment** feature generates an HTML website with hyperlinks to navigate through the exported files. If you have access to a web server, you can upload the website with the exported file and make it available for other team members to view in a web browser.

- The **Plot** option is set up for plotting multiple large, format layouts. You can revisit *Chapter 3, Documentation – A Residential Project*, for more information about plotting layouts or drawings.

- You can either publish or upload a BIMx Hyper-model to the web by selecting **Upload BIMx Hyper-model**. You need to have access to a cloud service when you want to upload a BIMx Hyper-model.

It's worth mentioning here that there is a difference between the BIMx 3D model, which is saved from an ArchiCAD file, and the BIMx Hyper-model, which can be created using Publisher. Unlike the BIMx 3D model, the BIMx Hyper-model includes documentation of the project as well. In other words, the layouts and interactive links between the drawings in the layouts and model are saved within the BIMx Hyper-model.

We will go into more detail about exporting various file formats later in this chapter. For now, you can click on **OK** to close the **Publisher Set Properties** dialog.

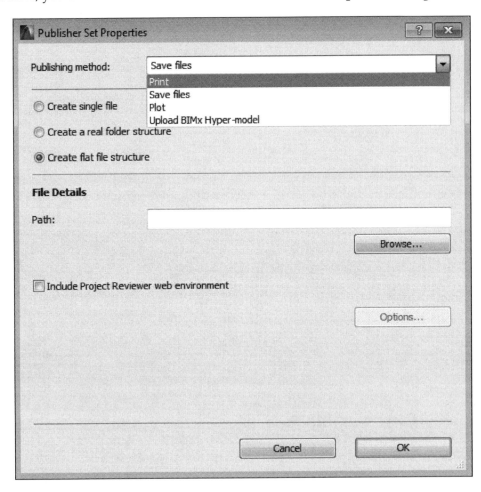

The publishing item list or folder structure will appear when you double-click on a publisher set. You can go back to the publisher set list by clicking on the **One Level Up** button with an upward pointing arrow, at the upper-right area of the window.

We mentioned that some of the specific settings are addressed in a different area. The **Format** area under the publishing item list includes drop-down options to select the specific export file format and a translator, if applicable. The **Format** area will include the settings for printing when you choose the **Print** publishing method.

Once you are satisfied with your settings, you have one more option to choose before you click on the **Publish** button. The **Sets to output** button, next to the **Publish** button allows you to choose if you would like to print only the selected items in the publishing item list, or the entire publishing set.

Finally, clicking on the **Publish** button will bring up the **Publishing** dialog, which you can use to monitor the publishing process. You can click on **Close** after all the items are published.

Exporting to CAD and other file formats

ArchiCAD has the ability to open and save various file types that are commonly used in other CAD and BIM programs. The recognition of out-of-the-box file types can be further extended with add-ons, enabling you to save additional file types. Communicating and coordinating with consultants who use other programs is an important part of project development. This is why the ability to read and write different file formats is valuable.

Where you save from matters

It is important to be aware of where you are in the project structure when you export or import non-native file formats. Depending on how you would like to use the information in these files, you can reference them in various parts of your modeling and documentation process.

Let's look at the basic examples of this concept next.

Project map and view map

Perhaps the most common file reference today is still in the form of 2D floor plans, even though we are working in the world of 3D BIM. Room layouts, structural grids, and equipment placement are relatively simple to coordinate with 2D floor plans. This is why they are a frequent choice of vehicle to send information between designers, structural engineers, and other consultants.

When you activate a project map or a view map element and want to export the displayed content, you have three main export options, as follows:

- Exporting 2D content
- Exporting 3D content
- Exporting other kinds of data, for example, lists, schedules, or indexes

In all of these cases, the whole content of the displayed information will be exported in one file. For example, when you activate **1st FLOOR PLAN** from the `Schematic Design Floor Plans` folder of the view map, you can export the entire first floor plan as a 2D DWG file. We will explore the details of the last two options mentioned earlier in the *Exporting 3D content* and *Other File Formats* sections of this chapter. For now, let's keep focusing on exporting 2D content.

Layout Book

The **Layout Book** is the digital representation of the printed document set. By its definition, elements of the **Layout Book** display 2D information and, therefore, the files exported while you view a **Layout Book** item will always be 2D. This does not mean that you can only create static file exports, in which the information is difficult to navigate and comprehend. As we will see later, there are useful interactive features that can be used to enhance the usability of the files exported from **Layout Book**.

Publisher

The Publisher is designed to automate the printing and file-export process. With a properly set up publisher set, it literally takes the click of a button to export numerous files and complex document structures. Whether you need to print or save your document set, the Publisher is a useful tool to extract the information that you built up though the modeling and documentation process in ArchiCAD and make it available to other participants in the project.

In the following exercise, you will save a 2D DWG file of the **1st FLOOR PLAN** in three ways from the three different areas of the project structure that we discussed earlier.

Saving files from the project map and view map

To save files from the project map and view map, perform the following steps:

1. First, open the view map in the **Navigator** palette.
2. Click on the plus sign next to **Schematic Design Floor Plans**.
3. Then double-click on **1st FLOOR PLAN** to activate it.
4. Go to the **File** menu and select **Save As** or press the key combination of *Ctrl + Shift + S*. The **Save Plan** dialog will open.
5. Select **DWG File** from the **Save as type** drop-down menu.
6. Navigate to your choice of folder in the browser section of the dialog.
7. Under the **Translator** heading, select **01 For further editing**.

8. Name the DWG file 1st FLOOR PLAN in the **File name** section.

9. Click on the **Save** button.

10. Then, the **Locate txt.shx** dialog will appear. This dialog will allow you to specify a vector-based font assigned to the DWG, which is not essential for our purposes.

11. Click on the **Skip All** button to finish the saving process.

Saving files from the Layout Book

To save files from the Layout Book, perform the following steps:

1. First, open the Layout Book in the **Navigator** palette.

2. Then click on the plus sign next to the **A-1 PLANS** subset if the tree structure is not unfolded.

3. Next, double-click on **A-101 1st FLOOR PLAN** layout, under the **A-1 PLANS** subset, to activate it.

4. Repeat steps four through seven from the preceding heading to set up the **Save Plan** dialog.

5. Name the DWG file 1st FLOOR PLAN layout in the **File name** section.

6. Repeat steps nine through eleven from the preceding heading to finish the saving process.

Publishing files from the Publisher

To publish files from the Publisher, perform the following steps:

1. First, open Publisher in the **Navigator** palette.

2. Then select the **Layouts to DWG**.

3. Click on the **Publishing Properties** button at the lower part of **Navigator**. The **Publisher Set Properties** dialog will appear.

4. Specify a file path of your choice by clicking on the **Browse** button under the **File Details** section of the dialog.

5. Click on **OK** to close the **Publisher Set Properties** dialog.

6. Double-click on the **Layouts to DWG** to reveal the content of the **Layouts to DWG** publisher set.

7. Click on the plus sign next to the **A-1 PLANS** folder if the tree structure is not unfolded.

8. Select **A-101 1st FLOOR PLAN** under the **A-1 PLANS** folder.

9. Click on the **Set to Output** button, next to the **Publish** button at the bottom of the **Navigator** palette and select **Selected items**.

10. Click on the **Publish** button. The **Publishing** dialog will appear.

11. Once the publishing process is finished, you will see a green check mark next to **A-101 1st FLOOR PLAN published**.

12. Click on **Close** to finish the saving process.

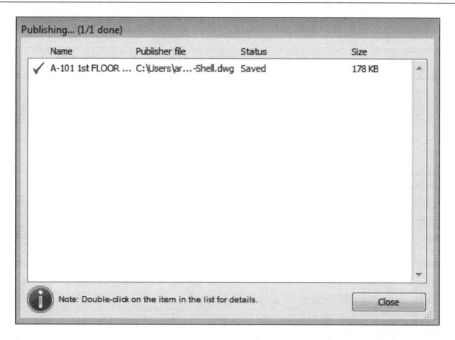

The previous steps highlight the difference between the export options. If you open three different DWG files in AutoCAD, you will notice that the **1st FLOOR** PLAN. DWG file will be in **Model Space**, while the **1st FLOOR PLAN** layout.DWG and the **1st FLOOR PLAN** published.DWG files will be in **Paper Space**. This is the result of saving files from different areas of the project structure.

Activating the **1st FLOOR PLAN** in the view map brings up the entire floor plan, which is the equivalent of **Model Space** in AutoCAD. The Layout Book is similar to **Paper Space** in AutoCAD, which is why saving the **A-101 1st FLOOR PLAN** layout and publishing the **A-101 1st FLOOR PLAN published** layout will create DWG files that will activate **Paper Space** in AutoCAD. The difference between the last two DWG files is only in the process of creating them.

List of file formats

To have a high-level overview of ArchiCAD's file format translation capabilities, let's look at the list of file formats that are available in the **Save Plan** dialog based on the basic installation of the software. As we mentioned before, installing third-party add-ons can extend this file list. There are similar options available when you go to **File | Save As** with a section or elevation view active; however, there are significantly different options available saving with a 3D view active. We will discuss 3D file formats later in more detail.

We already discussed how the active environment of the project structure has a fundamental influence on the available exportable file formats and the type of content in the exported files. The other factor that defines what kind of information you can export is the type of format itself. From this perspective, there are two main groups of file formats available, with two additional groups in one of them:

- Raster file formats (2D)
- Vector file formats (3D and 2D)
    - ○ BIM type file formats
    - ○ Basic vector-based file formats

The concepts of raster and vector file formats mentioned earlier need some further explanation.

Raster file formats store information based on pixels. When you zoom in to the content of a raster type file, the view will "pixelate" at a certain zoom factor and the onscreen resolution will decline. You will need high-resolution raster files to print sharp and readable drawings. Raster files can only store 2D content.

Vector files store information based on vector coordinates. You can zoom in to the content of a vector file theoretically and infinitely without losing any resolution. Vector-based files are often smaller and more appropriate for printing drawings because of their nature. Vector files are not appropriate to save renderings or photographs however. This is why raster files still have a distinct function even in mostly vector-based projects. Vector files can store both 2D and 3D type content.

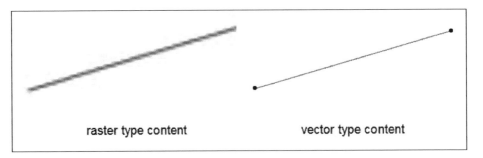

raster type content   vector type content

The BIM type file formats store information based on the attributes of individual content elements. For example, a BIM type file recognizes whether a wall it is saved from a 2D, 3D, or floor plan view.

Basic vector-based file formats, on the other hand, simply recognize the geometry of the displayed content based on vector coordinates. If you save a basic vector based file from a 2D floor plan view, it will store only 2D information. If you save a basic vector-based file from a 3D view, it will store the geometry in 3D.

Now that we have established the definition of these basic concepts, it is important to address the fact that, even though we save a certain file type from a 2D and floor plan view, it can either store only 3D or 2D content. For example, a BIM type file format will "understand" that a wall is a 3D element, which is based on the wall's attributes, even if it is represented in 2D projection in the floor plan view.

Certain vector-based file formats capture 2D drawings if they are saved from a 2D floor plan view and store 3D geometry if they are saved from a 3D view. The DWG format is a good example of this behavior. On the other hand, if you save a PDF file from either a 2D or 3D view, in both cases the vector content will be 2D. The 3D view will be "flattened" into 2D graphics if you save a PDF file from a 3D window.

The following screenshot illustrates the available file formats in the **Save Plan** dialog. As we mentioned earlier, similar file export options are available when the **File/ Save As** command is accessed while the other 2D type views are active (for example, sections, elevations, or interior elevations). The **Save Document** dialog is activated in those cases that refer to the non-floor plan type content.

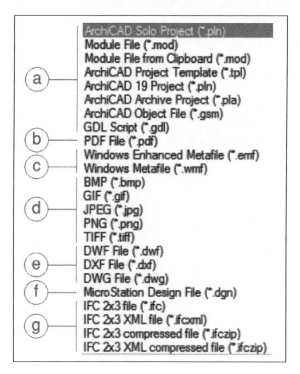

The details of the preceding screenshot are as follows:

a. These formats are native ArchiCAD file formats. We will discuss the **Module File** type later in this chapter.

b. PDF files saved from a 2D type view (floor plans, elevations, sections, and so on) will contain 2D graphic elements. PDFs can also include raster elements, for example, **Figure** images inserted on the floor plan.

c. Windows metafiles are legacy formats that can contain both raster and vector 2D information.

d. These are raster-based image file formats (also referred to as bitmap files) that can be edited in raster graphics programs.

e. Autodesk DXF and DWG files are the most frequently used formats because many CAD and BIM software are capable of handling these types of files. A 2D vector line drawing of the view will be saved when you select either of these file types. We will discuss saving and opening DWG files in more detail later in this chapter.

f. ArchiCAD has a long history of collaborating with Bentley products. MicroStation is a 3D CAD design and modeling software.

g. IFC is an open-source BIM exchange file format. We will also address IFC files in more detail later.

Exporting 3D content

We have referred to the fact that 3D content is handled differently in file exports. This is true when saving basic vector-based file formats because the definition of 3D geometry is dependent upon actually generating content in 3D view. Otherwise the basic vector based file formats would not have any reference to 3D content. This is not necessary with BIM type file formats, which means that 3D content can be saved from either a 2D or 3D view.

You can activate a 3D view by double-clicking on **Generic Perspective** or **Generic Axonometry** under the 3D section of the project map.

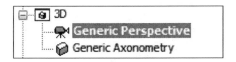

An even simpler shortcut is to press the *F5* key, which is the shortcut key for the **View/ Elements in 3D View/ Show Selection/ Marquee in 3D** command. If nothing is selected, the whole content of the project will be generated in the 3D view when you press *F5*.

3D file formats

Once the 3D content is generated, you can go to **File | Save as** to export the model in various file formats. The following screenshot illustrates the available file formats in the **Save 3D** dialog, which is activated when you select the **File/ Save as** command:

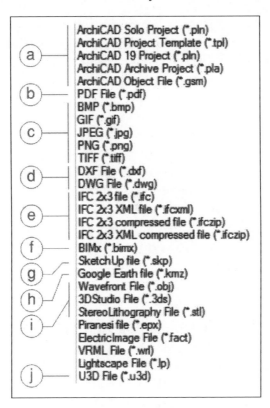

The details for the preceding screenshot are as follows:

    a.   These formats are native ArchiCAD file formats. We will discuss the **ArchiCAD Object File** type later in this chapter.

    b.   PDF files saved from a 3D view will contain a projected 2D vector line drawing of the 3D view.

c. These are raster-based image file formats that can be edited in raster graphics programs. A projected 2D raster image of the 3D view will be saved when you select these file types.

d. Autodesk DXF and DWG files are the frequently used formats because many CAD and BIM software are capable of handling these types of files. Saving DXF and DWG files from a 3D view will generate a file with 3D geometry in these formats.

e. IFC is an open-source BIM exchange file format. 3D model content with element attributes will be saved in IFC format when you select this option.

f. BIMx is Graphisoft's own BIM exchange format. An interactive BIMx Hyper-model will be saved when you select this option. We will discuss the BIMx Hyper-model format in more detail later.

g. Selecting the **SketchUp file** format can be useful when you want to communicate 3D information with consultants who do not have more access to robust BIM solutions. There is a free version of SketchUp available, which makes this a very accessible file format.

h. With the **Google Earth file** format, you can display your model in Google Earth. This can be useful at client meetings and site design discussions. Interesting presentations can be made by using the **Tour** option in Google Earth as well.

i. Visualization experts commonly use OBJ, 3DS, and STL files. STL is a standard format in 3D printing.

j. You can save PDF files with 3D model content in them. U3D is the standard format for 3D model content in PDF files.

Saving model elements as a library part

ArchiCAD allows you to create library parts without GDL scripting, which is the basic coding language of the program. This is a useful feature in generating repetitive elements as well as collaborating with other members of the design team. For example, a simple representation of a 3D chair can be easily modeled with the **Slab** tool and saved as a library part. The saved library part can be made available for the rest of the design team members, enhancing the productivity of the team. You can revisit *Chapter 5, Project Setup and Modeling Part 2 – Healthcare Building Project,* for more information on library parts.

You can save a selection of model elements as a library part in two ways:

- First, you can go to **File | Libraries and Objects | Save Selection as** with a floor plan view active. Choose **Object** from the available options to create a generic library part. The other options allow you to create custom library components. For example, you can design and model custom door leaves or cabinet doors, which you can use to create detailed, model-based interior elevations. You can also create custom drawing titles with one of the available options by drawing a custom drawing title with 2D elements and saving them as a library part.

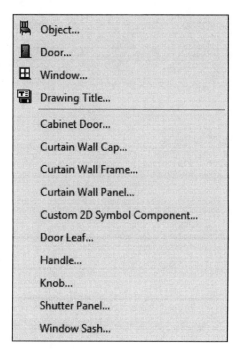

- You can select **File/ Save as** and choose **ArchiCAD Object File** from the **Save as type** drop-down list, with a 3D view active. When you view the model elements in 3D, ArchiCAD will prompt you to select a top, side, or bottom view to visualize the model elements in 3D. This feature allows you to define the default orientation of your library part in 3D space. For example, if you view and save the model elements from a side view and place the new library part on a floor plan, you will notice that the model elements will be placed sideways.

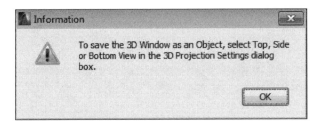

Specific file formats

Understanding the basic concept of how ArchiCAD handles different file formats is important in order to collaborate effectively with design team members using other programs. The process of exchanging content between different software packages is called interoperability. Now that we have covered the basics, let's look at specific file formats and their export setting in detail.

DWG

As we mentioned previously, DWG is perhaps the most commonly used file format to exchange information with consultants. ArchiCAD has a robust DWG translation system, which is partly due to a long history of developing the translation capabilities of the program. Although DXF is a separate format, the translation settings are similar. We will focus on the DWG format, since it is more likely that you will use them.

Translators

The core of the DWG file interaction within ArchiCAD is **Translator**. When you save or open a DWG file, you assign a DWG/DXF translator to the process. A translator is a predefined collection of settings that ArchiCAD uses to translate the information in the DWG file. You can customize these settings and save them as a custom translator. You can access the **DXF-DWG Translation Setup** dialog by clicking on the **Settings** button, next to the **Translator** in the **Save Plan** or **Save Document** dialog.

We used a prebuilt translator called **01 For further editing** when we saved and published DWGs earlier in this chapter. You can access the settings of this translator by going to **File | File Special | DXF-DWG Translation Setup**. This will activate the translation setting dialog. You will notice that the **01 For further editing** translator is listed at the top of the **Available Translators** list with blue and green arrows. The blue arrow indicates that this is the default translator for exporting DWG/DXF files and the green arrow indicates that this will be the translator used in the current setting to export the file. A similar arrow pointing left indicates the default translator and the translators in use for importing DWG/DXF files.

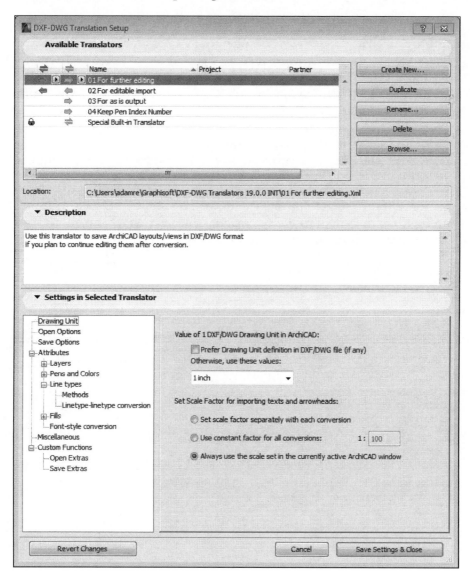

The setting to customize translation is in the **Settings in Selected Translator** area of the dialog. As you will see, there are many options and details that can help you fine-tune the translation process. We will now highlight a few important settings that define how the DWG file will be handled.

Drawing Units allow you to specify what a DWG unit will be equal to in ArchiCAD. Typically, the default **Working Units** are specified in feet and fractional inches, in which case you need to select feet in this area.

There are various versions of DWG files and some programs only handle older DWG types. You can select the **File Format** in the **Save Options** area.

The **Attributes** area lists the detailed setting options to customize the DWG translation. You have the ability to create custom conversion tables for **Layers**, **Pens and Colors**, **Linetypes**, and **Fills**. One specific setting can make a difference to how the converted DWG file will look in AutoCAD. Enter 4 in the **LTScale value in output File** area, under **Line-types | Methods**, to achieve an optimum line type scale conversion. This means that the length of dashes in a dashed line type will remain the same after converting your file into DWG. Although there is a detailed explanation about why this value needs to be set, the end result is more important for our purposes.

There are more options, such as the ability to convert ArchiCAD labels to AutoCAD leaders under **Custom Functions | Save Extras**. You can review and adjust these settings to achieve the optimal translation process of your choice.

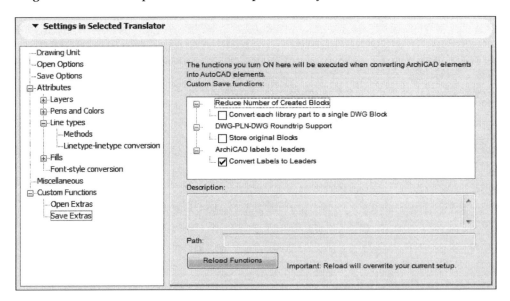

The dialog has a feature that is useful in setting project standards. Adjusting all the settings would be time consuming if we needed to do that in every project file individually. You can export the combination of settings—a translator—as an XML file by selecting the translator in the **Available Translators** list and clicking on the **Create New** button; import it in to other projects by clicking on the **Browse** button at the upper-right side of the dialog (see *Chapter 9, Visualization and Model Management*, for more information on standards and model management).

PDF files

PDF files are also important tools of collaboration for several reasons. PDFs are compact. They can include both vector and raster content, and multiple-page PDFs are easy to navigate. The only software that is needed to view and interact with PDF files is the free Adobe PDF Viewer, which is already installed on nearly everyone's computers.

Project managers and clients, who don't necessarily want to work in the BIM environment, can easily mark up PDF sketches saved from ArchiCAD. This makes this file type a popular choice of collaboration platform outside the modeling software.

Save or print?

We need to distinguish between two different methods of generating PDF files in ArchiCAD. They are as follows:

- If the Adobe PDF printer driver is installed on your computer, you can create PDF files the same way as you would send a drawing or layout to a printer. Selecting the Adobe PDF printer driver as the "printer" will allow you to save a PDF file instead of physically printing the content.

- ArchiCAD has its own built-in PDF driver. You can create PDFs with ArchiCAD's PDF driver by selecting the **PDF File** type directly in the **Save Plan** or **Save Document** dialog as mentioned earlier. This method will usually create a better and more compact file because Graphisoft has integrated this driver into ArchiCAD.

Publishing multiple layouts into a single PDF file using the built-in PDF driver will generate an interactive digital document set. This means that ArchiCAD will automatically create hyperlinks in the document for navigating through the pages. You can click on an elevation marker on the floor plan view in the PDF file and it will automatically jump to the page of the referenced elevation. This feature is particularly useful when you want to create a software agnostic representation of your work which has multiple layouts.

Let's look at how this works in action:

1. Open the Publisher in the **Navigator** palette.

2. Select the **Layouts to PDF**.

3. Click on the **Publishing Properties** button at the lower part of **Navigator**. The **Publisher Set Properties** dialog will appear.

4. Specify a file path of your choice by clicking on the **Browse** button under the **File Details** section of the dialog.

5. Click on **OK** to close the **Publisher Set Properties** dialog.

6. Double-click on **Layouts to PDF** to reveal the content of the **Layouts to PDF** publisher set.

7. Click on the plus sign next to the **A-1 PLANS** and **A-2 ELEVATIONS** folders if the tree structure is not unfolded.

8. Select the following layouts while holding down the *Ctrl* key:
   - **A-101 1st FLOOR PLAN**
   - **A-102 2nd FLOOR PLAN**
   - **A-201 NORTH ELEVATION**
   - **A-202 EAST ELEVATION**
   - **A-203 SOUTH ELEVATION**
   - **A-204 WEST ELEVATION**

9. Then click on the **Set to Output** button next to the **Publish** button at the bottom of the **Navigator** palette and select **selected items**. The **Publishing** dialog will appear.

10. Once the publishing process is finished, you will see a green check mark next to the published layouts.

11. Finally, click on **Close** to finish the saving process.

You will be able to click on the elevation markers on the two floor plan pages of the PDF file. Clicking on the markers will bring up the referenced elevation page.

BIMx Hyper-model

Graphisoft developed its own BIM presentation format called BIMx Hyper-model. The company is aiming to share content in a rich and interactive way with this format, which is more reflective of the complex BIM environment than other previously existing file types.

The main advantage of the BIMx format is that it allows someone who is not working in the BIM modeling environment to interact and view the model in 3D as well as 2D. The different views of the model are connected with interactive links and presented in the intuitive interface of the free BIMx Viewer.

BIMx Hyper-models can be viewed on desktop computers as well as mobile devices. In addition, the format supports stereo 3D viewing with 3D headsets.

You can publish a BIMx Hyper-model of your project by selecting **File** | **Publish BIMx Hyper-model**.

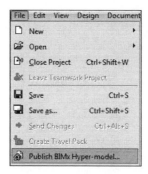

IFC files

The **IFC** (stands for **Industry Foundation Classes**) file format is an open-source BIM file format. You can share the building information model and its attributes with ArchiCAD and other BIM authoring software (for example, Autodesk Revit) using this format. IFC files are required by some large public clients because of their software agnostic and open structure. There are also free IFC model viewers available, making it simple to share your model with non-ArchiCAD users.

When you convert an IFC model that originated from another software, walls will be converted to ArchiCAD walls, slabs will become ArchiCAD slabs, and so on. The program can recognize these elements' natures based on the attributes saved in the IFC file.

As well as the advantage of the format being software independent, it's worth mentioning one of the disadvantages. This drawback is related to how the IFC format stores information about the equivalent of library parts.

The productivity and efficiency of using multiple library parts of the same kind is due to creating instances of the same model element. The IFC format does not recognize instances. The content of the individual library parts converted in an IFC file is achieved by repeating the geometry multiple times as separate elements. Although the developers are working on a solution for this problem, it is not yet available.

Even with this disadvantage, the IFC format is useful in collaborating with consultants using other BIM software.

Similar to the DWG/DXF translators, ArchiCAD has a detailed translator system available for IFC files. You can access the IFC translation settings by going to **File** | **File Special** | **IFC 2 x 3** | **IFC Translation Setup**. With multiple preset translators and the ability to customize your translation, you can exchange BIM content that is specifically formatted for structural engineers, MEP, or other consultants.

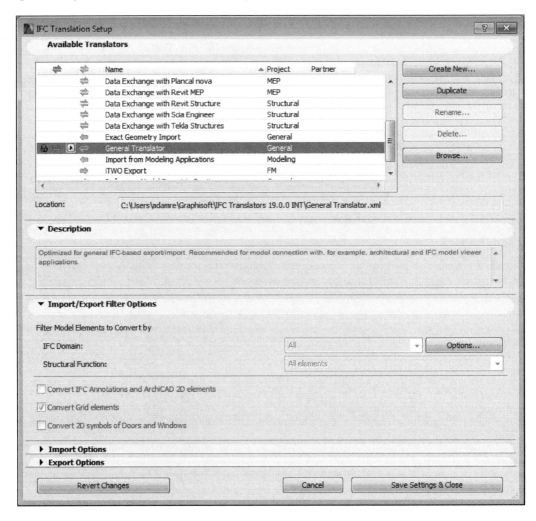

Other file formats

ArchiCAD can translate other file formats besides the ones we highlighted in the previous section. In particular, we should address XLS and TXT formats here because you can save **Schedules** and **Lists** in these formats for further editing or just sharing with others. When you activate **Door Schedule** by double-clicking on **Door Schedule** under **Schedules | Element** in the project map, you can save it in **Excel Workbook** (XLSX or XLS) or **Tabbed Text** (TXT) format. You can import these file formats directly in Microsoft Excel for viewing or editing. Lists of elements, components, or zones can be saved as TXT files.

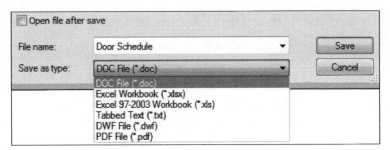

Collaboration

Collaboration is bidirectional by definition. So far in this chapter, we have discussed how you can export certain file types. Let's review the second half of the collaboration process, which is receiving information and importing it into ArchiCAD.

Many of the settings that we mentioned previously apply to importing as well as exporting different file types with slight variations. The active project environment and the nature of the specific file type also define how you can reference the information in your project.

Let's look at DWG files again in this context to illustrate some of the slight variations of the importing process.

Referencing DWG files

We will discuss four different ways that you can use to reference a DWG file next. Each of them relies on an assigned translator, similar to the process of exporting DWGs. They are as follows:

- Perhaps the most straightforward way of referencing a DWG file is by going to **File | Open**. This will bring up the **Open File** dialog, where you can choose the **DWG File** format from the **Files of type** drop-down list. You can then browse to the particular DWG file and specify the translator of your choice from the **Translator** drop-down list. Notice that the **02 For editable import** translator is selected when you open the dialog, which is the default translator for importing DWGs. Opening a DWG will close the previously opened project file and ArchiCAD will create a new project based on the DWG file.

- You can go to **File | File Special | Merge** if you would like to import the content of the DWG file as editable elements into an existing project. Once selected, the **Merge DXF-DWG** dialog will appear. You can specify here whether you would like to merge the content of Model Space into the current view or append paper space(s) to Layout Book. This part of the process is unique to importing, since you need to link the concept of AutoCAD's **Paper Space** and **Model Space** to the ArchiCAD project environment.

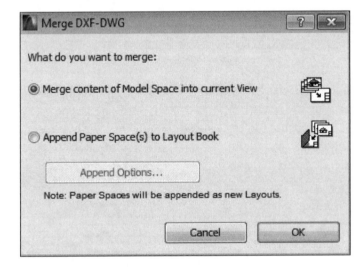

- ArchiCAD has an Xref management system to support the concept similar to external references in AutoCAD. You can attach a DWG file as an Xref by navigating to **File | External Content | Attach Xref**. This will bring up the **Attach Xref** dialog, where you can specify the DWG file; you can also specify where you would like to reference the file and translator of you choice for the process. Xrefs have their own management system in ArchiCAD, which can be accessed by going to **File | External Content | Xref Manager**.

- The fourth option for referencing a DWG file is using the **Drawing** tool or by going to **File | External Content | Place External Drawing**. In either case, the DWG will be handled as a drawing element in ArchiCAD with an assigned layer and properties. The **Place External Drawing** command will use the default settings specified in the **Drawing Default Settings** dialog. You can access this dialog by double-clicking on the **Drawing** tool icon.

The **Drawing** tool is also useful in referencing other types of files, for example, scanned sketches in JPG format or PDF files. A good way to keep your views clean and organized is by creating **Independent Worksheets** and placing drawings or sketches that you would like to use as reference on them.

Using worksheets

You can imagine these worksheets as individual sketches in your model structure that you can reference in virtually any view using ArchiCAD's **Trace** tool (**View | Trace**). Once you have created the worksheet and placed the sketch or drawing from another file on it, you can right-click on it in the project map, and select **Show as Trace Reference**.

Let's look at how that works in action. We will use the Xref process for this exercise to reference a DWG file on the worksheet:

1. Open the project map in the **Navigator** palette.
2. Right-click on **Worksheets** and select **Create New Independent Worksheet**.
3. You can leave the default values for **Reference ID** and **Name** in the **New Independent Worksheet** dialog. Then click on the **Create** button.
4. Navigate to **File | External Content | Attach Xref**.
5. Browse the 1 SECTION.DWG file.
6. Uncheck the **Specify On-Screen** option under **Insertion Point**. This way we will place the DWG based on its own origin.
7. Click on the **Attach** button.

8. Leave the layer settings unchanged in the **DWG/DXF Partial Open** dialog and click on **OK**. When you zoom out, you will see that the section is placed on the worksheet.

9. Activate the 1st floor plan view by double-clicking on **1st FLOOR PLAN** in the **Navigator** palette.

10. Right-click on the newly created worksheet and select **Show as Trace Reference**.

11. The section will appear aligned under the floor plan.

12. Then, navigate to **Window | Palettes | Trace & Reference**.

13. The **Trace & Reference** palette will appear, which you can use to adjust the visibility of the referenced worksheet.

14. You can turn off the visibility of the referenced worksheet either by clicking the top left button of the palette or by pressing *Alt + F2*.

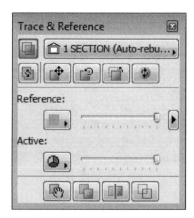

Collaboration with IFC files

As we previously mentioned, we can use IFC files to exchange models with consultants using other BIM platforms. A typical example of such a scenario is working with structural engineers. Structural engineers often use Autodesk Revit, which can export their models in IFC format. The structural model is an important component of the building and it is a good practice to keep an updated copy of it referenced in the architectural project.

You can merge the structural model directly into your project (**File | File Special | Merge**) but it is better to open it in a separate file and reference that file into your project by selecting **File | External Content | Place Hotlinked Module**. This way you can keep your project clean and organized no matter what the content of the structural model includes.

IFC management

ArchiCAD has IFC management features that are helpful for updating IFC files. For example, when you receive an updated version of the structural model in IFC format, you can open the separate file that you used to originally convert the model and automatically update its content.

Of course, you could create a new separate ArchiCAD file altogether from the updated structural model, but that way you would lose the original elements that you might have already linked in to your project. For example, if you dimension the structural column that is referenced in to your project from the separate file and recreate the structural model in a new separate file, the dimension will lose its dynamic connection to the original structural column and will be deleted.

Instead of recreating a separate file, you can open the original converted structural model and select **File | File Special | IFC 2 x 3 | Update with IFC Model**. Only new elements will be added and the original elements will be updated in this way, maintaining all references and dynamic links in your project.

You can even review changes before updating the IFC model by navigating to **File | File Special | IFC 2 x 3 | Detect IFC Model Changes**. After merging the changes this way, the difference will be highlighted with the **Mark-Up** tool.

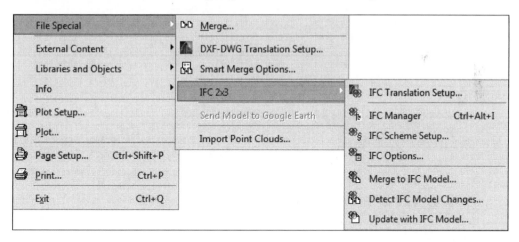

Teamwork

We will discuss two meanings of the word *Teamwork* in this section. First, we will look at the details of how ArchiCAD's Teamwork function works and then address a broader definition of teamwork. The second, broader definition refers to how design teams collaborate and share work in the BIM environment from the user's perspective.

Before we get into discussing the task-related details, let's shed some light on a few of the important elements of the underlying technology, which is called the **Graphisoft BIM Server.**

BIM Server

The Graphisoft BIM Server technology has a true server approach, which means that the information is managed securely in a database form. The server backs up the data automatically. In case of a system failure, the project file can be recovered or a previously saved state can be regenerated.

Another advantage of this technology is its speed. Only a small amount of data needs to be transmitted over the network when you save your work in a Teamwork project. For example, if you place a wall on the 1st floor plan and save your work, only the data related to that one wall will be transferred back to the server, as opposed to the whole project file. This feature reduces related time delays to the point where you will almost feel that saving the work happens instantly. Of course, this depends on network connection speed and other factors as well.

Users

The BIM Server Manager allows the registration of multiple users with various predefined roles. User roles can be established based on the level of interaction with the BIM project, ranging from advanced users capable of changing project level settings, to project managers only reviewing the work of the other team members. Every user has a unique **Login name** and **Password** that needs to be entered when logging in to the BIM Server.

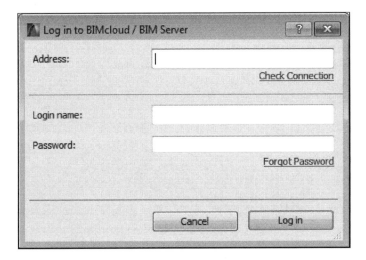

Teamwork projects

After logging in to the BIM Server, the **Open/Join Teamwork Project** dialog will appear, listing the available Teamwork projects under the selected BIM Server. You can select a project of your choice from the list and click on the **Open** or **Join** button at the lower-right corner of the dialog. Depending on whether you had joined that particular project in the past or not, the same button's function will change accordingly. The list of Teamwork projects will also include information about whether you had already joined the project, in the **Status** column.

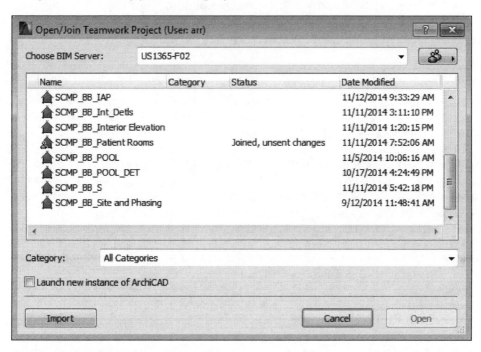

Teamwork libraries

We need to mention here that the BIM Server can host BIM Server libraries as well, to allow multiple users to work on the same content. You can see the list of available BIM Server Libraries by going to **File | Libraries and Objects | Manage BIM Server Libraries**. Your user status needs to be **Server or Project Administrator** in order to make any changes in the **Manage BIM Server Libraries** dialog.

Working in the Teamwork environment

When you join a Teamwork file for the first time, ArchiCAD needs to download the whole project on your local computer. This process can take several minutes but it only happens once, at this point. When you open the project the next time, only the changes made by the other users need to be downloaded and synchronized with your local copy, which takes significantly less time.

It is useful to have the Teamwork palette open when you work with a Teamwork file. You can bring up the Teamwork palette by going to **Teamwork | Teamwork Palette** or **Windows | Palettes | Teamwork Palette**. You can review the areas of the Teamwork palette in the following screenshot.

The **Teamwork** palette consists of three main parts. You can interact with the Teamwork project in the **Workspace** area of the palette. You can send your changes to the server and receive the changes made by other users simultaneously by clicking on the **Send & Receive** button. This command will effectively synchronize your local copy of the Teamwork project with the server.

You can also select a free element in the project and reserve it for modification by clicking on the **Reserve** button. While an element is reserved by you, no other team member can work on it. Once you are done adjusting an element, you can click on the **Release All** button to make it available for the rest of the team.

As you work with other team members in the Teamwork environment, don't forget to click on **Release All** at the end of the day. Surprisingly, many project management issues stem from ignoring this common step.

ArchiCAD allows you to visually filter the project elements on the screen with the options listed in the drop-down list under **Colored workspaces**. You can highlight your reserved elements and color other users' elements with this option, which is useful in effectively working with others. Clicking on the **My Workspace** button will reveal the areas where you have elements reserved for your work.

The **Users** list shows all active and inactive users working on the Teamwork project. You can send a message, change the user's color on your screen, and look at the user's settings by selecting a user and clicking on the respective button at the lower-right, under the **Users** list.

The **Messages** feature works as ArchiCAD's internal text messaging application, with the additional function of managing reservation requests between users. If you need to work on an element that is reserved by another user, you can notify that user and request the element with this tool.

Working in the Teamwork environment is intuitive and supportive of complex production processes. Coordinating the work of large teams requires other considerations as well, which we will discuss next. The **Teamwork** palette is shown in the following screenshot:

Division of work

One of the challenges of managing a BIM project is related to assigning work to individual team members and coordinating their efforts. Even though ArchiCAD can technically handle a large amount of content and many users working at the same time on a single file, the effective division of work can be hindered when multiple users try to adjust the same elements.

A solution to this problem is dividing the project into different files or Teamwork projects, representing logical sections, and linking the files or Teamwork project into each other.

Using module files

Module files are useful in creating and placing repeating parts of the building. For example, you can save the repeating model and annotation elements of a patient room and link it into the project several times. You only need to make changes affecting all the linked patient rooms once in the module file and the change will be reflected in all of the placed instances. This concept is similar to using repeating library parts but it's extended to a collection of the elements that you want to keep separately editable.

Using Hotlink Manager

With **Hotlink Manager**, you can view the list of placed module files, change their links, and even break the links making the module's content regular, editable elements of the project. You can access **Hotlink Manager** by going to **File | External Content | Hotlink Manager**.

Efficiency with module files

Let's look at a useful technique to save a module file in action:

1. Open the view map in the **Navigator** palette.
2. Click on the plus sign next to **Design Development Floor Plans**.
3. Double-click on **1st FLOOR PLAN** to activate it.
4. Zoom in to the top-left area of the floor plan.
5. Select the following library parts in **1001A BATHROOM** by holding down the *Ctrl* key:
    ° **Shower Cabin 17**
    ° **Towel Bar 01 17**
    ° **Basin 17**
    ° **Grab Bar 01 17**
    ° **WC 17**
6. Navigate to **File | External Content | Save Selection as Module**.
7. Navigate to a folder of your choice.
8. Enter `Bathroom Module` in the **File name** field.
9. Make sure that the **Replace selection with this hotlinked module file** option is checked.
10. Lastly, click on **Save** to save the module file.

You can quickly create modules from a collection of elements with this technique. Once the module files are created, you can place instances of them at other locations of your floor plan. Notice that the placement anchors of the library parts change from round to square, indicating that the library parts belong to a placed module file.

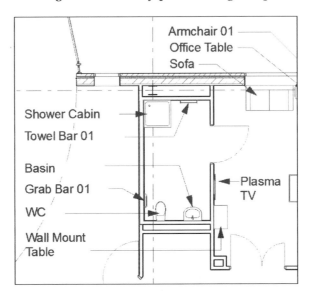

Collaboration between offices

Working with other team members in the same office has its own challenges, but sharing work between different geographic locations adds a whole other level of complexity to the process. ArchiCAD's BIM Server, Teamwork process, and some of the additional techniques we mentioned earlier on can be useful in supporting inter-office collaboration. Aside from technical solutions, talking to other team members in different offices on the phone can save a lot of time when you want to resolve issues.

Summary

In this chapter, you learned about the Publisher and its functions in the documentation and collaboration process. We explored how different project environment areas are related to various file types and how non-ArchiCAD files can be used as references in your work. You also learned about the Teamwork environment and how the Graphisoft BIM Server technology can support your team's collaboration efforts. We will conclude our lessons with model management concepts and visualization in the next chapter.

9
Visualization and Model Management

In this chapter, we will look at ArchiCAD's material system in detail and the basic concepts of architectural visualization. We will learn about:

- The basics of visualization
- Different rendering techniques with ArchiCAD
- How to create different types of presentation graphics
- How model management and troubleshooting are closely related to each other

Issues with display settings and file management can be often resolved simply, if you know how the elements and their attributes are connected.

Visualization concepts

Architectural visualization is a large topic, which alone is the focus of many books that are available today. We will have an overview of ArchiCAD's visualization capabilities in order for you to have a basic understanding of them. You can learn more about this subject from various online resources and publications. There are video tutorials available at `https://www.youtube.com/user/Archicad` about rendering with ArchiCAD.

The purpose of rendering

Rendered views of a proposed building have been important tools for centuries to communicate the design to clients and users. The process of translating the designer's ideas into visual representations is an important early step toward realizing a building. It can secure support for the project or stop it altogether. It requires skills that were traditionally related to hand drawing and painting. Good visualization is based on considering viewpoints, colors, light, shapes, and other basic graphic concepts.

In past decades, the use of computers has substituted the manual process of drawing and painting. Nevertheless, it is still important to understand the basic graphic concepts in order to create good renderings. One of the challenges of creating computer visualization is related to softening the inherent mechanical and lifeless look of the renderings, which we will discuss later in this chapter.

Rendering programs

A good way to approach realistic computer rendering is to consider it as virtual photography. You can create realistic representations of the smallest parts of the building and its surroundings with ArchiCAD and take a virtual photograph of the overall effect from a specific view point. While it is still important to understand the basic graphic concepts of composition, colors, and so on, learning about the basics of photography will support you in your work as well.

Realistic computer rendering programs are based on two methods:

- Simulating the effects of light on geometry and materials
- Calculating the effects of light on geometry and materials

Rendering programs that simulate the effects of light are also referred to as biased rendering software and programs that calculate the effects of light are also known as unbiased rendering programs. Both methods can generate high quality results and are available in the ArchiCAD workflow. ArchiCAD has two internal rendering engines that are based on simulating effects. With the use of add-ons, third-party programs are available to render to building model as well. An example of programs based on calculating the effects of light is Maxwell Render, which has a well-established add-on for ArchiCAD.

Programs based on the calculation of the physics of light have settings that tend to be simpler and closely resemble the use of a real camera. The simulation of the effects of light relies on approximating algorithms, which can be complex. The detailed settings of the simulation programs require additional knowledge of these algorithms. To simplify this issue, ArchiCAD has preset scenes for various scenarios as we will see later on.

Even the simulation-based programs have settings that are based on the use of a physical camera, with which you can treat the process as virtual photography.

The basics of photography

Let's review some of the basic settings of a real camera next. This knowledge will be useful for us when we adjust some of the rendering settings. The most commonly used camera type that allows the user to manually adjust settings is called the **Singe Lens Reflex (SLR)** camera. Its name refers to a mirror in the body of the camera that allows the user to see directly through the lens, which tilts out of the way to expose the film or digital sensor when the shutter is released.

The lens has an aperture, which can open or close, letting more or less light pass through the lens. The shutter can control the length of time through which the aperture is open, regulating the amount of light that enters the camera. The combination of the aperture size and the shutter speed has a fundamental effect on what the picture will look like.

The settings of rendering programs are related to SLR camera settings and their names follow the standards of photography.

Shutter speed

In bright and daylight conditions, we would typically set a fast shutter speed because there is plenty of light around our subject. On the other hand, if we were in an interior of a building or in night time conditions, we would probably need to set a slower shutter speed to allow more time for the exposure because the amount of light is significantly less. The value of shutter speed is measured in seconds.

To illustrate this, in the following set of images, the first image in daylight is rendered with 1/250 seconds shutter speed, which is considered fast. The third image in night time is rendered with 1/2 seconds shutter speed, which is much slower. The shutter speed is considered in combination with the aperture size as you will see in the next section.

The next image shows examples of aperture size - shutter speed combinations. Note that the two values are inversely proportional to each other.

APERTURE SIZE/ F-STOP	○	○	○	◎	⊙	⊙
	f 1.8	f 2.2	f 3.5	f 5	f 8	f 11
SHUTTER SPEED	1/250 s	1/60 s	1/60 s	1/15 s	1/4 s	1/2 s

Aperture size or f-stop

In theory, regardless of the lighting conditions, you can set a small or a large aperture size. Imagine setting a large aperture size and therefore, creating a wide opening for the light to enter the camera without adjusting the shutter speed. In such a scenario, your film or sensor will be overexposed because too much of light will be captured by it. If you set a small aperture without adjusting the shutter speed, then your image can be underexposed. In both the cases, you will lose the clarity of the details of your subject because they would either be too bright or too dark to see.

The shutter speed and aperture size both seem to control the amount of light; however, there is a significant difference in the effect of adjusting one or the other. With a small aperture size, all of the details of your subject will be in focus regardless of their distance from the camera. With a large aperture size, parts of your subject around the camera's target will be sharp and the parts that are farther behind or in front of the target will be blurred.

Depth of field

The area around your camera's target where the objects are sharp is called **depth of field**. If you would like to achieve a shallow depth of field with a large aperture size, you will need to counter balance with a fast shutter speed in order to reduce the amount of light entering the camera. This could be desirable if you would create an interior, rendering to focus on a furniture arrangement and blurring out objects in the background or in the foreground.

The shallow depth of field effect is more pronounced when the camera is close to its target. Focusing on close objects in interiors tend to produce more blurred backgrounds than exterior views of the building.

If you would like to create an overall sharp image, you will have to choose a small aperture size and slow shutter speed. A typical example of this would be an overall exterior image of the building. Let's take a look at the following images:

Shutter speed: 1/250 s, F-Stop: 1.8, ISO: 100

Shutter speed: 1/2 s, F-Stop: 11, ISO: 100

ISO or exposure value

The ISO or exposure value refers to the camera's overall sensitivity to light. This value also reflects the combination of the shutter speed and aperture size. As we discussed before, the same exposure value can be achieved with different shutter speed and aperture size combinations, however, the effect will not necessarily be the same. Higher ISO values allow the shift to lower light conditions. We can use ISO 100 in a typical daylight condition and ISO 1600 with an evening image.

Let's imagine that we want to create a sharp exterior image in the middle of the day, using the combination of shutter speed 1/250, f-stop 11, and ISO 100. If we want to take the same image in the evening with the same f-stop, we would need to allow for a much longer shutter speed to compensate for the low light conditions.

This could create a problem in physical photography because long shutter speeds would require the camera to be stable for the time of exposure. If we didn't have a tripod to stabilize the camera, we could have used a higher ISO value (for example, ISO 1600) to set a higher overall camera sensitivity and maintain the shutter speed of 1/250 with the same f-stop of 11. This way, even if we held the camera in our hand, the image would be sharp.

Shutter speed: 1/2 s, F-Stop: 11, ISO: 1600

Although the virtual camera in ArchiCAD does not need to be stabilized, this concept is carried over from the world of physical photography and represented in the ISO or exposure value.

Active virtual environment

Although our main subject is the rendering of still images with ArchiCAD, this is a good place to mention that we can create active virtual environments of our model as well. The active virtual environment is one of the visualization concepts that can be utilized to present your ideas. Let's discuss two options that are available in the program. Both of them could be useful in presenting your design intent.

3D Document

ArchiCAD's **3D Document** feature allows you to create a specialized 3D view, which you can use as a locked background for annotation. A newly created 3D Document will be listed under **3D Documents**, in the project map.

When you add annotation to a 3D document, you can snap to the elements in the view and orientation of the annotation, which will be adjusted to the view's 3D settings. This means that dimension lines will be presented parallel to the dimensioned elements. If the 3D Document is based on a perspective view, the dimension line will be displayed in perspective as well.

When you update the model, the content of the 3D document will be automatically updated as well, including dimensions that are linked to model elements. You can create a new 3D document or adjust the default 3D document settings by going to **Document** | **3D Document** | **New 3D Document** or **3D Document Settings**.

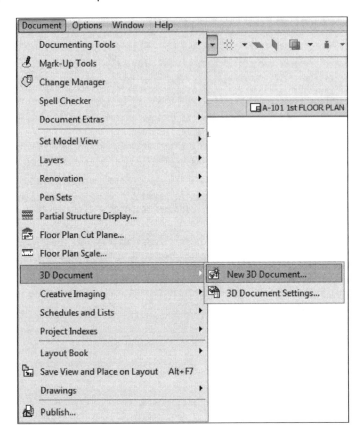

Active 3D models

We discussed several 3D output file formats in the previous chapter (see *Chapter 8, Work Sharing with ArchiCAD*, for more information). Let's look at two of them that you can use to create an active visualization of your model.

VRML stands for **Virtual Reality Modeling Language**. The VRML file format is designed to carry 3D model information, independently from any particular software packages. There are numerous free VRML viewers available that can run on desktops or as plugins to web browsers. You can even create websites with a dynamic representation of your model with the web plugin. You can zoom, orbit, and pan around the model directly in the website, making your building design easily accessible to your target audience.

The **3D PDF** is a somewhat more updated version of the same concept. PDF files can contain 3D models and only require the free Adobe Acrobat Reader to view and navigate around them. ArchiCAD can save your model in a U3D file format, which is the preferred format for 3D content in PDF files. Adobe Acrobat Reader has several lighting and rendering options to customize the viewer's experience. Perhaps, one of the most important benefits of this format besides the widely available free viewer is that it can contain large models at a fraction of the original file size.

After reviewing the basic concepts of visualization, let's look at some of the specific rendering settings next.

Rendering

Before you can click on the rendering button, you need to address three components that contribute to the look of the final image:

- Content (materials assigned to geometry)
- Light (artificial and natural lights)
- Camera (views)

It is recommended that you consider material assignments at the beginning of the project when you first start modeling the elements. It's even better if you create a template file that has most of the commonly used elements setup with proper material assignments.

Rendering also refers to non-photo realistic visualization. For example, materials can be displayed in line-based elevations and sections to create a detailed representation of the building. We will see later in the chapter that ArchiCAD has the option to create sketch style renderings that simulate hand-drawn effects. Sketch style visualization also falls into the category of renderings.

Content

We will look at the setting of the modeling elements next, as they relate to rendering. We will review the material assignment of the parts of the building model and additional elements (for example, planting) that can enhance the presentation of your project.

Material assignment - attributes

ArchiCAD has a comprehensive system for representing different materials in different views. The following map describes the structure and relationship between the material representation concepts in the program:

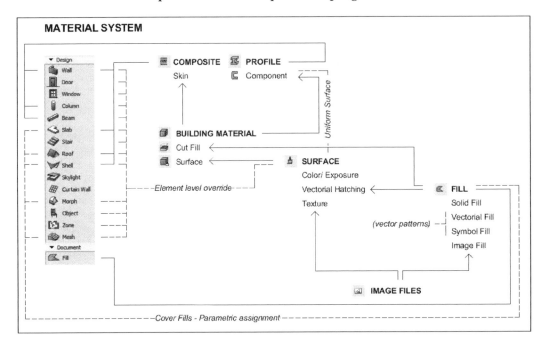

Building Materials in ArchiCAD consist of two components. The **Cut Fill** is a 2D representation of the material, which will appear in floor plans and sections when the element is cut. The **Surface** is a 3D representation of the same material, which will define the look of the element in sections, elevations, 3D documents, and 3D views when the element is not cut as well as in renderings.

You can access the **Building Materials** settings by navigating to **Options** | **Element** | **Attributes** | **Building Materials**. You can assign additional information to the material in the **Building Materials** settings dialog. For example, you can specify a manufacturer or **Physical Properties** of the material, which could be used in energy modeling.

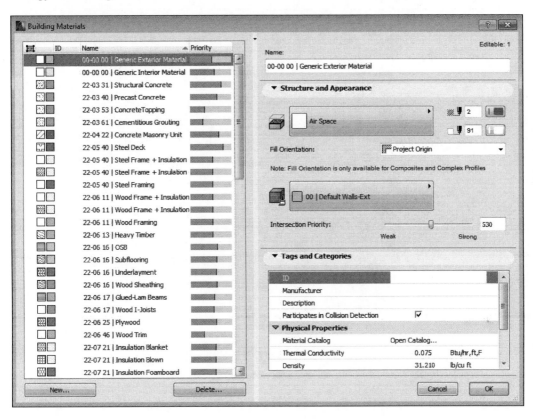

Surface refers to the visual qualities of the element's surface in different views when the element is not cut. The **Surface** settings define what kind of texture will be assigned to the element and how it will interact with light. You can access the **Surface Settings** dialog by navigating to **Options | Element Attributes | Surfaces**.

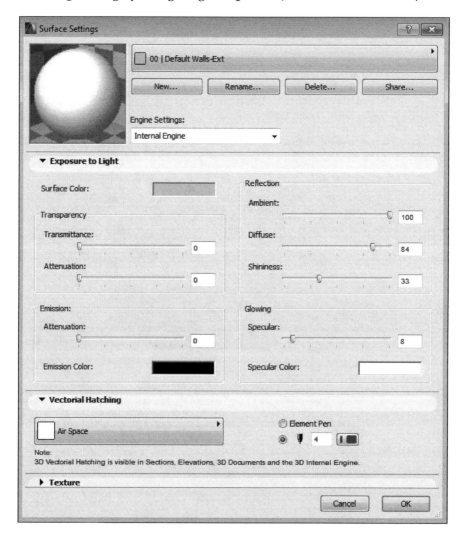

In the **Surface Settings** dialog, you can adjust the color and exposure settings in the **Exposure to Light** area. You can select an image file as a texture map and adjust the surface qualities in the **Texture** area. You can select a fill in the **Vectorial Hatching** area, which will be displayed in sections, elevations, 3D Documents, and 3D views when the Internal Engine is used to project the model. For example, you can assign a brick pattern fill here for a brick material and the lines of the brick pattern will be displayed on an elevation.

You can create a new surface by clicking on the **New** button in the top area of the **Surface Settings** dialog. This will activate the **Add New Surface** dialog. You can duplicate an existing surface and adjust its settings by selecting the **Duplicate** option.

It is useful to play with the different **Exposure to Light** settings of the **Surface Settings** dialog with a new surface. You can study the effect of different setting combinations this way without unintentionally affecting an already assigned Surface in you project.

You can also access predefined surfaces with the **New from Catalog** or **Replace Settings from Catalog** option. There are more than 500 predefined surfaces available in the *Standard ArchiCAD Catalog* and you can also download surfaces from http://www.BIMComponents.com. If you have a software service agreement with Graphisoft, you can access the *Additional Surface Catalog* as well.

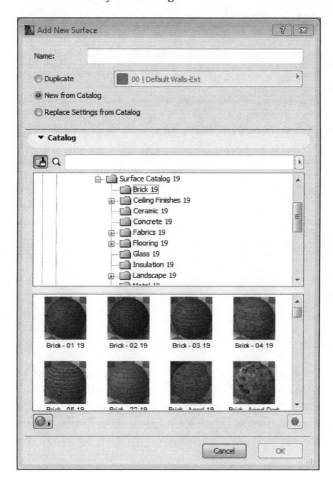

The basic modeling tools are listed under the **Design** section of the **Toolbox** palette. Typically, you can assign Building Materials in the **Geometry and Positioning** area of the tool's settings dialog with the exception of walls, library part type elements (doors, windows, skylights, stairs, curtain walls, and objects), and zones.

The material assignment of the library part type elements are primarily driven by parameters that are coded in the GDL script. These parameters are listed in the tool's **Settings** dialog. You can also make exceptions to the default material parameter settings by overriding the **Surface** assignment. The **Override Surface** setting is available in the **Model** area of the tool's **Settings** dialog.

Walls, **slabs**, **roofs**, and **shells** in ArchiCAD have a designated system to represent their structure. This system is called **Composites**. You can access the **Composites** settings by navigating to **Options | Element Attributes | Composites**. The **Edit Skin and Line Structure** area of the **Composites Structures** dialog allows you to create layers (**skins**) within elements and assign appropriate **Building Materials** to them. You can also define the thickness of the skin and type of lines separating them here.

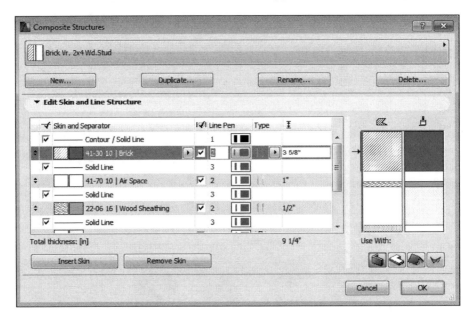

Walls, **beams**, and **columns** can have **profiles** assigned to them, which will define their shapes as extrusions. For example, you can assign the W8X31 standard steel profile to a beam that will specify the beam's cross section shape and size. You can access the **Profile Manager** by navigating to **Options | Element Attributes | Profile Manager**.

The **Components - Default** area of the **Profile Manager** allows you to assign a specific **Surface** to the **Profile**, which will be extruded along the element. The type of fill used to create the profile will define the look of the cross section.

When the **Use Building Material** option is selected, the profile will inherit the **Surface** and **Fill** properties of the fill's **Building Material** that is used to create the profile. This is a unique area in ArchiCAD, where **Fills** represent **Building Materials** instead of **Fill Patterns** due to the nature of profiles.

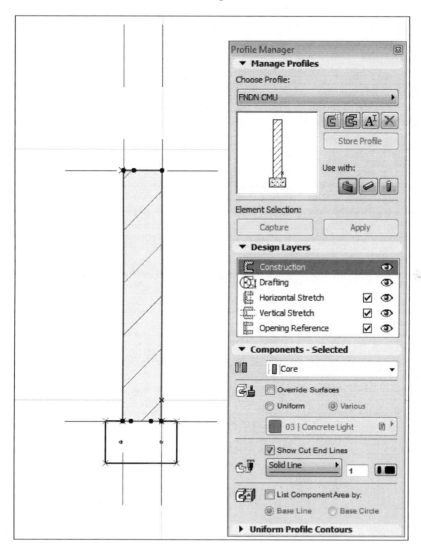

Using fills

There are four **Fill Types** available in ArchiCAD:

- Solid Fills
- Vectorial Fills
- Symbol Fills
- Image Fills

You can access the **Fill Types** settings dialog by navigating to **Options | Element Attributes | Fill Types**.

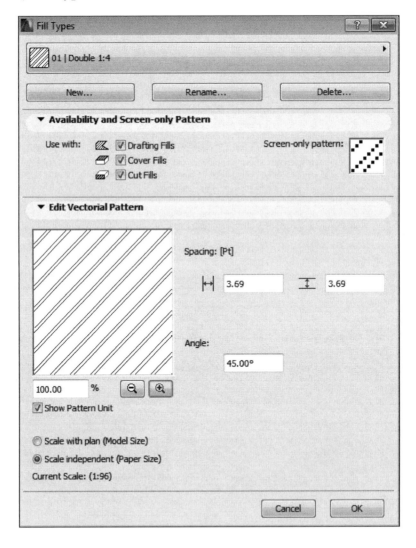

The top portion of the **Fill Types** settings dialog allows you to select, create, rename, and delete a fill type. The **Availability and Screen-only pattern** area includes the settings to select the use of the fill type and a window to create a pixel-like screen-only pattern.

Except for the **Image Fills** type, you can use these fill types as **Drafting Fills, Cover Fills,** or **Cut Fills**. **Image Fills** can only be used as **Drafting Fills** or **Cover Fills**.

Drafting Fills

You can select **Drafting Fills** when you want to use the fill type with the 2D **Fill** tool as an annotation or drafting element. **Cover Fills** can be assigned as **Vectorial Hatching** in the **Surface** settings dialog.

Cover Fills

Cover Fills can also be assigned to **Slabs, Meshes, Roofs, Shells,** and **Morphs** in the **Floor Plan and Section** area of the tools' settings dialog and **Zones** in the **Floor Plan** area of the **Zone Default Settings** dialog, if the **Use Fill from Surface** option is not selected. The **Vectorial Hatching** of the assigned **Surface** will be applied if you select the **Use Fill from Surface** option.

To simplify these concepts, imagine that **Cover Fills** can be used to create visible patterns on the surfaces of the elements of your building model in various views. **Cut Fills** can be visible patterns on a cut surface of a model element.

Cut Fills

Cut Fills can be assigned to **Building Materials** in the **Structure and Appearance** area of the **Building Materials** settings dialog. You can also use **Cut Fills** as 2D fills. For example, you can add 2D Cut Fills to the details, to enhance the definition of your documentation.

The **Screen-only pattern** window is an 8 x 8 pixel grid. You can create a simplified representation of your fill in this area by drawing the individual pixels. When you un-select the **Vectorial Hatching** options under **View | On-Screen View Options**; all vectorial hatching will be visually substituted by the simplified version of the fill from this window. This requires fewer resources from the computer. The purpose of this feature was more relevant years ago, when computers were not as powerful as today.

The lower area of the **Fill Types** settings dialog includes settings specific to setting up Solid, Vectorial, Symbol, or Image Fills. You can adjust the size, scaling, and the angle of your fill patterns among other settings here.

Solid Fills, as the name suggests, are solid color fills. You can adjust the transparency of these fills.

There are several Vectorial Fills available in the basic ArchiCAD library. You can adjust the spacing of these fills, which essentially means changing the size of them. You can also set the angle and the scaling of Vectorial Fills.

Creating new fill types

When you create a new fill type, you will notice that the **Vectorial Fill** option is not available. You can duplicate an existing **Vectorial Fill** and modify its settings to create a new one. To create an entirely new vector type fill, you will need to select the **Symbol fill** type, which is a special type of **Vectorial Fill**.

In order to create a new **Symbol Fill**, you can draw a pattern in a floor plan or worksheet window using simple **lines**, **circles**, and **hotspots**. You can copy the pattern to the clipboard and paste it in the **Fill Types** settings dialog by clicking on the **Paste** button in the **Edit Symbol Pattern** area of the dialog. Once you have pasted the custom pattern, you can adjust the new fill's size, angle, and scaling here.

Image Fills are based on image files. For example, you can use the texture image of a floor pattern to create an Image Fill from it. You can adjust the size, angle, and scaling of the Image Fill in the **Fill Texture** area of the **Fill Types** settings dialog. A unique setting option for Image Fills is the **Mirroring Method** setting, which allows you to adjust the way the image file will be repeated in the fill. You can fine-tune the tiling effect of the image by selecting one of the available **Mirroring Methods**.

The following image illustrates the **Mirroring Method** settings using the **Wood Parquet** fill type, which is a part of the basic ArchiCAD library. Note the different tiling effects as a result of selecting one of the available four options:

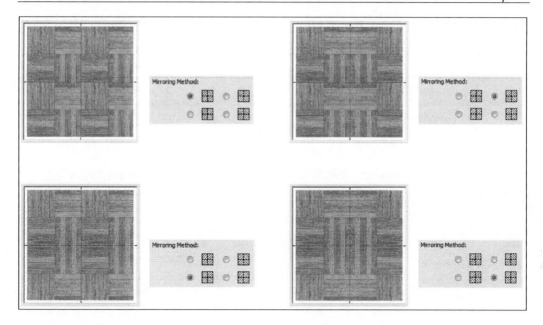

The **Element Attribute** settings that we have discussed so far are connected to each other and are applied in a coordinated fashion. You can override these settings at the element as well as at view level. Although this means that you have a great amount of freedom to set up your project, it can also lead to file management issues especially with a larger design team.

We will discuss the override options later in this chapter, as they relate to management (see *Chapter 9, Visualization and Model Management*).

Exterior improvements

The basic ArchiCAD library includes objects that are designed to add the details of the building's surroundings. You can select these objects under **2. VISUALIZATION | 2.2 Site Improvements** in the library.

These objects make it easier to relate to the building's scale and soften the sterile look that is typical of some lower quality computer renderings. 3D computer artists spend a significant amount of time developing small and realistic details. For example, details of gutters or wet pavement surfaces with puddles can all enhance the quality of a computer rendering even if the viewer perceives those details in their peripheral vision.

While your project's schedule may not allow you to spend as much time as 3D artists spend on enhancing the details of your renderings, you can still add a few elements that will make a difference. A few strategically placed objects in a good composition will help you to achieve a reasonable quality for your renderings.

For the purposes of this chapter, we will discuss exterior renderings. The basic ArchiCAD library has objects to improve the details of the interior images as well.

ArchiCAD Library elements for rendering

An important issue to address before you select the exterior improvements is the complexity of your model. The complexity of your model is directly related to the time it takes the computer to develop the rendering.

3D tree objects that simulate the look of real life trees can be composed of many polygons; and adding only a couple of them to the model can significantly lengthen the rendering time. It is advisable to consider the size of the individually inserted objects because they can significantly contribute to the overall project file size as well.

A set of special objects is available in the basic ArchiCAD library to address these issues. For example, the **Deciduous Trees** object under **2.2 Site Improvements | Garden** represents trees with 2D images that are automatically oriented vertically and toward the camera. You can create the look of a realistic tree with this object without having to burden the model with a great amount of polygons, representing the individual leaves of the tree.

One disadvantage of these types of objects is that they can only cast the shadow of the vertical rectangle, which is the bounding box of the tree image. While it might be acceptable to place them farther away from the camera, it is recommended to avoid placing them in the forefront of the view where their shadows would be clearly visible.

An alternative option to consider is placing them in the shadow of the building where the objects' own shadow will not create an issue.

Tree Model Detailed and *Deciduous Trees*

The **Tree Model Detailed** object has a feature that is based on the capabilities of GDL. The object can recognize its distance from the camera and change its shape accordingly. If you place these objects farther away from the camera, for example, modeling a line of trees in the background, it will simplify its 3D crown model automatically and therefore, reduce the count of polygons required to represent the trees.

The trees in the distance can create a realistic look even with the simplified model.

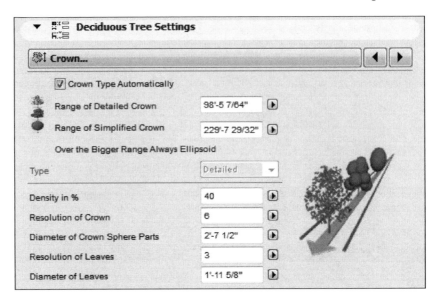

Plants, people, and vehicles are helpful in visually clarifying the scale of the building. The human eye can naturally relate to the scale of these elements and in return relate to the scale of the building that is adjacent to them.

You can find people models under **2. VISUALIZATION | 2.3 Site People and Vehicles | People** and vehicles under **2. VISUALIZATION | 2.3 Site People and Vehicles | Vehicles** in the basic ArchiCAD library.

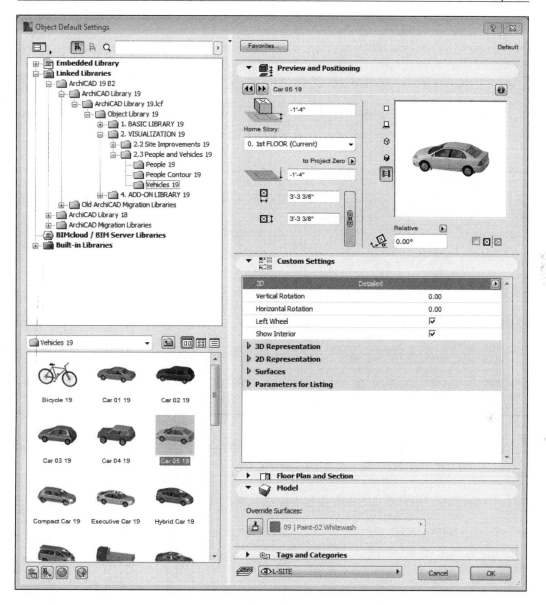

Representing people is one of the most challenging aspects of computer renderings. The human face recognition is very sensitive. This is why a computer-generated person's face is easily recognizable as artificial. A good technique to take this problem into account is to have the models of people face away from the camera whenever possible.

Light

For exterior images, you can adjust the position of the sun as the main light source in the **3D Projection Settings** dialog. You can access the **3D Projection Settings** dialog by navigating to **View | 3D View Options | 3D Projection Settings**.

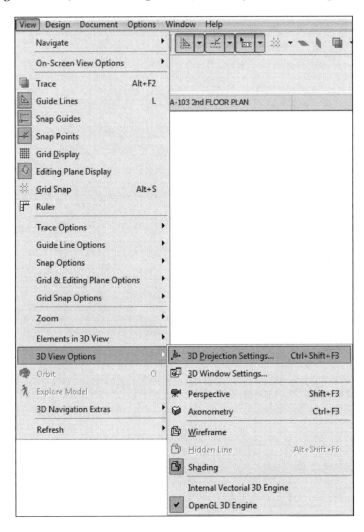

You can create interior and exterior artificial lights with the **Lamp** tool, which you can find in the **Toolbox**, under **More**. The basic ArchiCAD library has a collection of light fixture models and light sources.

Some of them have settings to simulate the real physics of light distribution and color properties based on photometric files (for example, **IES Light** under **16 Electrical**, in the library). You can also download Photometric Data Files (**IES** is an abbreviation of **Illuminating Engineering Society of North America**) from many light fixture manufacturers. For example, you can download Philips IES files from http://www.colorkinetics.com/support/ies/.

The **3D Projection Settings** dialog has two modes, which are **Perspective Settings** and **Parallel Projection Settings**. You can switch between the modes by clicking on the button at the top-right area of the dialog. In both the modes, an icon represents the sun and its position, which is relative to the camera and the building model. You can drag the icon to a position of your choice and adjust the sun to fit your desired lighting conditions.

You can also change the **Azimuth** and **Altitude** parameters of the sun parametrically in this dialog. If you would like to set the sun position accurately according to a certain day and time of the year, you can access the **Sun** dialog by clicking on the **More Sun** button at the lower part of the **3D Projection Settings** dialog. You can specify the exact time and date relative to the geographic project location here. Specifying the precise location and time is necessary for creating Sun Studies. The **Light Parameters** area of the dialog has options to specify the intensity and color of the **Sunlight**, contribution to ambient light, and intensity and the color of the **Ambient Light**.

You can also specify the color and intensity of **Fog** and whether you want to use fog in your rendering.

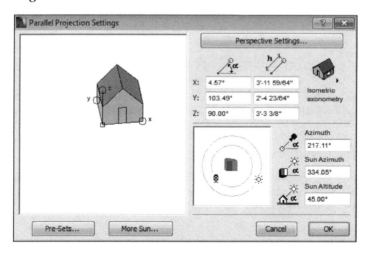

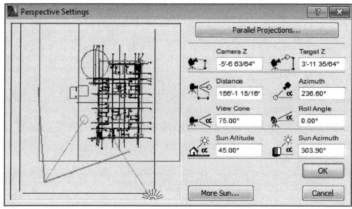

Camera

You can set up a specific 3D view by either using the **3D Projection Settings** dialog or placing a camera with the **Camera** tool. You can find the **Camera** tool under **More** in the **Toolbox**.

The **Camera** tool allows you to place a camera and point to its target in a floor plan view. Once you have a camera placed on the floor plan, you can see its icon appearing in the **3D Projection Settings** dialog **Perspective Settings** mode, which is similar to the icon of the sun. You can adjust the position of the camera and its target in this dialog as well by dragging them to a new location. You can fine-tune the position and orientation of the camera by adjusting the camera parameters in the **Perspective Settings** dialog.

The position of the camera of an axonometric or parallel projection 3D view can be adjusted similarly with the camera parameters in the **Parallel Projection Settings** dialog. There are also preset parallel views that you can activate by clicking on the button at the top-right corner of the dialog.

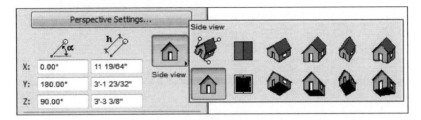

Once you have placed a camera on the floor plan, you will notice that it appears in the project map under **3D** along with its assigned camera path. You can access the camera and path settings by right-clicking on the camera icon in the project map and selecting **Camera Settings**.

The top area of the **Camera Settings** dialog allows you to create and manage camera paths consisting of several cameras. We will mention these paths later in this chapter as they are used to create multiple instances of **Fly-Through**.

 You can use the keyboard shortcut *Ctrl* + *Shift* + *F3* to access the **3D Projection Settings** dialog.

Rendering parameters

Now that we have covered the three basic components of rendering (that is, content, light, and camera), we can discuss the actual process of rendering in ArchiCAD. We will review the available rendering settings next with the help of practical exercises.

For the purposes of this chapter, we will focus on exterior scenes and perspective views. As we referred to it earlier on, you can create interior renderings as well as renderings of parallel projection views (for example, elevations, axonometric views, and so on).

Let's start with opening the **PhotoRendering Settings** dialog, which you can access by navigating to **Document | Creative Imaging | PhotoRendering Settings**.

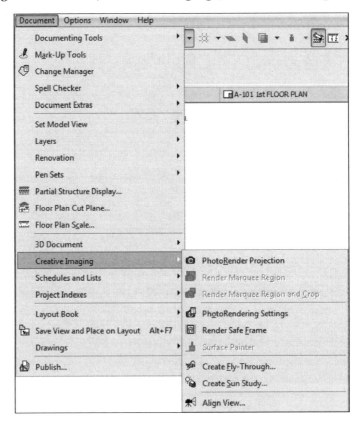

ArchiCAD has three built-in rendering engines that you can use to generate presentation images. These engines are:

- The **Internal** engine
- **CineRender by MAXON**
- The **Sketch** engine.

The **Internal** and the **CineRender by MAXON** engines can be primarily used to create photorealistic images. ArchiCAD also has a **Sketch** engine, which you can use to simulate hand-drawn sketch renderings. We will use the **CineRender** and the **Sketch** rendering engine for our examples.

We have mentioned the issue of the "sterile look" of computer generated renderings before. In addition to that issue, designers using computers are also challenged by specific, inaccurate details too early. For example, you can use a preset window object on the exterior of your building, which the computer will render in full details.

At the beginning of a design phase, you might not necessarily be able to decide if the modeled window will end up being of the actual type that you would like to select for your project. If your team members or clients see a rendering of that particular window object, it might mislead them into believing that this is the specific choice for the project.

The **Sketch** engine can be useful in early design phases because you can create renderings with it that do not look very specific in detail. On the other hand, you need to balance the sterile, or even the fake look of the sketch renderings. It is recommended that you use the sketch renderings as backgrounds for actual hand-drawn sketches. This way you benefit from the rapid generation of perspective as well as the outline of sketches, and yet you can always add the necessary natural touches by hand.

Let's see how the **Sketch** rendering engine works in action next. When you activate the **PhotoRendering Settings** dialog, you can see two main tabs on the top of the dialog under the preview window. The **Settings** tab includes all of the settings for the selected scene and engine.

The **Size** tab allows you to set the size of the image. You can also apply a **Render Safe Frame** here, which helps you to visually identify the area of your rendering in the 3D view. You can avoid unexpected elements being cut off from your rendering with this feature.

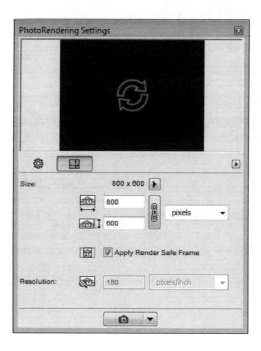

The top area of the **Settings** tab consists of two drop-down menus. The **Scene** drop-down menu allows you to select, save, and manage a combination of rendering settings. The **Engine** drop-down menu lists the available three rendering engines that you can choose from.

The **Basic settings** area of the **Sketch** engine allows you to specify the main **Line Style** and **Line Color**. The other setting areas include options to adjust the paper roughness, line, shadow line thickness, background selection, as well as other adjustments. It's recommended that you play with the various settings to achieve a desired sketch rendering style. Once you are satisfied with a setting combination, you can save it as a scene in the **Scene** drop-down menu.

We will start with a preset scene to test the Sketch engine. Open the `Commercial_Bldg-Shell-Rendering.pln` file. You will see exterior improvements already placed in this file as well as a camera that we will use in the following examples.

Sketch rendering

1. Open **Project Map** in the **Navigator** palette.

2. Double-click on **Camera 1** under **3D/ 00 Path 1** to activate the 3D exterior view.

3. Go to the **Document** menu and select **PhotoRendering Settings**, under **Creative Imaging**. The **PhotoRendering Settings** dialog will open.

4. Select **Koh-I-Nor** from the **Scene** drop-down menu. This will activate the Sketch engine with preset options.

5. Click on the **PhotoRender Projection** button at the bottom of the **PhotoRendering Settings** dialog to start the rendering.

A new window titled **Picture # 1** will open where you can see the rendering developing. Your rendering will look similar to the following image. Notice that the brick vectorial hatching is displayed on the wall of the building. The **Sketch** engine can render the **Vectorial Hatching** of **Surfaces**.

Once the rendering process is done, you can save the image as a JPG file. To do this, perform the following:

1. Go to the **File** menu and select **Save as**. Or press the key combination of *Ctrl + Shift + S*. The **Save Picture** dialog will open.

2. Navigate to a desired location and enter a name of your choice in the **File name** field.

3. Click on the **Save** button to finish the process.

Keep the **PhotoRendering Settings** active on your screen because we will continue working with it in the next exercises.

Rendering with CineRender

We will use the CineRender by MAXON engine to create a photo realistic image. MAXON has developed an advanced rendering solution and integrated it into ArchiCAD. We need to mention, that the **CineRender** engine works with its own set of specialized materials that are different from ArchiCAD's internal materials.

The CineRender and ArchiCAD materials are synchronized and appropriately matched in the basic ArchiCAD library. You can review and adjust the **CineRender Settings** of a material in the **Surface Settings** dialog by selecting **CineRender by MAXON** from the **Engine Settings** drop-down menu.

We will use **Physical Camera** in CineRender to see an example of how the basic photography concepts we discussed earlier work in action. We will modify a preset scene to achieve the desired results, as follows:

1. Turn on the **L-SITE** layer. This will reveal the plant objects around the building.

2. Select **Outdoor Daylight Medium** option from the **Scene** drop-down menu. This will activate the **CineRender** engine with the preset options.

3. Make sure that the **Detailed Settings** option is selected.

4. Select **Use Physical Render** under **Detailed Settings**.

5. Click on the plus sign next to **Use Physical Render** if the tree structure is not unfolded.

6. Click on **Physical Camera** under **Use Physical Render**.

7. Check the box next to **Camera Exposure** and set **Camera ISO** value to **100**.

8. Set the **Camera F-Stop** value to **f/11.0**.

9. Set the **Camera Shutter Speed** value to **1**.

10. Click on the **PhotoRender Projection** button to start the rendering.

The camera settings mentioned here are appropriate for a daylight condition if we want to create an overall sharp image. You can experiment with different camera settings to achieve different effects. Once finished, your rendering should look like the following image. You can save it at this point.

HDR rendering

HDR stands for **High Dynamic Range**. HDR background images in the basic ArchiCAD library are panoramic images that have a higher bit depth than normal JPG files. HDR images can be used as environmental light sources because of this, which can be useful to create natural looking atmospheres in your renderings. To do so, do as follows:

1. Unselect **Sunlight** under **Render Settings | Detailed Settings | Light Adjustments**.

2. Click on **Environment** and select **HDRi Sky** from the **Sky Setup** drop-down menu.

3. Click on **HRDi Sky** and reveal the settings under **HDR Image**.

4. Click on the button with the three dots next to the **File Name** field. The **Load Image from Library** dialog window will open.

5. Select **Trees 02 GS.hdr** under **Libraries | ArchiCAD Library | [HImg] HDR Images | High Res Luminance**.

6. Finally, click on **OK**.

7. Click on the **PhotoRender Projection** button to render the image.

You may notice in your finished rendering, that the trees in the background HDR image are reflected in the windows of the building. There is also a green tint in the image and you can only see ambient shadows. The green tint and lack of sharp shadows are realistically contributing to the representation of a forest-like environment.

You can use HDR background images to simply create realistic lighting in your renderings. They also serve as backgrounds for your presentation images.

White model rendering

The **CineRender** engine has a feature that you can use to render images that look like scale models. This option along with the **Sketch** rendering engine's features can also be useful in rendering schematic images at the early stages of the design process:

1. Unselect **Sky Visibility** under **Render Settings | Detailed Settings | Environment | HDRi Sky**.

2. Click on the box next to the **White Model** option under **Render Settings | Detailed Settings | Effects**.

3. Click on the **PhotoRender Projection** button to render the image.

Your rendering will be similar to the following image:

The four images above illustrate the basic rendering concepts in ArchiCAD. You can explore the additional settings available in the different rendering engines and see their effects on the images.

 It is recommended that you start your exploration with a preset scene, modifying only one or two settings first, in order to understand the changes, resulting from adjusting the settings.

Fly-Through animation

Fly-Through is an animation in which the camera moves along a path around, or inside the building model. The cameras placed in a floor plan view define the path.

You can see **00 Path 1** under **3D**, in the **Project Map** in our `Commercial_Bldg-Shell-Rendering.pln` example file, which only includes one camera that we used for the exterior renderings. In order to make a **Fly-Through**, you can copy the existing camera, move it to a different location, and set a different target for it. Fly-Throughs require at least two cameras in a path, since they need a start and end frame.

You can right-click on the path and select **Camera Settings**. This will activate the **Camera Settings** dialog where you can adjust the settings of each camera assigned to this path separately. Clicking on the **Path** button in the lower left area of the dialog will reveal the **Path Options** window. This dialog has **Motion Controls** and **Display Options** as well as the **Motion Resolution** setting area. The **In-between frames** setting is important to mention for our purposes here. This is the setting that will specify how many frames ArchiCAD will add between each camera of this path.

You can access the **Create Fly-Through** dialog by navigating to **Document | Creative Imaging | Create Fly-Through**.

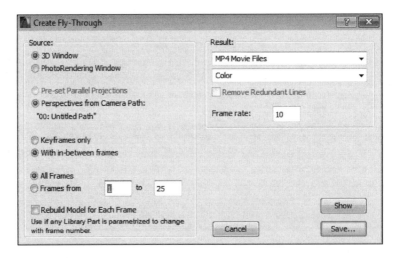

The **Source** area of the dialog allows you to set whether the animation will be generated in the **3D Window** or **PhotoRendering Window**. You can also specify the frames and select the **Rebuild Model for Each Frame** option here that is related to camera-position-sensitive objects.

We mentioned the automatic crown geometry adjustment feature of the **Tree Model Detailed** object. This object is a good example for illustrating the effect of the **Rebuild Model for Each Frame** option. When this option is selected, ArchiCAD will regenerate the tree model, adjusting the complexity of its geometry frame by frame. This means that the tree model geometry will be optimized throughout the whole animation.

The **Result** area of the dialog has options to set the file type, frame rate, and the color depth of the animation. The **In-between frames** of the **Path Options** and the **Frame rate** setting of the **Create Fly-Through** dialog define together the smoothness of the animation.

If the value for **In-between frames** is set to **60** and the **Frame rate** is **60**, it will mean that the animation will transition between the cameras in one second. A typical video has a frame rate of 24. This means that the video will display 24 frames per second. If we set the **Frame rate** to **24** and leave the value of **In-between frames** at **60**, the animation will transition between the cameras in 2.5 seconds (*60/24 = 2.5*).

You can finally show the animation on the screen or save it as a file by clicking on one of the buttons in the lower-right part of the dialog window.

Model management and troubleshooting

Model management and troubleshooting are advanced topics that are connected to each other. Mostly BIM managers handle tasks related to these subjects; however, the way you build and organize your work contributes to how the project is managed from the BIM perspective.

If the project model(s) are well managed, troubleshooting becomes easier. For example, the reason for elements showing incorrectly on your floor plan can be easily tracked down if standard visibility settings are applied in the project.

We mentioned earlier that it is recommended that you start thinking about materials and their visibility in different views and renderings from the beginning of the modeling process. Trying to assign and organize the materials of the individual elements of a complex model takes a lot of time after the elements have already been placed. This is an example of a model management problem.

Using project templates and attribute files

Template files are useful for starting with preassigned materials and visibility settings. ArchiCAD offers two basic templates to start with, for typical residential and commercial projects. If you don't have access to a custom project template, these templates are good starting points for your work.

There are other useful features to help you keep a well-managed project besides template files, which we mentioned earlier in this book. Attribute sets can be saved as Attribute Manager Files (AAT) from the **Attribute Manager** dialog. You can access the **Attribute Manager** by navigating **Options | Element Attributes | Attribute Manager**.

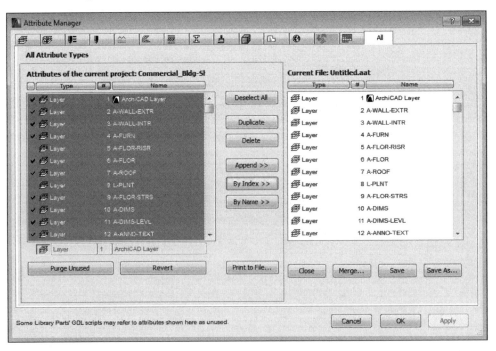

You can also import individual, or sets of attributes with the **Attribute Manager** and override existing settings in your project file.

Many of the model management issues are related to the appropriate visibility of the elements in different views and therefore, troubleshooting is often necessary when elements are displayed incorrectly.

From the user's perspective, a thorough understanding of ArchiCAD's model and document structure (see *Chapter 7, Documentation – A Commercial Project*) and material system (see *Chapter 9, Visualization and Model Management*) is important to maintain and build an organized model.

Large projects and project teams require model management and troubleshooting tasks related to linking files, updating referenced content, and managing users, which are typically performed by BIM managers (see *Chapter 8, Work Sharing with ArchiCAD*).

For example, referencing and updating model content from IFC and DWG files can be streamlined by saving export and import settings in XML files as we discussed in the previous chapter.

Controlling visibility

Let's look at an example and illustrate a visibility issue. As we saw earlier in this chapter, you can override the Surface assignment of elements on an element level in the **Model** area of the elements **Default Settings** dialog.

There are two other ways to override attribute assignments. Knowing about these concepts can help you in basic visibility troubleshooting.

You can override **Cut Fills** on a view level with the **Model View Options** dialog. You can access the dialog by navigating to **Document | Set Model View | Model View Options**.

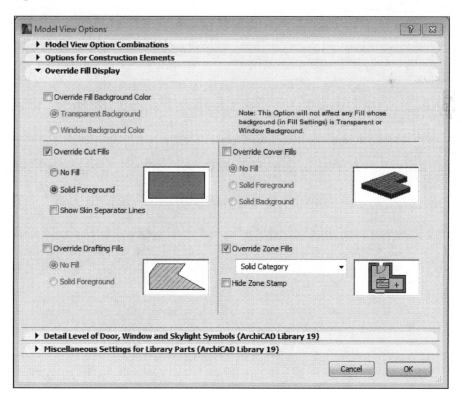

The **Override Fill Display** area of the dialog includes an option for overriding cut fills. For example, you can select a **Solid Foreground** fill for all the walls in the view regardless of their individual settings and turn off the visibility of the **Skin Separator Lines**.

On an element level, you can select a specific **Cut Fill Pen** for an object that is different from the assigned fill in its GDL script. Unless you know about this option, it is hard to find out why a single object is not displayed with a proper cut fill in some cases.

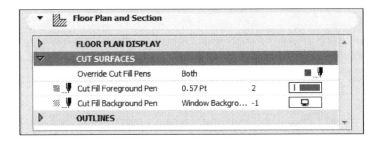

You can select the **Override Cut Fill Pens** in the **Floor Plan and Section** area of the object's settings dialog at some point for an individual element and forget about it later. It is easy to forget these kinds of individual settings when you are preparing for a deadline. This is why it is recommended that you avoid them and use global attribute assignments as much as possible.

Summary

In this chapter, you learned about visualization concepts including some basic knowledge about photography. We saw examples of ArchiCAD's rendering capabilities and reviewed the material system that drives the visibility of elements in different rendering styles. Finally, we discussed model management and troubleshooting issues that you, as a user, need to consider in your work.

We hope you have found this journey through *ArchiCAD 19 - The Definitive Guide* to be enjoyable and beneficial. Whether you went step-by-step through every task, in every chapter, or just went to the more advanced subject matters, it was our goal for you to become enlightened and educated.

The best way to learn ArchiCAD is to use it on a project. If you have finished the exercises in this book and want something else to work on, put your home in ArchiCAD, or a friend's place, or the building that you work in; something that you will feel good about creating.

For more tutorials on ArchiCAD, there are plenty of short videos available at ArchiCAD's YouTube channel `https://www.youtube.com/user/Archicad`.

To keep up with the latest in learning about ArchiCAD, go to `http://www.graphisoft.com/`, click on **Support**, and go to the Help Center. This should keep you busy. Enjoy your adventure in the world of BIM and ArchiCAD!

Index

Symbols

3D content
exporting 260
file formats 261, 262
model elements, saving as library
part 262-264
reception desk, viewing 197
3D Document 289
3D PDF 291

A

active 3D models 290, 291
active virtual environment
3D Document 289
about 289
active 3D models 290, 291
adjustments
Drawing Manager 244
multiple layouts, setting up 246
annotation
about 71
Dimension tool 73
Label tool 72, 73
Text tool 71
ArchiCAD
about 1
exporting to 253
GUI 1
project workflow 77-79
selection methods 5
URL, for video tutorials 283

ArchiCAD GUI
about 1, 124
Attributes toolbar 124
Info Box palette 1
Navigator palette 1
panning interface 2
Quick Options palette 124
Toolbox palette 1
view, toggling 3
zooming interface 2
ArchiCAD Library elements
for rendering 302-305
ArchiCAD project, settings
about 3, 4
files, using 320
for stories 4, 5
Renovation Filter feature 5
units 5
attributes
about 209, 292-297
Building materials option 211
Composites option 211
Fill Types option 210
Layer Settings option 210
Line Types option 210
managing 212
Mark-Up Styles option 211
Operation Profiles option 212
Pens & Colors option 211
Profile Manager 211
Renovation Override Styles option 211
Surfaces option 211
Zone Categories 211

B

basement
element modification 14
floor slab, creating 13
garage, adding 15, 16
basement casework layer
about 62-64
Beam tool 68, 69
Column tool 68, 69
Mesh 2 64-67
bathroom
about 103, 104
annotations, adding 104
bathroom casework layer
about 50
mirror, adding 52
toilet, placing 52
tub, placing 52
vanity, adding 50, 51
Beam tool 68
bedrooms casework layer
about 53
beds, placing 53
furniture, placing 54
BIM Server, Teamwork
about 276
libraries 277
projects 277
users 276
Building Information Modeling (BIM) 2

C

camera 308
casework and plumbing fixtures
adding 187, 188
ceiling plan views
about 82
folder, cloning 82
layer, preparing for reflected
ceiling plans 82
CineRender
rendering, performing with 314, 315
clone folders
about 179, 180
deleting 181

collaboration
about 271
DWG files, referencing 272, 273
IFC files, using 274
IFC management 275
worksheets, using 273, 274
columns and grids
about 139
Grid tool 144
profiles, using 139
Column tool 68, 69
composite
about 140, 296
creating 166
layer combinations, adjusting 167
composite type, ceilings
creating 19
first floor ceilings 20
second floor ceilings 21
Computer-aided design (CAD) 2
content 291
Cover Fills 299
Curtain Wall tool
about 127
used, for creating curtain walls 127-130

D

depth of field 286
dimension
creating 74
editing 75
Dimension tool 73
dining room casework layer 58, 59
documentation workflow
about 229
drawing placement 229
sheet setup 229
view adjustment 229
Drafting Fills 299
drafting tools
about 213
dimensions, editing 217, 218
fills, modifying 213-216
text, editing 216
Drawing Manager 244, 245

E

enlarged plan
about 89
Detail tool 90
for bathroom 95
for kitchen 92
for laundry room 93, 94
layer, preparing 91
views 91
exterior improvements
about 301
ArchiCAD Library elements, for
rendering 302-305
exterior walls
about 125
creating 8, 13
Curtain Wall tool 127
elevation marks 125
Renovation Filter, setting 8
Wall tool 125, 126
Wall tool, using 9
Extrusion method 135

F

file formats
3D content, exporting 260
exporting to 253
Industry Foundation Classes (IFC)
files 269, 270
Layout Book 254
list 257-260
other file formats 271
PDF files 267
project map 253, 254
Publisher 254
saving, locations 253
specific file formats 264
view map 253, 254
files
exporting 114
multiple files, exporting 115
fills
using 298, 299
fill types
Cover Fills 299
creating 300, 301

Cut Fills 299
Drafting Fills 299
Find & Select tool
about 7
modification commands 8
floor slab
for basement, creating 13
Fly-Through animation 318

G

garage casework layer 70
Graphisoft BIM Server 276
Grid System tool
additional grid lines, creating 152, 153
column grid, adjusting 149, 150
using 145-148

H

High Dynamic Range (HDR)
about 315
rendering 315, 316
hotlinks
about 120, 160
applying, to core 160-162
applying, to interior model 166
applying, to shell model 160-162
attribute settings, exporting 121
attribute settings, importing 121
elevation marks, moving 163, 164
layer, preparing 160
Xrefs, attaching 164, 165

I

Industry Foundation Classes (IFC)
files 269, 270
Interior Elevation tool 98
interior walls
ceilings, creating 19
creating 17
doors 34-37
layers, managing 28, 29
layers, managing with Quick
Layers palette 29
pet palette, using 19
roofs 22

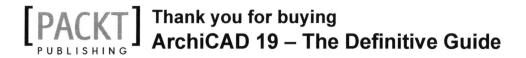

About Packt Publishing

Packt, pronounced 'packed', published its first book, *Mastering phpMyAdmin for Effective MySQL Management*, in April 2004, and subsequently continued to specialize in publishing highly focused books on specific technologies and solutions.

Our books and publications share the experiences of your fellow IT professionals in adapting and customizing today's systems, applications, and frameworks. Our solution-based books give you the knowledge and power to customize the software and technologies you're using to get the job done. Packt books are more specific and less general than the IT books you have seen in the past. Our unique business model allows us to bring you more focused information, giving you more of what you need to know, and less of what you don't.

Packt is a modern yet unique publishing company that focuses on producing quality, cutting-edge books for communities of developers, administrators, and newbies alike. For more information, please visit our website at www.packtpub.com.

Writing for Packt

We welcome all inquiries from people who are interested in authoring. Book proposals should be sent to author@packtpub.com. If your book idea is still at an early stage and you would like to discuss it first before writing a formal book proposal, then please contact us; one of our commissioning editors will get in touch with you.

We're not just looking for published authors; if you have strong technical skills but no writing experience, our experienced editors can help you develop a writing career, or simply get some additional reward for your expertise.

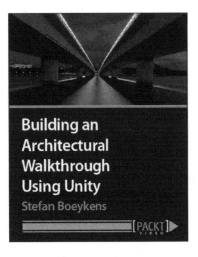

Building an
Architectural
Walkthrough
Using Unity

Stefan Boeykens

Building an Architectural Walkthrough Using Unity

ISBN: 978-1-78355-990-9   Duration: 02:51 hours

Walk around in your own architectural design with the Unity Game Authoring system

1. Enliven static images and technical drawings with an interactive Unity app.

2. Walk around freely, climb stairs, open doors…explore!

3. This is a practical and useful tutorial covering exactly what you need to know to use architectural design in your own projects.

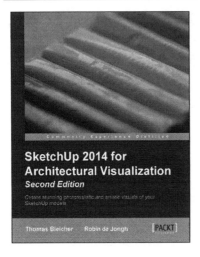

SketchUp 2014 for
Architectural Visualization
Second Edition

Create stunning photorealistic and artistic visuals of your
SketchUp models

Thomas Bleicher   Robin de Jongh

SketchUp 2014 for Architectural Visualization

ISBN: 978-1-78355-841-4   Paperback: 448 pages

Create stunning photorealistic and artistic visuals of your SketchUp models

1. Take advantage of the new features of SketchUp 2014.

2. Create picture-perfect photo-realistic 3D architectural renders for your SketchUp models.

3. Post-process SketchUp output to create digital watercolor and pencil art.

4. Make the most of SketchUp with the best plugins and add-on software to enhance your models.

Please check **www.PacktPub.com** for information on our titles

Blender 3D Basics Beginner's Guide Second Edition

ISBN: 978-1-78398-490-9   Paperback: 526 pages

A quick and easy-to-use guide to create 3D modeling and animation using Blender 2.7

1. Explore Blender's unique user interface and unlock Blender's powerful suite of modeling and animation tools.

2. Learn how to use Blender, and also the principles that make animation, lighting, and camera work come alive.

3. Start with the basics and build your skills through a coordinated series of projects to create a complex world.

WebGL HOTSHOT

ISBN: 978-1-78328-091-9   Paperback: 306 pages

Create interactive 3D content for web pages and mobile devices

1. Simple, ready-to-use interactive 3D demonstrations and explanations for a variety of popular and innovative websites.

2. Detailed overview of how to build 3D environments including features such as designing, navigating, and interacting in 3D scenes.

3. Instantly deploy 3D websites for a variety of applications including e-commerce, social media, visualizing big data, and mobile devices.

Please check **www.PacktPub.com** for information on our titles

28715193R00201

Made in the USA
San Bernardino, CA
05 January 2016